Ceremony and

Ceremony and Civility

Civic Culture in Late Medieval London

BARBARA A. HANAWALT

OXFORD
UNIVERSITY PRESS

UNIVERSITY PRESS

Oxford University Press is a department of the University of Oxford. It furthers the University's objective of excellence in research, scholarship, and education by publishing worldwide. Oxford is a registered trade mark of Oxford University Press in the UK and certain other countries.

Published in the United States of America by Oxford University Press
198 Madison Avenue, New York, NY 10016, United States of America.

© Oxford University Press 2017

All rights reserved. No part of this publication may be reproduced, stored in a retrieval system, or transmitted, in any form or by any means, without the prior permission in writing of Oxford University Press, or as expressly permitted by law, by license, or under terms agreed with the appropriate reproduction rights organization. Inquiries concerning reproduction outside the scope of the above should be sent to the Rights Department, Oxford University Press, at the address above.

You must not circulate this work in any other form
and you must impose this same condition on any acquirer.

Library of Congress Cataloging-in-Publication Data
Names: Hanawalt, Barbara A., 1941– author.
Title: Ceremony and civility: civic culture in late medieval London / Barbara A. Hanawalt.
Description: New York, NY: Oxford University Press, 2017. | Includes bibliographical references and index.
Identifiers: LCCN 2017002194 (print) | LCCN 2017021601 (ebook) | ISBN 9780190490416 (Updf) | ISBN 9780190490423 (Epub) | ISBN 9780190490393 (hardcover: acid-free paper) | ISBN 9780190490409 (paperback: acid-free paper)
Subjects: LCSH: London (England)—Social life and customs—To 1500. | London (England)—Politics and government. | City and town life—England—London—History—To 1500. | Political culture—England—London—History—To 1500. | Immigrants—England—London—History—To 1500. | Acculturation—England—London—History—To 1500. | Citizenship—England—London—History—To 1500. | Courtesy—Political aspects—England—London—History—To 1500. | Political customs and rites—England—London—History—To 1500. | Power (Social sciences)—England—London—History—To 1500. | BISAC: HISTORY / General. | HISTORY / Europe / Great Britain.
Classification: LCC DA680 (ebook) | LCC DA680 .H36 2017 (print) | DDC 942.1/204—dc23
LC record available at https://lccn.loc.gov/2017002194

Contents

Preface and Acknowledgments	vii
Introduction	1
1. The Urban Environment	13
2. The City and the Crown	33
3. Civic Rituals and Elected Officials	52
4. Rebellion and Submission	81
5. Gilds as Incubators for Citizenship	106
6. Civic Lessons for the Masses	134
Conclusion	157
Glossary	165
Abbreviations	167
Notes	169
Bibliography	205
Index	221

Preface and Acknowledgments

MEDIEVAL LONDON DEALT with challenges of immigration from the countryside and the Continent. These problems may seem similar to those of today, but the solutions were rather different. In place of newspapers, television, and other media, the actual visual contact in ceremonies and other public occasions made the city officials familiar to the population. Distinctive dress (liveries) also help to identify the authority figures to both the literate and nonliterate inhabitants. In a society in which oral statements and slanders could cause unrest, those who misspoke about the authorities had to be publicly punished as a lesson to others. Punishments meted out to offenders were also rituals, including pledges of large quantities of wine as retribution or parades through the streets to the stocks. Ceremonies and rituals were a show of power, but they were also didactic lessons for the large immigrant population. One lesson we might take away is that London's civic culture emphasized that men's privilege of living and working in London also came with the obligation to conform to the behavior required in the city and to respect the governing officials.

In this final book on London I have extended my inquiries into the activities of the men in London. My previous studies have been on childhood and women in London. Like all of my books, the research is based on extensive work in archives. Much of the material appears in court records. I have used both quantitative and qualitative methods to digest archival material and analyze individual cases that appear in the records. The records of cases are illuminating even if filtered by court scribes. The sources for this book provided exceptional opportunities to hear the voices of the elite men of London as they expressed their horror at the miscreants who opposed them or broke the laws of London. Their official oaths are recorded as is the manner in which they were elected. Being educated, the elites compiled books that were collections of events that they witnessed, the mythical history of London, and even a treatise on good governance.

The court records even tell us the words of defiance used by those who opposed the elite. Unlike children, women, and the poor, these men had the power of the pen and oratory with which to express themselves. London was a vibrant place in the late fourteenth and fifteenth centuries. It has been entertaining to read the records of the period. I hope, in this book, that the voices of these Londoners give a flavor of how the elite ruled the city.

The elite were colorful men, both in their personalities and in the brilliant clothing they wore. The clothes "made the official," and they took serious delight in them. It would have been an experience to sit in on the meeting of the committee of aldermen as they determined the livery to be worn at the next swearing in of the mayor or at a royal entry. Did the discussions revolve around the availability of cloth and dyes or the latest fashions seen in Calais, Bruges, and Ghent? On at least one occasion, colors had to be changed because the men of Lincoln were going to wear the color the aldermen had chosen.

Over the years I have used a number of archives in England. For this project the Guildhall and the London Metropolitan Archives have been my chief base. I have always found the staff most helpful in producing records and helping to locate those that I would need for various projects. The requests for photographs was handled with great efficiency. Historians would be at a loss without archivists, and I thank them for their work and their kindnesses. For photo enhancements, thanks to Garth Pootinga of Green Hat Media.

Extended periods of time at archives require funding, and I have been fortunate and grateful for what I have received. The initial funding for the larger study of London came from the Guggenheim Foundation in 1988–1989. I have revisited the archives periodically since thanks to the funding from the National Endowment of the Humanities, the University of Minnesota and The Ohio State University, including monies through my chair at Ohio State, the King George III Chair of British History. I also received a special grant from the Mershom Center for International Studies at Ohio State University to read through the *Journals of the Common Council*. I have been twice honored with a National Humanities Council Fellowship, the last one in 2010. I chose to take it to the Newberry Library in Chicago. I found wonderful community of scholars there among the staff, the other fellows, and the library community. I also thank the History Department at Indiana University, which made me a visiting professor when I retired back to Bloomington so that I could use the library.

Unfortunately, Anne Lancashire's three-volume *Civic London to 1558* for the Records of Early English Drama series came out after my book was finished. For those who would like to pursue these topics further without going to the archives, I highly recommend it.

My research and writing has brought me wonderful graduate students. The joy of seeing students flourish, develop their own research agendas, and publish their results is one of the great pleasures that a teacher has. I appreciate their return of respect in the Festschrift that they published in my honor, *The Ties that Bind*. Indeed, working together does bring close ties, and what is so gratifying is that although they earned their graduate degrees from the three different universities, they are all friends and help each other. Perhaps more than they realize, I have a strong emotional investment in their success.

I must also honor an old friend, Lawrence Clopper, recently deceased, who was a scholar of medieval English drama. Although he did not contribute to this book, he has been very much an intellectual companion for many years, since I first started teaching at Indiana University. I miss his intellect, his companionship, and his gourmet cooking. He cannot be replaced for me and for his many friends.

Ceremony and Civility

Introduction

LONDON WAS A magnet for people from all over the British Isles and the Continent. They came, men and women, young and old, rich and poor, seeking employment, alms, or excitement hoping to better their lot. Some were hired servants and apprentices who would live with their masters, but many were footloose soldiers, sailors, journeymen, merchants, students, clergy, thieves, and desperate women. Nobles, royal servants, and wealthy aliens were also among their number. While some were literate in Latin, French, and English, many were illiterate in any language. They spoke in foreign tongues, but also in impenetrable dialects from the far reaches of the British Isles. The population was a shifting one, with immigrants staying a short while and leaving and others dying of plague or from diseases contracted in the unhealthy city environment; new immigrants arrived daily. The immigrants were far more numerous than the small population of elite and long-term residents. The newcomers had to be instructed about the laws and customs of the metropolis, the governing hierarchy, and the civic virtues that the elite hoped would permeate the urban mentality. Civic lessons had to be ongoing.

London had a variety of institutions, both formal and informal, that helped to establish the authority of officials and educate the immigrants. The elite used elaborate civic ceremonials and parades to inform the masses about who were the powerful officials and city's elite and to establish hegemony. The oath taking of the new mayor was followed by parades that included civic officials and the powerful city gilds. Another group of ceremonies were public shaming rituals that were intended not only to punish those who violated civic ordinances or insulted officials, but also to inform bystanders of the behavior expected of urban residents. The ceremonial life of London was an active performance of power by the London elite to establish the social and governmental hierarchy. Other institutions, such as wards, parishes, and gilds, helped to instill the behavior expected in a civil society. London's twenty-four wards, each headed by an alderman, expected all nonclerical, non-noble male residents to participate in ward governance and peacekeeping. The wards, the basic units of city government, taught men the city's laws and power structure. The trade gilds had their own ceremonies of oath taking, elections, induction of apprentices, and shaming rituals that informed members of correct behavior. Parishes and parish gilds welcomed only those who could pay the dues, but they, too, had their own forms of governance and ceremonies that instilled a respect of order, hierarchy, and civility.

Fourteenth- and fifteenth-century English society, like all of European society, was hierarchical. The nobility gained their status at birth or by being ennobled. Within their ranks there were many levels, partly dependent on ancestry, but also on landholdings. The church also had a hierarchy, based on ordination and one's rank within the church. The urban hierarchy—the mayor, aldermen, sheriffs, and city oligarchs—stood outside these more established ones. Part of the goal of the ceremonial show was to maintain the elites' status in the English realm as a whole. London's mayor held a rank that was equivalent to that of an earl, which placed him among the very elite of the nobility. The mayor had to keep up the appearances of this rank and, at times, defend it. The ceremonial welcoming of the king or queen into the city was a lavish affair, indicating the wealth and importance of London and its officials to the crown.

As in most preindustrial cities, the environment of London was unhealthy, and the city struggled to replenish its reduced population. Within the walls, enclosing about a square mile, residents lived in crowded neighborhoods where infections could spread rapidly. In addition, plague and famine could decimate the population. Infant mortality was high, even among the wealthy. Added to the population shortfall was the problem that many inhabitants could not afford to marry, or their apprentice or service contracts prohibited marriage, or they stayed only long enough to acquire a skill or money to go home to their villages and marry there, or they died without reproducing. As a consequence, the city's population was always in flux. Even among the elite, many lines died out, or the members bought property in the country and left the city. London was a city of opportunity for the immigrants but could also be a dead end. The newly arrived, if they hoped to make a success of their stay in the city, needed to learn to function according to the rules of behavior.

Most of the instruction was directed toward men. The male population and its participation in ceremonies, rituals, and government is the subject of this book. Women did not have a role in the wards, because their behavior was assumed to be guided by and under the control of their fathers, husbands, or masters. For them, correction took place in the home. Women participated in the parish, but had very limited official roles either there or in the gilds, and had none in the government.

If one of the purposes of civic ceremony and ritual was didactic, what lessons did the elites hope to instill? The term "civil society" was used in the Middle Ages to mean both a socio-economic unit and an idea, or mentalité, of urban life. The values of the civil society were the peaceful possession of private property, personal security, access to legal means of settling disputes, loyalty to the city, and obedience to officials. The term also evolved to imply urbane and polite behavior among those living in the city. An ideal of personal freedom in trade, marriage, and property ownership, as well as a commitment to the community, was fundamental to the medieval meaning of civil society.[1] The goal of civil society was to preserve the common good. Shared, self-imposed codes of behavior made the enforcement of laws easier, because the expectation was that those dwelling and trading in a community would conform to the norms. Rational self-interest impelled people to follow the code of behavior because they feared that failure to do so could lead to a loss of business partners or employment.[2] The businessmen who ran London's government shared these precepts of acceptable behavior and appealed to them when infractions occurred. Records from court cases, civic ordinances, and chronicles illustrate the civic values that London's citizens strove to defend when they were violated. Emotive language signaled the betrayal of the common good.

London, of course, experienced unrest of various sorts from its inhabitants. A shared sense of the common good did not stop quarrels from breaking out or insults against officials from being voiced. These tremors and signs of disrespect had to be dealt with quickly to avoid destabilizing the elite. Factions among the elite could lead to serious street fighting for control over the city government. Violent fights among the gilds occurred. Negotiations could be tricky among the elites, and the various means of calming them involved ceremonials. Insults to the mayors and other officials by fellow elites were treated with forbearance. The oligarchy knew that too violent a punishment could lead to factional strife. Miscreants and hotheads usually came to the Guildhall to offer atonement. Punishment was reduced to a bond to be paid if the man offended again, and he had to produce sureties for his good behavior. Occasionally, a public ceremony of contrition was also required, such as forcing the offender to walk bareheaded around the city. Gilds used similar means to punish offenders, sometimes requiring them to bow down to the masters in the gildhall to cement their apologies. The more humiliating and physical punishments, such as being paraded through the streets on a hurdle and being made to stand in the pillory, as well as being sent to Newgate prison, were reserved for the non-elite.

By far the most serious challenge that the city governors faced came from the crown. London's franchise to govern itself and elect its own officials was established in charters granted by the king. This dependence put the government of London in a precarious position, because the king could revoke the charter if he was displeased with the city. If the mayor and aldermen were not able to contain disruptive skirmishes, then the king would use that as an excuse to revoke the charter. Various kings in the late Middle Ages threatened to take the governance of the city into their own hands or ended up doing so. This was a frequent occurrence in the thirteenth century, but it became less common in the fourteenth century and ceased in the fifteenth century. Ceremonies to propitiate an angry sovereign required lavish gifts of precious gold and silver objects and large quantities of money.

The ceremonies and rituals of London used many types of symbols. One of the most prominent was clothing. The aldermen had a special committee to determine the livery the city officials wore each year for the city's grandest procession, the oath taking of the mayor. The committee also determined the livery to be worn for royal entries into the city and for the various ceremonial processions throughout the year. The livery distinguished the officials' positions and made them easily recognizable. Each gild had a livery that was changed yearly or biannually. The livery was distinctive in color, but did not differ from the regular male clothing—the clothes were not uniforms. Cloth was expensive in the Middle Ages, and these outfits were vibrantly colored and made of costly fabrics. Livery was so important as an indication of rank that there were rules to prohibit the disposal of the garments after their year or so of use. Nonelites in parish gilds also had a distinctive livery, and when the yeomen of gilds tried to form their own gilds, part of their assertion of organization and power was to adopt a distinctive livery. As the historian Martha Howell has observed, in the late Middle Ages "the exterior was a sign of the person and inseparable from it; the social, visible self was the entire self." Sartorial display was a key vehicle in establishing social hierarchy.[3] Clothing, or the removal of it, was also important in shaming rituals. To walk bareheaded in the streets was a symbol of humiliation. Bakers taken to the stocks had both their shoes and hoods removed. Prostitutes had their hair cut off, and were clothed in a distinctive dress. Male bawds also had the hair shorn to within an inch of fringe.

Other physical symbols were the mace and the sword. The sword, symbolic of the rank of earl, was carried before the mayor in processions, and along with it the ceremonial mace. The sheriffs also had staffs that distinguished them in processions. Gilds, both trade and parish, had distinctive banners. Many also had badges and coats of arms. Gild masters wore garlands on their heads for elections. For the trip to the stocks, a very potent symbol in itself, the man being punished rode through the streets of London on a hurdle pulled by a horse. In addition to the public announcement of his transgression, the fraudulent item was hung around his neck (a loaf of bad bread for dishonest bakers); the liar or slanderer wore a whetstone indicating his sharp tongue.

Music accompanied the ceremonies. For royal entries, a group of children dressed as angels might sing. Horn players accompanied the procession of the mayor and sheriffs to Westminster. The number of horns could be a source of rivalry among gilds and had to be limited because of the noise. The trip to the stocks was accompanied by music as well, including tabors (a type of drum).

The terms *symbol*, *ritual*, and *ceremony* are used somewhat interchangeably in this book. Many disciplines have laid claim to these terms, but anthropology in particular made them a subject area of research.[4] Clifford Geertz's observations of the drama of Balinese ceremonies led him to speak of the "theater state." The dramaturgy of state rituals is an important element of the governing power of the state.[5] A more recent anthropologist, Catherine Bell, has argued in favor of a theoretical model—practice theory—that concentrates on how ritual is performed, because it permits the observer to map relationships of power.[6] The movement of actors in a specially constructed space imparts a sense of the ritual power relations and the meaning it is to convey. Bell's analysis is valuable for studying London's rituals and is adopted in this book.

The ceremonial spaces in the city, including the streets, the Guildhall, the cathedral, the halls of the various gilds, and the parish churches were utilized to help establish the hierarchy. In the procession for the mayor's oath taking at Westminster, the space around him was ceremonially protected. In the gildhalls, seating at the table separated the elite from the regular members. In the parish church, the rood screen kept the parishioners separate from the area of the priest. London was very conscious of the hierarchical uses of space. Major fights broke out among gilds over the prominence of their place in ceremonies in St. Paul's Cathedral.

Historians were quick to pick up the study of ritual and ceremony without distinguishing between the two.[7] Marcello Fantoni's recent summary of historians' uses of symbols, ceremonies, and rituals points out that the study of ritual has become so popular that "everything is 'ritual'—revolts, religious liturgy, festivals, family life, diplomatic protocol, public executions, etc.—and entire civilizations have ended up being considered 'ritualistic.'"[8] But his survey does not resolve the problem or recommend a way to distinguish between ritual and ceremony. This book follows the same approach used by other historians and does not draw sharp distinctions. Both follow prescribed formulas, and the symbols that were used by those performing them and their meanings were known to the viewers as well as the participants.

Historians, unlike anthropologists, must rely on written directions or descriptions of rituals. Contemporary illustrations of medieval London's ceremonies do not exist, but the written sources are so rich in description that the colors and sounds of each come alive. Relying on the written scripts for ceremonies presents problems, since those directions may not actually have been followed. Still, the very formulaic words used in the written records, including those of oaths and the directions for a ritual performance, were essential for the efficacy of the ceremonies. Medieval law and practice required that oaths be repeated word for word in order to legitimate and to confer power and obligations. In most cases, chronicles or court records confirm that the prescribed rituals were actually carried out or were not carried out properly, and in other cases it is through the court records that we know that a ritual existed.

Rituals that had developed during the fourteenth century were recorded in the *Liber Albus* of 1419, thus giving a formal status to the practice. John Carpenter, the common clerk of London, compiled it, drawing on earlier compilations and cartularies. The book also included the oaths sworn by officials of all ranks and by men who joined the wards. These spelled out not just the duties but also the behavior and attitudes expected of the oath takers. Numerous ordinances, gleaned from the Letter Books and the mayor's court rolls, called upon citizens, craftsmen, and the general public to behave honestly, think of the reputation of the city, avoid fraud and the creation of nuisances, settle disputes within their crafts or within the city courts, honor the civic officials, and generally support the common good of the city. The mayor's court provided examples of the punishments of those who did not follow the laws and rules. The Letter Books, so called because each was assigned a letter of the alphabet, were compilations of important cases and their resolutions, royal correspondence, ordinances, and matters that the city wanted to have available for ready reference. The Assize of Bread recorded the frauds of bakers. The Coroners' Rolls, sporadically preserved, described the investigations into violent deaths. The *Journals of the Common Council* for the fifteenth century provide a wealth of details about running the city, ritual preparations, and information about major civic events. Taken as a whole, these London records provide scripts for ceremonials, show the role of officials in enforcing ordinances and respect for officers (often through ceremonies), and paint a picture of the goals of a civil society. Added to the rich municipal archives used in researching this study are those of the gilds, of parishes, and the private accounts of citizens and observers. All these sources speak to the need to maintain a civic culture that would contribute to the peace and prosperity of the city.

The compilation of the *Liber Albus* was a sign of changes in London and the consolidation of power in the hands of the elite that occurred in the last half of the fourteenth century and the first half of the fifteenth. Several crucial factors contributed to these changes, but perhaps one of the most important was the depopulation caused by the Black Death of 1348–49 and the periodic revisitations that occurred almost every generation thereafter. The plague substantially reduced the population of London and concentrated wealth in the hands of a small group of men and women. The changes did not happen immediately. Some transitions were violent, with factions fighting each other and royalty involved in the process. Others were more gradual, such as the increased export of English wool, which enriched many Londoners in the merchant gilds engaged in long-distance trade. And some of the transition was social, resulting from marriage patterns among the elite that tended to concentrate wealth in the hands of a few men.[9]

The writing of history would not be complete without some discussion of time and how the city marked it. London, unlike Florence and Venice, marked time by regnal years. Londoners were part of the realm of England and a charter from the king granted their freedoms. But they also marked time by the mayoral office holder, whose term was a year. Liturgical time, however, played a different role in London than it did in the rituals of the continental cities. The mayors were elected on the Feast of the Apostles Simon and Jude, but other than a mass held before the election, the ceremonies were entirely secular. The same was true of the election of sheriffs. There were elements of religion in the ceremonies, but no ecclesiastical official participated in the elections. The mayor, sheriffs, and aldermen processed on major feast days, but, again, no bishop participated the procession. The Bishop of London played no major role in civic ceremonies. In Venice, the liturgical and political calendars were closely allied,[10] and the city of Bruges contributed heavily to the religious celebrations.[11] Florence tied both its economic and political power to its shrines and churches.[12] London, by comparison, was secular in its official ceremonies.

London was not alone among the cities of late medieval Europe that employed civic ceremonies as a tool for displaying power and reinforcing the authority of their officials. The Italian and Burgundian cities developed more ambitious civic rituals in the fifteenth and sixteenth centuries. London's late fourteenth- and fifteenth-century shows seem very modest compared to these. In England, much of the discussion about civic ceremonial has centered on the provincial cities, their theatrical performances in particular. One of the central questions has been whether or not theatrical performances and other ceremonies promoted harmony in the cities or served to underscore inequalities of wealth and power. Initially, the historians Mervyn James and Charles Phythian Adams made strong arguments for the integrative power of civic ceremony and the performance of plays; however, later scholars found that the plays, civic rituals, and ceremonies of civic office or royal and noble entries served to elevate the elite and reinforce the lesser denizens' lower place in the social hierarchy.[13] The argument that civic ceremonial, even in the religious plays of Corpus Christi, tended to separate the powerful from the middling and poor carries the weight of evidence.

One observation about late medieval English towns, however, is universal to the studies. Performative actions were the great teachers of hierarchical order and an honored tradition in urban centers. The ceremonies of installation to office, the maces and swords born before the mayor, and the liveries so lovingly described in the city records all announced the importance of officials. These were not empty theatrical effects, but were part and parcel of creating the official's power. Likewise, humiliation rituals were very visible to the population and taught lessons of behavior. Although literacy was becoming more common during the fifteenth century, oral and visual practices still conveyed powerful messages.

In exploring the use of ceremony and ritual for establishing a respect for hierarchy and in instilling a civic culture in medieval London, it is crucial to understand the urban environment. The physical landscape included residential, business, and market spaces, as well as governmental, religious, and social spaces. The major ones, civic and royal, were on the main arteries of the city. Their ceremonial routes are mapped in chapter 1. Rituals of humiliation occurred on the main thoroughfares and also in the offender's neighborhood. The sacred spaces were St. Paul's Cathedral and the parish churches. Governmental spaces included the Guildhall and also the halls of the various gilds, the pillory, prisons, and the Tower of London. The whole of the city was available and used for ritual and ceremony. The social landscape was of equal importance. The ranks in society included citizens, apprentices, yeomen, servants, and immigrants from the English hinterland, as well as from abroad. Of these groups, those who acquired citizenship, or became "free of the city" as it was called, were by far the smallest. Women were present in all these ranks, although they were few among the citizens unless through marriage and scarce among apprentices, and there were none among yeoman. But women made up a large proportion of immigrants, especially as servants. Londoners were proud of their city and wrote about its history, struggles against the crown, charters, and assets. Chapter 1 also discusses the myth that London was the new Troy.

Because London's relationship to the crown was so important to the city's identity and independence, chapter 2 gives a brief history of their clashes. The crown sought control over the city and required continual infusions of money, while the city sought to maintain its right to self-government. The mayor and other civic officials had to uphold the independence of London, but do so in a way that would not provoke the king to exert his authority over the city. The biggest threat to the city's independence was internal unrest that became violent and could lead the king to take the city into his own hands. If individuals or factions called upon royal aid, as happened at the end of the fourteenth century, then the charter was in danger. An adroit mayor had to negotiate among the fractious gilds, a restive commons, and the crown. Needless to say, not all mayors were so skilled. As always, London had to treat the monarch with the greatest of care, and this meant loans, lavish gifts, and elaborate royal entries. The relationship was symbiotic, but it required the city to be constantly vigilant.

Since the mayors of London were elected for a year term, their elevation to dignity of office required elaborate ceremonies that were convincing to the denizens of the city, as well as to the king. Chapter 3 describes civic ceremonials surrounding the urban elite as they went through the election of the mayor and his procession to Westminster and back. These ceremonies were well established, but the *Liber Albus* presented the script for the election, complete with stage directions for where everyone was to stand and move in the Guildhall and on the procession to Westminster and back. An early fourteenth-century Chamberlain, Andrew Horn, provided an excerpt from Bruno Latini, an Italian scholar, on the desirable attributes of the mayor. This excerpt in *Liber Horn* must have been well known to mayors and later recorders and certainly to Carpenter, because the advice seems to have been followed. To defend the dignity of office a mayor sometimes had to assert his rights against an earl, and fifteenth-century mayors were also insistent that they had the traditional right to participate in coronations.

The position of the mayor and civic officials also had to be maintained against inhabitants of the city who trespassed on their authority or who defied city laws. In chapter 4 the distinction of rank appears in the types of punishment administered to those people rebellious against the authority and person of the mayor and those of lower rank who defied the civic ordinances. Members of the elite who slandered the mayor or aldermen pledged vast quantities of wine, but these were usually reduced to a fine or the promise of a tun (265 gallons) or more if they offended again. A citizen could be stripped of his freedom for the most egregious offenses and barred from trading in London. Lesser people went to prison or were paraded to the pillory. To preserve the city of nuisance, such as streets not cleaned or buildings that overlooked other people's gardens and privies, the city had an Assize of Nuisances. Moral cleanness was also maintained through the punishment of bawds and prostitutes. Nowhere is the language of disapprobation clearer than in the cases of slander and the sale of fraudulent products. These offenders had no regard for the common good, the health of the consumers, the mayor, the king, and even God when they slandered or produced unwholesome food. Market morality had been transgressed.

By the end of the fourteenth century, the gilds had come to be active partners with the civic officials in enforcing apprenticeship contracts, determining citizenship, regulating the products they produced, and punishing members who offended. The major office holders, including the mayors, aldermen, and sheriffs, were drawn from the elite gilds. Chapter 5 discusses gild structure, hierarchy within the gilds, livery, gildhalls, and gild courts. Through apprenticeships, regulation of the quality of gild craft products, elections of wardens, and gild oaths and initiation rituals, gilds taught respect for hierarchy, but they also provided lessons in conducting trade and in social relations that were essential to the development of a civic culture in London. For the citizens (freemen) of London, the gild system was the most important indoctrination. Gilds faced serious problems regulating non-gild members, such as journeymen, who worked for wages, or skilled craftsmen from the Continent. But eventually they, too, imitated the gild structure and were assimilated into the gild, as lesser members.

Most of London's population, however, were not citizens or members of gilds. Chapter 6 explores the measures that officials undertook to educate these people into the laws and customs of the city. Civic ceremonial and public punishments were only one tool. The city also had public readings in English of the laws and customs. A variety of institutions helped to indoctrinate newcomers and noncitizens. Taverns and inns were often the place of first contact for strangers and aliens. The city essentially made taverners responsible for their guests and for informing them of the laws about bearing arms and curfew. After three nights, the person was no longer a guest and had to join the peacekeeping unit in the ward in which he resided. The wards, under the governance of an alderman, became vehicles for teaching the city ordinances. Parish churches welcomed not only long-term inhabitants but also newcomers. The parish was a place for a mix of population, but it, too, was hierarchical, the wealthier members serving as churchwardens. But the parishes and parish gilds provided an opportunity to learn something of governance. Finally, there were popular ballads and civic statuary that carried didactic lessons on behavior.

The wide use of public ceremonies indicates the fragile peace that the city managed to maintain. Only a small fraction of the population occupied the status of citizen, and they were outnumbered by a large majority of inhabitants. Of the free of the city, only a small elite participated in the civic offices or were members of the council. There was, therefore, a substantial portion of the city that could potentially turn to rebellion or at least disrupt the harmony of the city. Taken all together, London in the fifteenth century successfully managed to instill a sense of identity with city and teach lessons that promoted a civic culture. After a turbulent history in the thirteenth and fourteenth century, London negotiated the difficult politics of the Wars of the Roses in the fifteenth century with few challenges to the authority of the civic government or the hierarchical order of its denizens.

I

The Urban Environment

ONE OF THE court cases recorded in London in 1387 praised the preeminence of London in the realm: it "is the capital city and the watch-tower of the whole realm, and that from the government thereof other cities and places do take example." Furthermore, "there is greater resort, as well of lords and nobles, as of common people, to that city, than to any other places in the realm."[1] Late medieval London had a population of about 40,000 at the time. Decimated by the Black Death of 1348–1349 and subsequent visitations of the plague, its population had shrunk, from about 60,000 in 1300.[2] Although the city was smaller, it still drew people who came for the royal courts, to visit, and to settle. Because fewer people were seeking housing, the city was beautified, with gardens, commodious gildhalls, and comfortable houses for the wealthy merchants and nobles.[3] As wealth became concentrated in fewer hands, the conditions were ripe for the merchant elite to govern the city. Economic power and political access determined one's place in the social order. Citizenship brought political participation, and wealth conferred high social status and, with it, power.[4] By the late fourteenth century, heredity did not play a decisive role in the city, since most elite families did not perpetuate themselves beyond three generations, because they died out or moved to the country as gentry. London, unlike continental cities of Florence, Venice, and Ghent, did not emphasize vertical ties of patrilineage but horizontal ones among the merchant elite.[5] New men, such as the famous Richard Whittington, could rise to wealth and the mayoralty, although the story that he had arrived in London with just his cat is a myth.[6]

Although London was the largest and wealthiest city in England, compared to the powerful European cities it was something of a provincial town. Unlike Florence and Ghent, London did not have the manufacture of luxury woolen cloth. Much of its wealth came from exporting raw wool. Although London merchants imported luxury items, such as wine, spices, fine cloth, and mercery, they could not rival the vast shipping empire of Venice or the banking sophistication of Florence. London did have one market advantage: the king, nobles, and the court bought the products that London produced and imported. But London was not a freestanding city-state, and its dependent relationship with the crown was both symbiotic and fraught.

The composition of London's population was transient and far from homogeneous. Immigrants from other parts of the British Isles were referred to in the records as "foreigns" or "strangers," and those from across the seas were called "aliens." Within the city itself, a line was drawn between those who were "free of the city" (citizens) and those who were not. Citizens belonged to gilds and tended to be wealthier. The unenfranchised residents were usually poorer. The ranks of noncitizens, however, were mixed. Nobles, members of the royal administration, and wealthy foreign merchants lived in the city but were not citizens. Even Chaucer never became a citizen of London. Mixed in with the regular denizens were clergy, from bishops to chantry priests and friars.

Londoners took pride in their city, expressing a fascination with its history and laws. They wrote descriptions of the city, kept personal chronicles of events, and subscribed to the myth that Brutus, a refugee from the fall of Troy, had founded the city. Civic ceremonies expressed the city's pride in its wealth, its gilds, and its governance.

Practices and Divisions of the Urban Space

The very location of London, situated between two royal strongholds, the Tower and the royal court at Westminster, underscored the delicate balance that the city maintained in its relations with the crown. Both royal locations gave the king and his officials easy oversight of events in London. If the mayor seemed unable to control the city, the crown could take over governance or threaten to do so. The mayor's annual oath of office ceremony took place either at Westminster or the Tower, so that the newly elected mayor with the sheriffs and their entourages had to transverse the city to either the west or the east to receive the privilege of governing London from the king.

Proximity to the royal court, on the other hand, provided much of London's prosperity. The city profited from the suitors who came to the royal courts with their cases and needed housing, meals, and perhaps a bit of shopping. The court attracted a number of nobles who kept a residence in London for court appearances and business. Likewise, bishops had their establishments in or near London. The presence of all these wealthy consumers was good for the city's economy.

Viewed from the south bank of the Thames, the landscape of London was dominated by the Tower, to the east; London Bridge, with its shops and houses and the heads of traitors displayed on poles above the drawbridge; and St. Paul's Cathedral, to the west. Figure 1.1 shows a portion of Wenceslas Hollar's map of 1648. Seven gates punctuated the walls that outlined the city except on the Thames side. The whole area within the walls was dotted with the spires of various parish churches and filled with houses. The Guildhall was prominent even before it was enlarged, between 1411 and 1440. As trade increased, the wharf area was continually built up to accommodate more ships. In the fifteenth century, the wealthy gilds began to build halls with gardens and sometimes almshouses as well. Conduits carried fresh water into the city. During royal entries, the greater and lesser conduits served as stages for pageants, running with wine instead of water.

Although the city walls were expanded to accommodate the Dominican house (Blackfriars), London remained essentially within the Roman walls. These were reinforced continually in the Middle Ages, and at night the gates served as a barrier, keeping out those wanting to enter the city after curfew; they also served as prisons. Ludgate prison was meant for citizens involved in debt cases, but Newgate was the prison for indicted felons awaiting trial. Newgate was not a healthy environment; the coroners' inquest records people dying of prison fever and famine.[7] The city admitted as much in 1419, when it re-established Ludgate prison for debtors because some of the debtors who had been sent to Newgate had apparently died "by reason of the fetid and corrupt atmosphere that is in the hateful gaol of Neugate, many person who lately were in the said Prison of Ludgate ... are now dead."[8] It is no wonder that when the mayor wanted to wear down an offender, he sent him to Newgate.

Administratively and geographically the city was divided into twenty-four wards each under the leadership of an alderman. The aldermen mostly served for life. Their duties included recording frankpledge and apprenticeship contracts, holding wardmotes that gathered together the male inhabitants who had presented complaints about peacekeeping and nuisances in the ward, and supervising various officers who kept

FIGURE 1.1 Wenceslaus Hollar's 1647 view of London showing the Thames, the Bridge, numerous churches, and the crowded housing.

the peace in the ward. Every man seeking residence in London took the oath of frankpledge before an alderman in his ward. The frankpledge was made up of men who bound themselves to others to ensure mutual good behavior and peacekeeping. Wards performed the basic day-to-day activities of government and sanitation. The mayor and two sheriffs, elected annually, along with the aldermen and the members of the Common Council, administered the city. The mayor held a range of courts, arbitrated disputes, represented the city in the realm and with the king, and generally oversaw the smooth running of the city. The sheriffs tended to be younger than the mayor and the aldermen, and they answered to the king for taxes due and held courts for misdemeanors. The court of aldermen included the mayor and heard a variety of cases. It essentially governed the city. The Common Council worked in cooperation with the court of aldermen. It was made up of more substantial men of the wards, chosen by the aldermen. The Common Council's spokesman was the serjeant-at-arms, who also served as the common crier and mace bearer.

London developed a bureaucracy to manage the daily running of the city and the recording of its court cases and other business. The recorder had to be skilled in law, since he sat with the mayor in court and represented the city's legal cases with the crown. He was appointed by the mayor and aldermen and worked closely with them. The position was one of considerable power, since the appointment was renewable The chamberlain was the financial officer of the city. The common clerk was charged with keeping the city records, but since he held office for a number of years, he also became skilled in legal matters. A number of other lesser offices also formed part of the bureaucracy.

The city walls did not contain the growth of London. The jurisdiction of the city extended to the "bars." These were posts, perhaps linked by a chain across the way. The most famous of these was Temple Bar on the road to Westminster. Farrington Without to the northwest was made a ward, and Portsoken to the east had been a private jurisdiction. Expansion occurred at all the city gates to the north and west. These were known as the "suburbs."[9]

Much can be said about the aural, visual, and written aspects of London's ceremonial and civic culture, but it is not easy to re-create the smell of the city. Refuse from households found its way into the streets. On each side of the wider streets were gutters for carrying away rainwater running from the roofs, as well as the contents of chamber pots, kitchen refuse, and other waste. The narrower streets had only one gutter. The city provided public latrines, and private houses had latrines in their yards, but human excrement and manure in the streets was a constant problem. London had ordinances for keeping filth out of the streets and hired muck rakers to clean the streets, but the smell would have been omnipresent.[10] Coal came into increasing use in the late Middle Ages, so that the smell of burning soft coal mixed with the other odors of the city.

In contrast to the unpleasant odors, the smell of freshly baked bread coming from the numerous bakeries would also have permeated the air, and brewing gave off other yeasty smells. Public cookhouses were numerous, so that meat pies being baked and roasting meat would have added appetizing aromas. The smells of the cooking for gild feasts, church suppers, banquets, and even in private homes would have been enticing enough to make people on the streets feel hungry.

The city provided clean water for the inhabitants, piping it to the conduits from springs outside the city. The conduits provided water to people, who had to fetch it with buckets. The Greater and Lesser Conduits played a major role in ceremonies because at those times they ran with wine rather than water; they were also substantial enough to have wooden framed pageants on them.

In addition to the walls and the settlements beyond them, the River Thames provided a boundary of London and a focus of its trade. A major thoroughfare for local and long-distance boats and barges, it became a part of the ceremonial space of London. In fourteenth and fifteenth centuries London was a major trading center for both the importation of goods and the redistributive trade. Queenhithe and Billingsgate were the two public quays. The Gascons, the major wine importers, docked in the Vintry. Fish, including fresh, salted, and dried, came in to the docks of Billingsgate. The major trading partners were the Hanse merchants, who brought cloth, raw materials, wood, fish, grain, furs, and other items to their special district called the Steelyard. Venetians and Genoese merchants dealt in luxury goods and banking. The English exported wool, woolfells, and increasingly, woolen cloth to the continent. By the fifteenth century, a special quay and customs house were established for wool export.[11]

Crafts and commercial activity took place throughout London. The bridge, controlled and maintained by the city, served as a conduit for goods leaving the city to the southeast and for agricultural goods entering from that fertile area. The bridge connected London to Southwark. That borough was a separate jurisdiction and as such offered Londoners access to illicit trades, entertainments such as bearbaiting, and prostitution. On occasion, it served as an entry point for rebels. Wattling Street gave access to the north and west. The Cheap was the major market street and also important for royal entries and mayoral processions. Private individuals, in cooperation with the city, established specialized market structures, including Leadenhall.[12]

Within the walls, the city did not have undisputed control of its territory. St. Paul's Cathedral was exempt from city laws and ordinances. A number of religious houses, including the Dominicans, Benedictines, Augustinians, and Franciscans, had establishments in London. Perhaps the biggest problem was the chapel St. Martin le Grand near St. Paul's. It was designated as a royal chapel and had the right of sanctuary. The city complained because it did not pay tallage and offered shelter to felons and debtors. It was the location of the negotiations between the mayor and the royal officials when a disputed case arose between the city and the crown.

The official ceremonial space of London was concentrated around the Guildhall, Cheapside, St. Paul's, and the Thames. If a royal entry was involved, then the Tower and perhaps London Bridge were added. Coronation processions started at the Tower, where the uncrowned monarch would have spent the night. The royal party processed through Tower Street, up Mark Lane to Fenchurch Street, and along that street to Gracechurch Street as far as Cornhill. From there, the party entered into the heart of the city, where the uncrowned king would receive public acclaim from the citizens and the population. This route went along Cornhill and the Poultry and Cheapside to St. Paul's for a mass. From St. Paul's, the royal party went to Ludgate and out to Temple Bar on the way to Westminster. The city streets were lined with inhabitants in their finery, and the buildings were hung with tapestries. If the entry was one of an already crowned king, it usually started at the south entrance of London Bridge to Cornhill and so through Cheapside to St. Paul's. The ceremonial route passed the church of St. Thomas Acon, whose high altar marked the presumed birthplace of Thomas Becket, and ended at the St. Paul's, from which the royal party departed for Westminster by Ludgate.[13] Figure 1.2 shows the routes of royal processions and the mayoral inauguration procession. The Guildhall, the two conduits, and the cross are shown along the processional routes.

In contrast to the royal entries, the mayor's trip to his oath taking at Westminster started at the Guildhall and then proceeded west along the same route, going past St. Paul's and out Aldgate, down to Fleet Street, and so to Westminster. In the fifteenth century, when the trip was made by

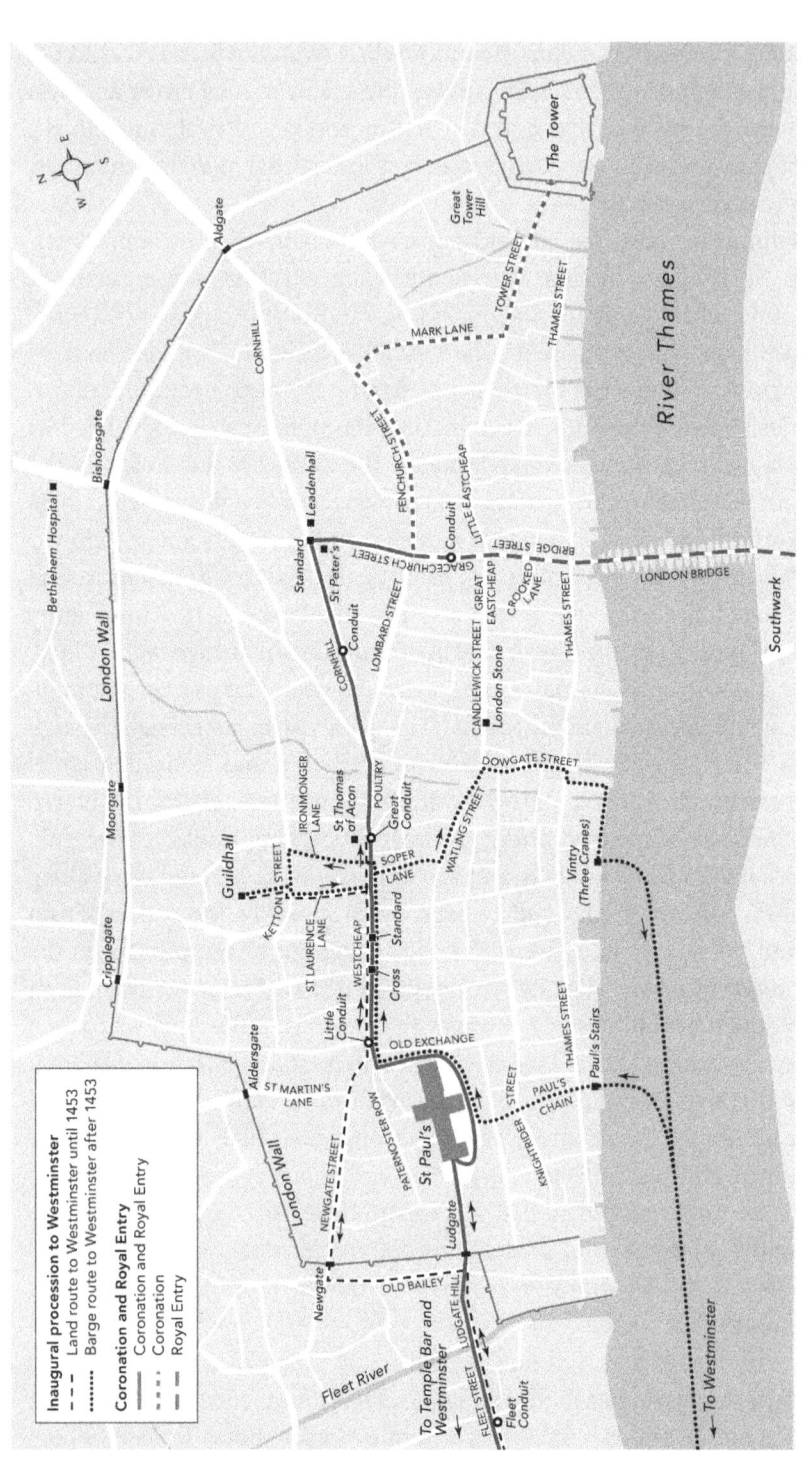

FIGURE 1.2 Map showing the royal and mayoral ceremonial routes through London. The Tower of London, the Guildhall, the conduits in the Cheap, St. Paul's Cathedral, and the Vintner's Warf. Map drawn by Nat Chase of INCaseLLC.

barge instead of horse, the procession started at the Guildhall and moved across Cheapside to Soper's Lane and so to the Thames, where the mayor boarded a barge at the Vintry. After the taking the oath at Westminster, the mayor made his entry, disembarking at Paul's Stairs and so up to Paul's Churchyard to the grave of William the Bishop, who was believed to have saved London from William the Conquerer, then to the Cheapside at the Little Conduit, and so to the Guildhall. The entire procession and the use of space were presented like a script in the *Liber Albus*.[14] The mayors also processed on major religious feasts, Whitsun Monday, and the Midsummer's Watch.

Other local ceremonies involved parish churches, churchyards, and the gildhalls and their gardens. Processions celebrating a patron saint's day, funeral processions, and major holidays were common to the London ceremonial scene. Trade and merchant gilds and parish fraternities all held processions and offered other forms of entertainment.[15]

The Social Milieu

The most important distinction among the population was between those who were free of the city and those who were not. A man could gain freedom (citizenship) three ways: by successfully completing an apprenticeship in a gild and being sworn in as a gild member and enrolled with the city; by patrimony; and by redemption, either by purchasing the right or as the gift of the mayor. The freemen were a select group. *Letter Book D* lists the names of those who gained citizenship between 1309 and 1312. In those three years, 907 men and two women gained the freedom.[16] If the population of London at the time was 60,000, these new citizens would have constituted 1.5 percent of the population. They joined the ranks of those who were already citizens.

Freedom of the city came with both privileges and obligations. The benefits, first and foremost, were that only freemen could buy and resell in the city and keep shops for selling retail. They alone had political rights in the city. But the obligations were also important. They were subject to taxation and obliged to serve in various capacities in the city. The oath of citizenship spelled out their duties. It began with the usual oath of loyalty to the mayor and the king "and to the franchises and customs of the city" and then outlined those obligations. Citizens were responsible to answer to all "summonses, contributions, watches, tallages, and other charges." Any apprentices that the citizen might take had to be freeborn, not serfs, and their terms had to last at least seven years. The apprentice had to be enrolled with the city in the first year of his contract and again upon completion of the covenant. One citizen could not sue another outside the city but had to take the disagreement to the mayor's court or to his gild. The oath also obligated the citizen to report to the mayor any assemblies that were contrary to the peace and to report any strangers trafficking in the city.[17]

Because of the great economic benefits citizenship status bestowed, it was subject to contentions and abuse. Freemen by birth caused some of the dissent. To obtain that status, the person of had to be the son of a freeman, not just born in the city. He had to take an oath when he came of age, just as did those who completed an apprenticeship.[18] Admission by redemption was another issue, particularly in the fifteenth century, when depopulation was adding to the competition for apprentices, and wealthy and skilled immigrants were coming to the city. The mayor was allowed to make six redemptions a year, but the king complained that when he did this, the royal government was deprived of the revenue from the customs that they as noncitizens had to pay. Finally, in 1434, the mayor gave up the privilege of granting redemptions in exchange for four casks of wine.[19] Parish clerks could be free of the city if they paid £20, but only twenty-eight would be admitted. They had to have continuous parish residence, could not take an apprentice, and had no governing privileges or obligations.[20] A woman married to a citizen had the right to trade, and that right continued in widowhood if she remained a resident of London and did not remarry.[21] By far the most fraught issue concerned strangers and aliens gaining the franchise. One merchant from Genoa bought the freedom of the city for his sons, and some aliens gained freedom under false pretexts, through gild membership.[22]

Freemen who ran afoul of the city government could lose their citizenship. The infractions might be that they refused to pay tallages, took cases outside the city courts, or behaved obstreperously to authorities.[23] John Corbet, a goldsmith, did not appear in court to answer for frequenting debates and conventicles of malcontents.[24] John Darby, a cloth worker with a shop near the Cheap, had his shop closed up for not removing a dead dog lying against his house. He could only avoid losing his citizenship by paying £50.[25] So valuable was citizenship for achieving economic success that one of the punishments that a gild could ask of the mayor was to have a recalcitrant gild member removed of his citizenship. Even the most defiant would hold out only a few days or months before humbly asking to be allowed back in and paying a large recompense.

The freedom of the city was closely tied to the trade and craft gilds since most men gained freedom through apprenticeship. Various gilds, however, fell into an additional hierarchy. At the top of the hierarchy were the great merchant companies that dealt in the long-distance trade of luxury goods, wool, and bulk items. Some craftsmen, such as goldsmiths and tailors, also gained prominence. The gilds that produced useful goods, such as bread, saddles, arrows, and tiles, and were further down the ladder. They formed their own regulatory trade gilds, but had less wealth and political power than the merchant gilds. Inside the gilds a further hierarchy prevailed; the wealthiest members wore the full gild livery and were referred to as the "men of the cloth." Those of lesser status might wear a hood but not the full array of a gown, and still others had neither distinction. Below them were men who had completed apprenticeships but did not have enough resources to set up their own shops or had failed in business. They worked as laborers and were called *yeomen* or *bachelors*.

Members in the upper ranks of the most prominent gilds formed horizontal attachments with other gild members of the same status. Their daughters married members of the same status group, and their widows tended to choose as second or third husbands members of their first husband's gild or one closely allied with it. The sons of prominent gild members might marry below their social status, but they counted on a large dowry to acquire capital for their business. Widows with children were particularly attractive marriage candidates since they had a dower for their life use, a third of the former husband's estate, and held their children's portion until they came of age, again a third. All told, this came to two-thirds of the former husband's estate. Widows without children received half of their former husband's estate on his death. Their wealth was kept within the gild by remarriage.[26] Members of the lesser gilds followed similar marriage strategies and formed a solidarity with fellow gild members or those in the same status group.

Finding evidence of London's poor inhabitants is much more difficult. The poor do not appear in city records unless they were in trouble with the law. The few surviving records of the wardmotes, the courts of the neighborhood, describe illegal activities, including as bawds and prostitutes, selling without being free of the city, hawking goods in the street, and other marginal economic activities they engaged in to stay alive. The very poor also appear in the records of coroners' inquests. During famines or severe winters, they were found dead in the streets and described as having frozen to death.[27] Cheap housing was hard to come by, and some of the poor most certainly lived in the streets. In the worst of the famines, in 1315–1316, nine paupers were crushed to death at a public distribution of bread when the chaplains were unable to stop the surging mob. Another famine occurred in 1322 and 1323, and in July a mob of desperate people appeared at the gate of the Friars Preachers for the distribution of alms from a will. Fifty-five men, women, and children were crushed to death. Some of the poor were named in the inquest, but many were unnamed.[28] London established graves for paupers in extreme circumstances such as plague. In the more routine cases of the death of an unknown poor person in the parish, a wealthier parishioner would step forward and offer to pay the burial expenses. Parishes and parish fraternities looked after those of their members who, through no fault of their own, fell into poverty. Likewise, the gilds had poor boxes, and the monies were used to take care of their indigent members. The Archdeaconry court in London offered to write wills for the poorer elements in the city. Among these wills are those of people described as paupers. They had little to give away, but some had wives, some were widows, and some were single men. They offered something to the church and had a residue to give to their surviving spouses. Like those who appeared in the wardmotes, they had eked out a living but had few possessions to show for it.[29]

As the historian of London Sylvia Thrupp has pointed out, the very language of the records indicates status differences in economic and political power. Whether written in French, Latin, or English, the language of status was obvious. Those who participated in ward politics were "the more sufficient (*pluis sufficeauntz*) the abler or more powerful (*potentiores, pluis vaillantz*)." Citizens who had achieved respectability, probity, wealth, prudence, and wisdom were grouped as *bons gens* and *probi homines*. These were the people who participated in the Common Council, in the wards, as churchwardens, and as gild masters. The words are repeated in gild ordinances, often in English, as "the more wise and discrete," "worshipful," "the worthy and notable," and so on. When political disturbances by the unprivileged are noted, those men are referred to as "plebs" or "lower people" (*de plebeis, inferiors*, or *populo minuto*). An observer of the followers of Northampton accused him of drawing support from "mochel smale people that konne non skyl of governaunce ne of gode conseyl." The terms of address to be used for the mayor and alderman underscored the respect for authority and hierarchy within the city. They were addressed as "gracious," "wise," or "worshipful."[30] I have applied the term *oligarchs* to this group.[31]

The division of the city by social status did not lead to an ideology of revolt. The notion of hierarchy was preached in the pulpits and accepted by the population. No ideological tracts proposing a wider franchise or different forms of representation appeared. Urban unrest revolved around economic, not political, opportunity.[32]

Observations on the City by Contemporaries

Pictorial representation of London was uncommon until the sixteenth century and later. A sketch by Mathew Paris in the mid-thirteenth century shows St. Paul's Cathedral and the walls. A late fifteenth-century miniature shows the Duke of Orleans in the Tower with London and the Bridge behind him. The earliest printed view of London was made in 1510, and it showed old St. Paul and the White Tower.

The city seals show the perceptions of those designing and adopting them. The thirteenth-century seal had on its obverse an image of St. Paul rising up from the walled city carrying a sword in one hand and the arms of England in the other. The legend is *Sigillum baronum Londoniarum*, a reference to Londoners' claim that the city's citizens were the equivalent of barons. The reverse showed Thomas Becket dressed as an archbishop, seated on an arch raised over the city. A lay figure and a clerical figure knelt on either side of him. The inscription read *Me que to peperi ne cesses Toma, tueri* (Cease not, Thomas, to protect me who brought you forth). The early seal therefore showed the river, the city walls, steeples, and city gates. The inhabitants are not suppliant to St. Paul, but kneel beside him. No single ruler appears on the seal. Perhaps fifty years later another seal, for the use of the mayors, was deemed essential. That seal showed St. Paul and St. Thomas beneath elaborate arches with the three leopards of England at the bottom. The inscription read *Sigillum Maioratus London*. The topography and the inhabitants were omitted. In 1381, Mayor William Walworth had a new seal made on the grounds that the old one was rude and decrepit.[33] The new one, shown on the right in figure 1.3, updated the architecture with rather elaborate gothic tabernacles containing the image of Mary flanked by angels. Saints Thomas and Paul are seated above the city arms (a cross with the sword of St. Paul), and in the Gothic structures next to them are two serjeants-at-arms.

The images on the city's seal were of great importance to London's inhabitants. In 1376 the recorder, eleven aldermen, and "an immense commonality" assented to the addition of a star (*molet*) in the river gate beneath

MAYORALTY SEALS OF LONDON.

The smaller dated 1280 was replaced in 1381 by that on the right which, save for the addition of two roses, is the same as that in use to-day.
The sword on the shield is generally accepted as the symbol of St Paul.

FIGURE 1.3 Seals of London from 1280 and 1381. Besides being larger in size, the more ornate seal on the right reflects the more stylish Gothic architectural elements.

Reprinted from an older illustration in Gordon Home in collaboration with Edward Ford, *Medieval London*. London: Ernest Benn Ltd., 1927.

the feet of the image of St. Paul.[34] The popular interest in the city arms and the seal indicates a high degree of identity with imagery that appeared on official documents. Since seals were so important to individual identity, it is no wonder that they were also important to citizens. Walworth's update of the mayoral seal made it larger and therefore more prominent and also gave it a more modern look.

The city kept the seal in a small box, which was put in the care of two aldermen and four commoners Figure 1.4 shows an elaborate key with a silk tassel. The appointment of the caretakers appears in the *Journals of the Common Council* and is indicated there by an ornate key drawn at the side of the entry. The elaborate precautions taken to protect this civic symbol indicate some suspicions about possible misuse, but also the importance of the seal for the authority of the city.[35]

Besides their claims as the birthplace of Thomas Becket and beneficiaries of the special protection of St. Paul, Londoners embraced the founding myth that Brutus, a descendant of Aeneas, had conquered the island and changed its name from Albion to Britain in honor of himself.

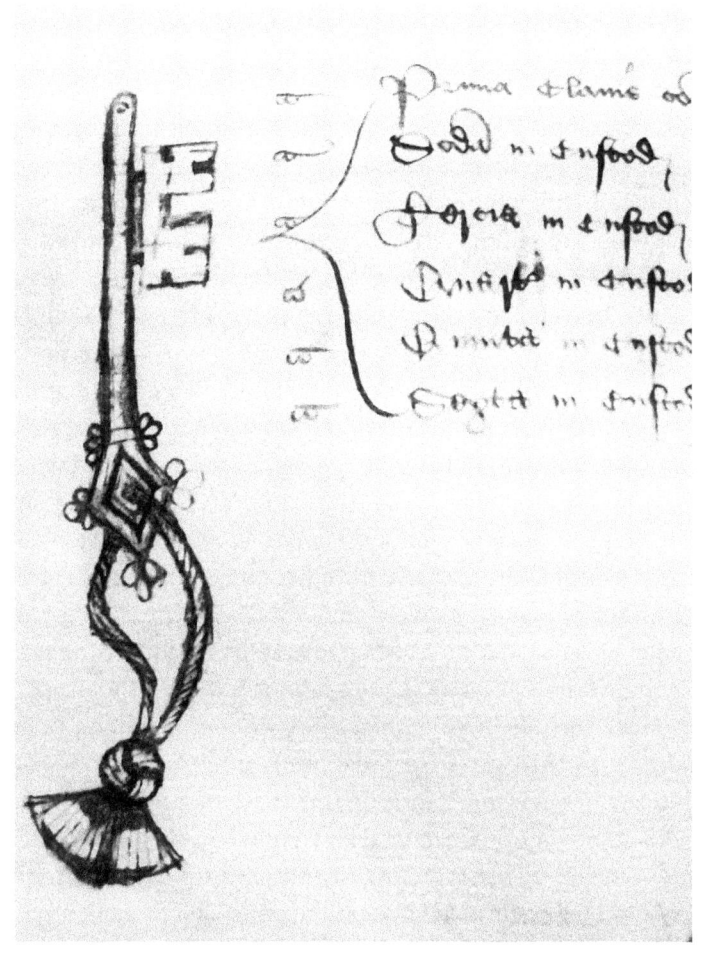

FIGURE 1.4 The ornate drawing of the key to the box containing the city's seal. The drawing was made by the clerk recording the appointment of the of two aldermen and two commoners to have charge of the key.

Photo by author from the *Journals of the Common Council*, COL/CC/01/01/05, with permission from the London Metropolitan Archives.

Brutus reputedly founded what would eventually be the city of London. True or not, founding myths provide a point in the history of a city that inhabitants can claim as their origin and are thus important to the collective civic identity. Geoffrey of Monmouth popularized the Brutus myth in *De gestis Britonum*, a history of the kings of Britain, completed circa 1130.[36] In Geoffrey's version, Aeneas fled the devastated city of Troy with his son and went to Italy. The grandson of Aeneas conceived a child who, by prophesy, would kill both his parents. That son was Brutus, and his fate was to have a series of adventures before finally landing on Albion, an island inhabited only by giants. The giants were driven into the hills or killed. Brutus then searched for a place to found a city and located it on the banks of the River Thames, calling it New Troy. The name was changed when Lud, who had fought Julius Caesar, came to the throne. Lud built walls around the city and changed its name to Lud's city.[37] The English were not alone in claiming descent from the mythical Aeneas and the Trojans; the Venetians also found the myth useful in adding luster to their city.[38]

Geoffrey of Monmouth's work was popular, serving as the basis for Wace's Anglo-Norman poem *Roman de Brute,* composed circa 1150–1155, and Laymon's *Brut* in Middle English verse, composed 1190–1215. A prose *Brut* in Anglo-Norman appeared sometime after 1272, and in about 1400, an English prose version appeared.[39] William Fitz Stephen, writing in 1183, accepted the Troy myth. In his preface to the life of Thomas Becket, whom he served as clerk and subdeacon throughout Becket's career as chancellor and archbishop, Fitzstephen declares that London is older than Rome because Brutus founded it after the Trojan War.[40] Andrew Horn included Fitzstephen's description of London in *the Liber Custumarum,* so that when Horn bequeathed his books to London, the founding myth came to be included in the London records.[41] In 1419, Carpenter, compiler of the *Liber Albus,* adapted Fitzstephen's description of London, including the founding myth, writing "that, even to this day, it possesses the liberties, rights, and customs of that ancient city Troy, and enjoys its institutions."[42] Carpenter claimed that granting the right of freedom to serfs who had lived peacefully in the city for a year and a day was a Trojan practice. The myth was so powerful that in 1428, it was included in an official document in *Letter Book K* about a case of two brothers who were serfs but had lived a year and a day within the city walls and were, therefore, free.[43]

The myth must have been well known among literate Londoners. The *Brut* prose chronicle circulated widely and was printed by Caxton in 1480. It was obviously a source of pride to establish the ancient lineage of the city and to claim to be older than Rome. Perhaps, however, the myth was not universally liked, because in the late fourteenth century, the chronicler Walsingham claimed that one of the charges against mayor Nicholas Brembre was that he had plotted to change the name of London to "Little Troy" and make himself a duke.[44] Walsingham, however, was not a Londoner.

The most eloquent summary of the physical and social space of London was that of William Fitz Stephen. Besides identifying London with the Brutus myth, Fitz Stephen provided an encomium of the city. A clergyman, he praised Londoners for "church going, honor paid to God, keeping of feast-days, giving of alms, entertainment of strangers, ratifying of betrothals, contracts of marriage, celebration of nuptials, furnishing of banquets, cheering of guests and likewise for their care in regard to the rites of funeral and the burial of the dead." The only faults he found were "the immoderate drinking of fools and the frequency of fires."[45] "The citizens of London are everywhere regarded as illustrious and renowned beyond those of all other cities in elegance of their fine manners, raiment and table, the inhabitants of other towns are called citizens but of this they are called barons."[46] Much of his joy in London, beyond the piety and dignity of the inhabitants, is evident in a recounting of the various sports of young men, including disputations, cockfighting, games, horse racing, tournaments, and ice skating. He seemed to remember his youth in London with considerable pleasure. As an older man, he praised the abundance of food and wine. He laid out the scenes of London life with a geographical memory of the city.[47] Given its small size, he and many others would know the city intimately by walking through it.

The fifteenth century saw an explosion of chronicles written by London citizens in English. The writers were merchants and tradesmen—at least one must have been a mayor—and they seem to have had access to city records and perhaps held civic and gild offices.[48] Figure 1.5 shows one such prosperous middle-class man at his desk. The chronicles are preserved in commonplace books that served as practical guides to prices, statutes, and ordinances and important events. The accounts, however, were not all of an instructive nature. Forty percent of the material dealt with regal activity and battles, but also included were descriptions of the weather; religious events; supernatural events, such as comets; plague; famine; and executions. Among the major historical events the chronicles recorded was the royal entry of Henry VI, fresh from his coronation in Paris, and they commented both on London's pageants and on the messages they should convey, while Henry's restoration to the throne led to reflections on the his failure to rule the realm.[49] Jack Cade's rebellion, in 1450, got a particularly full account because of the violence and the stand by the aldermen and men of the city at London Bridge. The trial of Eleanor Cobham, wife of

FIGURE 1.5 This drawing of a fifteenth-century window in a church in Islington shows a well-to-do man writing at a table. The chroniclers must have looked much like him. The clothing he wears presents a good image of the style at the time.
From John Carter, *Specimens of Ancient Sculpture and Painting Now Remaining in England for the Earliest Period to the Reign of Henry VIII*. London: Bohn, 1887.

Duke Humphrey of Gloucester, led the writers to describe and attempt to explain the sorcery involved in her accusation.[50]

The chroniclers were establishing their own style of writing history.[51] They drew information from firsthand experience, royal documents, pamphlets, ballads and poems, other chronicles, city records, and gossip and hearsay.[52] These literate Londoners wrote what they observed and shared the information with those who read their chronicles: family, heirs, and perhaps friends and fellow gildsmen.[53] The content provided information not only on business and law but also on citizenship.[54]

Recognized authors also wrote about London. Chaucer, surprisingly, did not write about the city, although he lived above Aldergate. The pilgrims in *The Canterbury Tales* start from an inn in Southwark, not London. Only a few of his characters have London roots, such as the Cook and the Gildsmen. The city itself is not explored. However, the poets Thomas Usk and Thomas Hoccleve wrote about their walks in London.[55] And William Langland wrote extensively about London in *Piers Plowman*. While agrarian settings make up much of the poem's allegories, London is very much present in the descriptions of its streets, people, churches, and law courts of Westminster. Langland wrote critically of the merchants and the gild struggles and the avarice that he saw in them and also condemned the corruption and bribery connected to the law courts. But he wrote sympathetically about his neighbors on Cornhill, a place of used-clothes markets and the stocks. In the tavern scene with Gluttony, Langland depicts a gathering of ordinary Londoners, including Cissy the shoemaker, Tim the tinkerer, and Clarice of Cock's Lane, along with a fiddler, a rat catcher, a rope maker, Rose the dish seller, and many others who led a marginal existence in London.[56]

A contemporary anonymous poem, "London Lickpenny," is more explicit about the corruption of the courts at Westminster. The protagonist went to various courts but could not get his plaint heard, explaining, "For lacke of money, I may not spede." As he mingled with the throng at the courts, his hood was stolen. Disappointed, he left for London. Here he was offered fresh berries and cherries and a range of spices, but again, he had no money. In the Cheap, he was offered fine linen and cotton. Then it was on to Candlewick Street, where drapers offered to sell him cloth. The street vendors' calls selling rushes, mackerel, ribs of beef, pies, and pewter pots reflected the sounds of the city. But he could not afford even to pay the minstrels for a song. Finally, he ended up at Cornhill and the frippery (used clothes) market, where he saw his stolen hood but could not afford to buy it back. He returned to Kent and to his plow.[57]

The Scottish poet, William Dunbar, writing in the late fifteenth century had nothing but praise for the city. He called the city "lusty Troy novaunt" and claimed that Julius Caesar had built the Tower. It was a city with strong walls, wise people, "blith" churches with "well sownyng" bells. "Rich be thy merchauntis in substance that excellis / Fair be their wives, right lovesome, white and small." He also mentioned seeing the nobles in their velvets and chains and the clergy in their garments. But he saved the last stanza of the poem for the mayor of London.

> *Thy famous Maire, by princely governaunce,*
> *With swerd of justice, he rulith prudently.*
> *No Lord of Parys, Venyce, or Floraunce*
> *In dignytie or honoure goeth to hym nye,*
> *He is exampler, loode-ster, and guye;*
> *Pryncipall patrone and roose orygynalle,*
> *Above all Maires and maister moost worthy.*[58]

2

The City and the Crown

KING JOHN'S CHARTER in 1215 granted "that the Barons of the city of London shall choose for themselves each year a mayor among themselves, who shall be a trusty man, discreet and proper" with the provision that he be presented to the king.[1] The mayors of London governed at the pleasure of the crown, but their position was not necessarily secure. Challenges to a mayor's hegemony could come from various political and social sectors, but the chief hazard to their rule was the crown. The king granted the right to govern, and the king could take it away. Charters did not protect the city government; the king could revoke them. Throughout the thirteenth and early fourteenth centuries, London's mayors and its elites struggled with the crown over their right to govern themselves. Various actions by the city or indications that the city could not keep peace among its inhabitants could turn a monarch against London and lead to the revocation of its charter. The city could become involved in royal dynastic struggles and pick the wrong side. The gilds could riot against each other, and the king would feel that the mayor could not control the streets. Or factional fights among the elites for control over the mayoralty and the government could lead to royal intervention. Even the monarchy's need for money could serve as an excuse for the king to take the government of London into his hands.[2] Forced loans, taxes, and ceremonies to entertain the royalty were often needed to propitiate the king. The city was very cognizant of the risks of inciting royal ire and sought to preserve stability in the city and in its relationship with the crown. By the fifteenth century, city officials had achieved a stable form of government and had won the respect of its population.[3]

Relations with the Crown

The basic freedom allowing the city to be self-governing was outlined in the charter that William the Conqueror gave to London. William had waited until he had taken the rest of the country to persuade London to submit. With the help of the Norman bishop William of London, the Conqueror granted the city a charter that established for the French and English burgesses (citizens) all the rights that they had formerly held. Londoners believed that Bishop William's intercession had been crucial, and for that reason the mayor and aldermen were accustomed to hearing a *De profundis* (Psalm 130) at his tomb after the new mayor had taken his oath of office at the Exchequer.[4]

London gained more privileges in the twelfth century, including the right to elect its own sheriffs, settle its own cases in the city instead of in royal courts, and for its citizens to prove their innocence by oaths rather than trial by battle. The citizens of London claimed that they were a collective *seigneury* and thus should be treated as peers of the realm. They called themselves "barons," and King John had referred to them by that title when he granted them the right to elect a mayor annually.[5] Unlike continental cities that established communes, London worked within the context of the English feudal system. The mayor held the rank of earl in the feudal hierarchy, its citizens were styled "barons," and the rights they demanded were those of peers of the realm.[6]

The turbulence of the thirteenth century intersected with factional strife in London. Some Londoners were loyal to the king, Henry III; while others sided with the rebels against him. The rebels lost, and London's charter was revoked. In 1285, Edward I resolved to punish the city for siding with the enemies of his father.[7] He revoked the city's charter, and for the next thirteen years appointed wardens to govern the city. Only by paying a fine of 2,000 marks was the city able to regain its charter in 1298.[8]

The number of new citizens grew substantially at the beginning of the fourteenth century, and many came from the crafts rather than the patricians. Strife between the elites and the commoners became violent, leading Edward II to issue a writ, in 1315, limiting the selection of the mayor to those who had been invited to attend the election. The commoners gained ground when the king approved the articles of 1319, which fixed the term of mayor at one year, committed the common seal to the care of two aldermen and two commoners, and gave the commonality control over weights and measures. Most important, the craft and merchant gilds were given control over citizenship since completion of apprenticeship in a gild was the route to citizenship.[9]

When Edward III took the throne, he chose to work with the mayors rather than against them. In the charter he granted London in 1327, he strengthen the mayor's powers. The mayor was now to be one of the royal justices to hear the cases of those imprisoned in Newgate. The new charter rectified the abuses of the past. The liberties of the city could no longer be revoked because of the actions of one of its officials. Only the offending officer would be punished, not the city as a whole. In 1354, Edward regularized, by statute, the causes that might provoke the withdrawal of the city's liberties.[10] The charter of 1327 had granted London a degree of autonomy. But royal interference was always a possibility, and coming out of the battle and strife of the thirteenth and early fourteenth centuries, London's mayors and alderman lived in fear of royal intervention.

The anxiety among the city elites about offending the king and the risk of revocation of the charter is illustrated in the case of William Hughlot, a teller of receipts of the Exchequer, who assaulted an alderman and a constable in January 1387. William had entered the house of a barber in the parish of St. Dunstan, in Fleet Street, and assaulted him with a dagger. The barber's wife saw that Alderman John Rote was passing by, and she called to him for help. The record explains that Rote, "by reason of the office which he held, whereby he was bound to the utmost of his power to keep and maintain the peace, as being an officer of the king" went into the house and commanded William to desist. William "well knew" that Rote was an alderman, but he assaulted him with the dagger, too. Rote grabbed William's hand and forced him to put the dagger back in its sheath. William then took his sword and assaulted Rote with it. A constable, hearing the tumult, came and tried to arrest the assailant. William drew his dagger again and wounded the constable. All of this, the record explains, was to the contempt of the lord king and the dishonor of the aldermen and mayor.

An unrepentant William was brought to the mayor's court from Newgate prison. He not only admitted that he had made the assaults, but proclaimed he had Mayor Extone to thank for his imprisonment and that the "court of the Guildhall of London was the very worst and most false court in all England." To make such an accusation against the mayor and the city court was also to slander of the king, "seeing that he [the mayor] is the immediate representative of our Lord the King within the City, which is the most excellent and noble city in the realm." Good governance had to be maintained in the city because of the proximity of the royal law courts and the upcoming meeting of Parliament. William Hughlot had to be punished as an example to other misdoers. By long tradition, the punishment for assaulting an alderman was the loss of a hand.

An officer of the sheriff brought an axe to the Guildhall, and William laid his right hand, the one that had drawn the dagger and sword against the alderman, on the block to be cut off. Alderman Rote, at the request of diverse lords, asked the mayor that this execution be remitted, and it was. For the contempt and wounding of the constable, it was adjudged that William should as well be imprisoned for a year and a day. Further, for his slander of the mayor and his false words, he was to suffer the "disgraceful punishment of the pillory, with a whetstone hung from his neck, in token of his being a liar." But William was an employee of Richard II, and through the intercession of the king and various lords, it was agreed that when William's prison sentence was completed, he would, instead of the pillory, carry a three-pound candle from the Guildhall through Cheap Street and Fleet Street to the church of St. Dunstan and make an offering of it there. After a short stay in prison, he was released on the surety of men who agreed to pay £100 pounds if he offended again. He did, however, carry the candle through London to St. Dunstan's church.[11]

The careful wording of the case illustrated the city's need to underscore its power as the king's representatives and officers of law enforcement in London and its suburbs. William Hughlot's case was a delicate balance between the crown and the city. Hughlot, in the employ of the king, had both royal and noble protection. At the same time, the king could not defy the legal powers of the mayor and aldermen, since he had granted them the right to administer his justice in the city. The mayor and aldermen were very careful to point out the important position of London in the kingdom, the presence of law courts and upcoming meeting of Parliament, the city's importance as a model of peacekeeping for other cities of the realm, and especially that they were acting on behalf of the crown. A compromise had to be reached that enforced the city's peacekeeping powers, but permitted the king to have his way in the case. Huglot had to do a public penance, but he avoided the discomfort of a long imprisonment in Newgate and the humiliation of standing at the pillory with a whetstone around his neck. His penance was more akin to that of someone committing a religious offense than that of a commoner who had been condemned by the mayor's court.

Gild Skirmishes Threatened Royal Intervention

Factional strife among the gilds was a constant challenge to peacekeeping efforts in London; only a few examples are needed to demonstrate how disruptive such affrays could be. If the intergild fights became violent and the king perceived that the mayor and aldermen could not resolve them, then he might use the disorder as an excuse to take the city into his hands. Trade rivalries accounted for many of the fights and tended to acerbate in periods of economic hardship, as the 1330s and 1340s were.[12] Skirmishes could also originate over such issues as who had precedence in civic processions or where the various gilds stood in St. Paul's on holy days, because these public displays indicated the prestige of the gild. Sharing ceremonial space became an occasion for brawls and riots. These clashes tested both the authority and the negotiating skills of the mayor.

Before Edward III went on military campaign in France, in the initial phase of what is now known as the Hundred Years' War, he added the power of conservator of the peace to the mayor's powers, in effect, giving him the right to hear and determine criminal cases. In April of 1338, Edward summoned the mayor and aldermen to his council and asked whether they were willing "at their peril to guard the city for the king and his heirs." They agreed. They returned with a plan providing that any person "making noise or cry near the windows or doors of shops so as to create a riot in the city should forthwith have judgment of life and limb"; that is, such persons would be treated as criminals and pay with their lives.[13] The measures proved necessary.

A large affray occurred between the Goldsmiths and the Fishmongers on the Saturday in Easter Week of 1339 (April 3) as a consequence of a dispute that had arisen on Good Friday. Easter Week was a time when the gilds turned out in their livery and accompanied the mayor and aldermen in public processions. Matters of gild honor, prestige, and precedence often came to the fore during such displays. Adding to the usual tensions that could arise on these occasions, London was on edge because the beginning of war with France and a shortage of coin had caused an economic depression. The Goldsmiths were among the powerful gilds in the city because they dealt in precious metals and provided the crown and nobility with jewels and plate. They also acted as pawnbrokers, had connections to the royal mint, and were involved in foreign trade. The Fishmongers, who had control over both the salt fish and fishing along the coasts, were a very wealthy gild in the fourteenth century. Since fish, particularly salt fish, was a staple of the medieval diet, their product was in demand. Furthermore, they had fleets that they used for more general trade and lent boats to the royal navy. To give some idea of their status: they had staged a grand procession to honor Edward I after he had defeated the Scots in 1298. Four gilt sturgeons were carried on four horses; followed by four silver salmon, also on horses; followed by forty-six armed knights on horses, which had been made to look like sea pikes (luces). An image of St. Magnus, the Fishmongers' patron saint, ended the procession. At the birth of the future Edward III to Isabella and Edward II, the Fishmongers produced miniature silver ship, "with all manner of tackle that belongs to a ship," and presented it to the queen on Candlemas, in 1313. The gild paraded it through London to Westminster, dressed in their finest and riding on horseback.[14]

On Saturday April 3, 1339, after the dispute on Good Friday, a great crowd of members of both gilds, armed with knives, assembled in the Cheap. The mayor gathered several aldermen and the sheriffs to go there and demanded that the responsible men of both groups resolve their differences before Monday. The effort was not successful, and the "next day [Tuesday] at the corner of Friday Street and the Cheap there was a terrible affray, in which several men were wounded." When the mayor appeared again, the rioters fled. The mayor then ordered the sheriffs to round up the guilty parties and bring them to the Guildhall on the following Monday. He also ordered a jury to come. None of the offenders could be found. But on the same day, the responsible members of both gilds presented the names of suspects; those men could not be found either. On April 12, the leaders of the two misteries agreed that they would keep the peace. A proclamation was made that unless the guilty parties appeared by Friday, they would be prosecuted as rebels. The proclamation was repeated on April 16 at the Stone Cross in the Cheap, naming names and giving the perpetrators until May 1 to turn themselves in. In the proclamation, the city officials cited their promise to the king to keep peace in the city while he was abroad. "And because riots in London, which was the mirror and exemplar of the whole realm, tended to encourage the king's enemies," the mayor had to act swiftly. That day, some of those named came forward and were put into prison. On April 21, a fishmonger and a goldsmith who had been proclaimed as suspects at the Stone Cross in Cheap turned themselves in and were imprisoned. Gradually, the suspects surrendered. As was the usual policy of the mayor and aldermen in such cases, most of the men were released to people acting as sureties for their good behavior and a promise to keep the peace. On May 1, one of those, John Frossh, was proclaimed to be a rebel and was banished from the city.[15] Yet even he seems to have been allowed back into the city, for he appears as a participant in the next riot of the Fishmongers.[16]

The Fishmongers were involved in a riot with the Skinners (Pelterers) a year later (1340). The Skinners were the chief suppliers of furs to the crown and nobility and had extensive trade with the towns of the Hanseatic League. These two prominent gilds clashed with each other over the issue of precedence in processions and civic government.[17] The ill will ended in several affrays on August 1, 1340. In one of these, Ralph Turk, the servant of the fishmonger, John Turk, was killed.

In reconstructing the events of August 1, the jurors of the Mayor's Court said that the problems arose between Nicholas le Leche, fishmonger, and John de Oxford, servant of Robert de Eynesham, a skinner, in front of the latter's shop. The cause was an old quarrel. Ralph Turk, Robert Halpenny, and John Haunsard, all fishmongers, had been accompanying Nicholas from the shop of Robert de Shordiche in the Cheap toward Bridge Street, where unknown skinners set upon them. Hugh Trappe, a skinner, attempted to stop the fight and was wounded by Robert Halpenny.

The mayor and sheriffs and their servants went to Walbrook to stop the affray and commanded that the Skinners deliver the offenders to the sheriff. The mayor then proceeded to Bridge Street to order the Fishmongers to do the same, but when he got there, Robert Halpenny accosted him with arms. The mayor arrested Halpenny and turned him over to the sheriff, but with the help of other fishmongers, Halpenny escaped. In the scuffle, Thomas, son of John Haunsard, "laid violent hands on the mayor," and another man hit the mayor's serjeant with a stick on the head, so that he fell and "his life is now despaired of." Further juries implicated other fishmongers and a chaplain of taking part in the assault. A group of young men and former apprentices were named, and the jurors said that William Turk, the fishmonger, abetted them. They were all implicated in the violence at Bridge Street.[18]

The coroner's inquest into the death of Ralph Turk did not occur until August 24. The inquest jurors said that after dinner on August 1, John de Oxford, a skinner's servant, assaulted Nicholas le Leche, a fishmonger, opposite his master's house. Ralph Turk and several other fishmongers came to the rescue, and John called a number of skinners to help him, including John de Cornubia, called "lyttle Jakke." In the affray that ensued, John de Cornubia struck Ralph with a poleax on top of his head, from which blow he died four days later. John de Cornubia and a number of others fled, and John de Oxford was put into Newgate prison. The jurors said, however, that it was not John de Oxford who had struck the blow. The sheriff was to find and arrest John de Cornubia.

The mayor ordered the sheriff to summon an inquest of the "best, richest and wisest men of the mistery of the Skinners for the following Wednesday, and the like inquest of the mistery of Fishmongers for Thursday next to enquire more fully into the death." The versions of the two gilds named different people and different times for the murder.[19]

With the king in France, the mayor had to quell the possibility of ongoing riot. Meeting in the Guildhall with the sheriffs, aldermen, and seventy-three commoners on August 3, the mayor read the king's charge to maintain order in the city during his campaigns in France. Taking the 1338 document as a mandate, the officials reviewed the affray that had taken place, the arrest of Robert Halpenny and the names of those who had rescued him. Thomas, son of John Haunsard, had assaulted the mayor, grabbing him by the throat. John le Brewere was accused of assaulting the serjeant. Thomas and John were brought in, and they acknowledged their guilt. Judgment, however, was deferred until August 29, after the delayed coroner's inquest. Taking safety in numbers, the mayor called together an "immense commonality" that included 528 men from all the wards. They agreed that Thomas and John should be beheaded immediately at the Stone Cross in the Cheap. The sheriffs carried out the sentence. John de Oxford, as the chief instigator of the fight, was sentenced to a year and a day in prison. After his release, he found sureties for his good behavior.[20]

The ill will between the two companies continued, and in 1343 the mayor summoned "the better men of the Fishmongers and Skinners to appear" before the mayor, sheriffs, and aldermen. The two groups appeared, including John Haunsard (father of the beheaded Thomas), Walter Turk for the Fishmongers, and Robert of Oxford for the skinners. They agreed to search for the misdoers of their misteries and turn them over to the mayor.[21]

The mayor, Andrew Aubrey, had handled the riot adroitly and had protected London from being taken over by the king. He went further to protect his use of punishment in life and limb by getting a letter from the Edward praising his swift action. The letter spelled out how Edward had asked the mayor and aldermen to present a plan for keeping the peace in his absence abroad. After hearing about the nature of the conflict between the Fishmongers and Skinners and learning that one of the fishmongers, with drawn sword, had seized the mayor by the throat, Edward commended the mayor for taking swift action. "We do greatly congratulate you; and you doing therein do accept, and, so much as in us lies, do ratify the same." The king goes on to say that, had the offenders not been punished, the franchise of the city would have been in jeopardy.[22]

These two major affrays were resolved by judicial acts of the mayor, aldermen, sheriffs, and the commonality, but the antiquarian John Stow, who had access to records that have since been lost, recounts additional ceremonial acts on the part of the mayor to bring peace among the gilds. The wardens of the Fishmongers and the Skinners were to dine annually with each other and drink a toast one to the other. The Goldsmiths and the Fishmongers were to do the same, and they were also to exchange their livery hoods.[23]

Any dispute between gilds threatened widespread disruption. When the Cutlers gild argued with the more powerful Goldsmiths over the right to work with precious metals, the mayor sought a solution that would satisfy both sides. The Cutlers had all the necessary tools and skills to work with metal and were in the habit of doing silver gilt and inlays of gold and silver on the handles and blades of knives and swords. The Goldsmiths claimed that they had the exclusive right to work in precious metals. After meeting separately and together with the representatives of both parties, the mayor resolved that the Cutlers should be allowed to continue their practice but that the Goldsmiths had the right to inspect their work and assay their gold and silver.[24] The acrimonious trade dispute between the Saddlers on one side and the Joiners (carpenters), Painters, and Lorimers (harness makers) on the other had led to street fights in 1327. After extensive negotiations and an enforced cooling off period, the mayor and aldermen had the representatives of the gilds meet together and arrange a compromise. To seal the bargain, the parties agreed that if any in their ranks started the fight again and were found guilty of doing so, the offender's gild would pay ten tuns of wine to the other party and ten tuns of wine to the mayor and aldermen.[25] These examples show that in the fourteenth century the mayor increasingly had sufficient respect to successfully quell intergild squabbles through arbitration or negotiation.[26] When the disturbances were between competing mayoral candidates, however, major problems still arose, and the crown, ever vigilant for an opportunity to intervene in London's affairs, did so.

Crises of the Late Fourteenth Century

Although the city government increasingly succeeded in keeping the peace, the city was not immune to the broader currents in the country. The kings' wars were costly to Londoners. The city was called upon repeatedly to send troops, supply equipment, and make loans and outright gifts. The plague in 1348–49 hit London more severely than the rest of the country; the city lost perhaps half of its population. Burial of the dead required the opening of new graveyards outside the city gates.[27] By the end of the century, houses and shops were reported to be in disrepair. The royal government's repressive measures in response to the depopulation—the Ordinance of Laborers (1349) and the Statute of Laborers (1351)—had an impact on London, as it did on the countryside. Both measures tried to fix prices and wages at the levels they had been before the plague. Although the statute was hard to enforce, its sporadic enforcement caused considerable tensions. A depleted work force should have caused the price of wages and goods to rise, but the statute tried to thwart the law of supply and demand.

The 1350 dispute between the Fusters, makers of the wooden frame of saddles (the saddletree), and the Saddlers, who provided the leather cover for the saddles, illustrates the tensions that arose in the immediate post-plague period. The Saddlers charged that the Fusters were selling saddletrees for 2s. or 30d. apiece, when they used to cost only 6d. or 7d., pointing out that the cost of wood remained at the pre-plague price of 3d. The Saddlers also complained that the Fusters had agreed not to take any apprentices, so that they could restrict the number of members in their gild and thereby control the prices. The Saddlers further alleged that the Fusters were trying to get a charter from the king that would restrict trade to those who were now in the gild. The Fusters pleaded not guilty, and one of them volunteered that he had taken an apprentice in the last year. The mayor's court jury, however, found that the Fusters were selling saddletrees for 40d. apiece, even though wood had not gone up in price.

The Saddlers argued that "owing the mischief caused by the Pestilence during the last two years" a new scale of prices should be adopted for a year or two until prices reverted to their former pre-plague levels and that the Fusters should take apprentices. The Fusters responded that "owing to a life of labor they were now feeble in strength, that they could not find apprentices or serving men to help them, and that at a time when they needed more comfort in the matter of food and clothing, conditions were so evil that a gallon of beer cost 2d. instead of 1d. and other necessaries had also risen in like proportion." They could not sell saddletrees at the price the Saddlers wanted because "they would be spending more in a year than they could earn in three." The mayor mediated the dispute and came up with an adjusted price that was acceptable to both sides.[28]

The mayor was called upon to make interventions in a number of similar disputes and attempted to set prices. The courts heard cases of violations of the Statute of Laborers, in which men accused one another of enticing away their servants. The hoped-for normalcy did not occur, and plague revisited virtually every generation, leaving London's population depleted. Furthermore, a new type of taxation, the poll tax on all people age fifteen and above, placed an undue burden on the poorer population of England. When the Poll Tax of 1380 did not garner as much revenue as had the previous one, and there had been no reoccurrence of plague to account for the loss of taxpayers, it became apparent that tax evasion was rampant. When the royal government then tried to re-impose the tax the next year, revolts broke out in June in the counties bordering London. Rebel groups from Kent, Sussex, and Essex converged on London. Either the disaffected commoners of London or perhaps even some of the aldermen let the rebels into the city. The Rising of 1381, or the Peasant Revolt, immersed London in violence. There were beheadings in the streets, as well as looting and drunken brawls. The Duke of Lancaster's Savoy Palace was destroyed, and the king's ministers were murdered in the Tower. Young Richard II, only fourteen at the time, made several attempts to placate the rebels. With the help of the mayor he managed to get them outside the city and to disperse by promising them manumission from serfdom. The whole story of the revolt need not be told here, since it has been well studied.[29]

London was experiencing its own crisis involving access to the major city offices. The election of John of Northampton, a Draper, as mayor in October following on the revolt brought to the fore tensions that had been riling the city elites prior to the revolt and had little to do with it. The governmental crisis had a number of causes. The war in France had gone very poorly. Issues over the lucrative wool trade had pitted the Grocers and Fishmongers, both belonging to the Merchants of the Staple,[30] who had the exclusive right to carry wool to Flanders by sea and bring back retail items in their ships, against the Drapers and Mercers, who exported English cloth and sold retail at home. The leader of the Staplers' party was Nicholas Brembre, and the leader of the Mercers and Drapers was John of Northampton. Bullion was in short supply, causing economic hardship.³¹ Richard II's uncle, John of Gaunt (Duke of Lancaster), played a large role in governing the kingdom, and his meddling in city politics had led to greater factionalization. Finally, there was growing resentment in the craft gilds against the oligarchy, who had gained control over the civic offices and the court of aldermen. Although historians no longer see the struggle between Northampton and Brembre as having been between the victualing trades and the nonvictualing trades, the high prices of food and goods that resulted from the economic problems added to unrest.³² John of Northampton, something of a demagogue, had been raising mobs of the discontented denizens and inciting violence in the city.³³

John of Northampton wanted to break the power of the Staplers, who held the offices of aldermen, sheriffs, and mayor, by limiting the term of alderman to one year and placing the election of the Common Council in the hands of the gilds instead of the wards. Since the wards elected the representatives to the Common Council, and the aldermen selected the candidates who would be elected, the elite controlled council membership. Northampton had the constitution revised to spread office holding around. Although the changes were in effect from 1376 to 1397, the new provisions were largely ignored. Being an alderman was financially burdensome, and few wanted to take time from their businesses or money from their purses to take the office. It was easier to keep electing those who were willing to serve. The election of common councilors from the misteries lasted only until 1384, when the king threatened to take matters into his own hands because of the disturbances and the incompetence of those running the city.³⁴

Both the initiation of Northampton's constitutional reforms and the gradual eroding and eventual abandonment of them took place amid the power struggle between John of Northampton and his party and Nicholas Brembre and his party. Both men were wealthy, although Brembre's wealth certainly outstripped that of his rival. Part of Northampton's power came from his alliance with the Duke of Lancaster, and it might have been in an attempt to propitiate the duke that Northampton was elected mayor after the revolt of 1381. Northampton immediately began a vigorous campaign to push his agenda of attacking the merchant elite.³⁵ His first target was the Fishmongers gild. Cloaking his attacks as an effort to lower the price of fish for the common people, he threw open the market for fish to everyone, citizen or not. He accused leading Fishmongers of slander and co-opted the Grocers to serve on the condemning jury. He threatened to bring one fishmonger before the Royal Council. Again, the threat of royal intervention through the duke was enough to stop the opposition party. Northampton was re-elected in 1382 with the support of both Richard II and the duke. Having gained a new term, Northampton pursued his goal of excluding the long-distance traders from the right to hold the offices of mayor and sheriff.

But Northampton went too far, alienating his allies the Mercers. Nicholas Brembre, the Duke of Lancaster's archenemy, was elected mayor in 1383. Northampton then reverted to rabble rousing and led a group of about five hundred Londoners on a march through the streets, assuming that the duke would welcome him. Instead, Brembre arrested Northhampton and imprisoned him in Bembre's home. The new mayor then had Northampton's chief confident, John Constantine, executed.[36] The situation was tense, but the population rallied around Brembre. Northampton's followers continued to cause problems, assaulting Brembre's house in an attempt to release their leader. Northampton was tried before the king and condemned to death, but the sentence was commuted to imprisonment. He was eventually released but took no further part in politics.[37] Brembre, however, ended up alienating the population. He was reelected in 1384 with the king's support, but when the nobility rose against Richard, Brembre was arrested and tried for treason. He was executed in 1388.[38]

Despite the political fights in the city and the shifting alliances with the nobility and the king, London managed to avoid being taken over by the king throughout the disturbances of the 1380s.[39] By 1392, however, Richard II was determined to bring London to its knees. Again, the conflict between the city and the crown could be put to a number of causes. Perhaps the primary one was that Richard needed money and London was the obvious source. In 1389, Richard arranged a truce with France. Parliament felt that its obligation to supply him money was at an end because he was no longer at war. Richard II, in desperate need of money both to carry out his foreign policy and to support his extravagances, tried to secure a loan from London by offering a valuable jewel as security. London refused, perhaps mindful of the fate of Brembre, who had tried to buy royal favor with loans and gifts. Indeed, neither London as a city nor individual merchants had made gifts to the crown for a couple of years.

In 1390, Richard held a tournament in Smithfield outside London. Tournaments were often an occasion for rapprochement with Londoners, but the arrangements only served to separate Londoners from the court and the nobility. The leading Londoners were not invited, although the city as a whole profited from the preparations and the presence of nobility from England and France.[40] Richard complained about a number of small annoyances, including the offal from butchering outside London, the continued unrest in the city being caused by unruly groups, arguments over the extent of privileges of London on the Thames, and so on. These irritants were excuses; the real object was to force London to give him money.

Richard removed the royal government to York, which meant that the Chancery, Exchequer, the law courts, and even the inmates of Fleet prison had to be moved as well. All the official documents were also moved. The removal of the court to York was a great inconvenience for Londoners taking cases there, but even more important was the loss of people coming to Westminster for their cases and thus the loss of customers for inns, victuals, and shops. Richard removed the elected city officials from their offices and arrested them. Taking the city into his hands and revoking its charter, he imposed a warden, Richard Whittington, on the city. The king ordered the city chamberlain to receive all the monies, issues, and profits of his office and give them to the Exchequer.[41] Citing the Statute of 1354, but applying his own misinterpretation of it, he imposed a fine of £100,000 on the city, to be raised from the monies collected by the chamberlain.

Richard's plans did not run smoothly. General unrest had followed the removal of the courts to York. By taking over London's government and resources, the king was in danger of killing his cash cow rather than being able to milk it. A compromise was reached, and Richard agreed to return the court to London. A lavish royal entry greeted Richard II and Queen Anne, including fresh livery, water conduits running with wine, and choruses of youths dressed as angels.[42] Richard granted pardons to the former mayor and sheriffs, and reduced the fine to only £10,000. Finally, he allowed Londoners, at his pleasure, to elect their own mayor and sheriffs, but he did not restore the franchise. The king required that Londoners erect a statue of him and the queen to be displayed on London Bridge. Londoners also provided lavish gifts to the king and queen. By the Parliament of 1394, however, Richard began to reverse his policies, allowing aldermen to serve in office for consecutive years, reversing Northampton's constitutional reform. He also revised the Statute of 1354 to make it less burdensome on the city. But the city's charter was still not restored. In 1397, he made a move that no monarch had made before; he appointed the warden Richard Whittington to be mayor. The king had appointed wardens before, but never a mayor. But Whittington was able to get the charter restored with a "loan" of 10,000 marks to the king.[43]

After the experiencing the fickleness of royalty during Richard's reign, both on the part of dukes and the king, London was cautious about embracing Henry Bolingbroke, King Henry IV. The city sent delegations to Henry and, when the deposed Richard was finally in custody, the mayor, aldermen, and gildsmen went out in their finery to meet Henry and escort him into London. He was given the usual royal coronation procession. Henry was eager to win over London and reconfirmed the city's charter and encouraged the trade in wool.[44] London had had to relearn the lessons of the thirteenth century that meddling in royal discord was fraught with danger. By the fifteenth century, the mayor and aldermen were more interested in maintaining stability in the city than in king making. The long reign of the unstable Henry VI and the subsequent Wars of the Roses kept the civic authorities guessing about which side to support. They were careful to keep out of the fray as much as possible.[45]

The fight between Northampton and Brembre and the showdown with Richard II had left the elite of London not only craving stability but also creating it. The merchants and capitalists of the city had won out and gained control of the government. Aldermen could now serve for life and the ruling elite strictly controlled the election of the mayor. The elite merchants' victory was recorded in the *Liber Albus,* with its brief commentary on the disturbances of the past and its emphasis on the orderly transfer of power. The mayor's position in the city and in the country was secure, and the city's charter was not revoked. Only once more did the trade gilds mount a challenge to the domination of the elite. Ralph Holland, a Taylor, tried to take over the mayoralty with the help of the trade gilds between 1438 and 1444, but his effort failed. On this occasion, the city managed the dispute without royal intervention.[46]

Royal Entries and Civic Displays

Among the city's expensive obligations to the crown were royal entries on the event of the coronation of the king or queen, victories such as that at Agincourt, the birth of an heir, and Richard's reconciliation with the city. The ceremonies, however, were as important to Londoners as they were to the monarch. On these occasions, the city showed its importance to the realm, its elite members displayed on their persons the wealth that accrued to their status, and the commoners enjoyed the free wine that flowed from the city's conduits. The monarch displayed his power over the city. To paint a picture of oppressive expense and competing opulence, however, would distort the symbiotic relationship of the two political entities on such occasions. The parades, pageants, and tournaments were occasions for a large civic party enjoyed by the inhabitants and the honorees alike.

Some of the entertainments were performances. In 1377, on the Sunday before Candlemas, a group of the elite citizens came, disguised and carrying torches, to visit Richard II. One was dressed as an emperor, another as a pope, twenty-four as cardinals, and some wore black masks. They came with minstrels and danced with the lords present. In accordance with the mumming tradition, they played dice with the young king and let him win. They also presented him with valuable gifts.[47] Religious plays performed at Clerkenwell and Skinners' Well drew crowds, and by the late fourteenth century, even the monarchs attended. The town did not sponsor these plays nor were they designed for royalty, but the fact that kings attended indicates the fluid relationship between the crown and the city.[48]

The crown provided some civic entertainments at its own expense. Edward III held several of his tournaments in London. Stow gives a description of the 1331 tournament, explaining that it was held in the widest part of the Cheap. The cobbles were covered with sand so that the horses would not lose their footing. The tournament lasted three days. Edward had a scaffold built across the street so that Queen Philippa and the ladies could watch the event. Unfortunately, the scaffold collapsed, throwing the ladies to the ground and injuring the knights below. Queen Philippa generously requested that the London carpenters not be punished for the collapse of her viewing place. After this incident, the king had a permanent stone structure built on the south side of the Cheap from which royalty could view tournaments and civic processions.[49] Edward favored disguises at his tournaments. In 1331, he and his nobles dressed as Tartars; the theme in 1343 was the pope and twelve cardinals; and in 1359, the king along with four sons and nineteen nobles dressed as the mayor and aldermen. In 1374, Alice Perrers, the king's mistress, dressed as Lady of the Sonne, rode from the Tower through the Cheap accompanied by many lords and ladies, the ladies leading the lords' horses by their bridles.[50] On the whole, the tournaments provided Londoners with an opportunity to make some profit from the preparation and provisioning and also the considerable entertainment. Whereas there was no hint of dissatisfaction with the tournaments of Edward III, that of Richard II in 1392, as we have seen, did not mend relations between the crown and the city.

The city hosted grand entries for the monarch and his family on special occasions.[51] Figure 1.2 shows a map of the royal processions. Already in the thirteenth century, a tower was placed on the great conduit in the Cheap, and red and white wine flowed from it. For the coronation of Edward II, in 1308, the chronicler says that the city was hung with tapestries and looked like "New Jerusalem."[52] The populace broke into spontaneous dancing. There were other royal entries, in addition to tournaments, during the reign of Edward III, but it is the coronation of Richard II that receives the most notice from chroniclers. The tower had become a castle with four towers, each with a maiden who scattered gold leaves and fake florins. A mechanical angel on top of the castle bent down and gave a crown to Richard.[53] One of the most elaborate of the royal entries was the celebration of Henry V's victory at Agincourt in 1415. The mayor, aldermen, sheriffs, and twenty thousand citizens met Henry at Blackheath and accompanied him to the London Bridge with songs. At the bridge was a giant, and on the turrets were a lion and an antelope and many singing angels. The usual rich cloths and tapestries were hung on the buildings, and at Cornhill there was a tower with patriarchs and kings. At the Cheap conduit, which ran with wine, there was another castle with angels singing. Figure 2.1 is a section of the Aggas map of 1560 that shows the Cheap, the Guildhall, the city walls, and the close housing. They progressed to St. Paul's, where the bishops met the king and sang *Te Deum Laudamus*. Londoners obviously had expanded their ceremonial repertoire for royal entries. Not only did they put on a magnificent procession for the monarch and his consort, they also gave a very valuable gift of money or precious objects.[54]

When the young Henry VI made his entry into London, in 1432, after his coronation in Paris, the dress and the pageantry celebrated the mayor's power. Londoners offered a mixed message when they met the king at Blackheath: they were opposed to the war with France but wished to honor the king. They also did not want to be outdone by the Parisians, who had put on a magnificent display for Henry's coronation. The mayor was splendidly dressed in crimson velvet and a great velvet hat that was furred, a gold girdle, and a gold symbol of office around his neck. He looked more like an earl than a merchant. The mayor stood out because the gildsmen wore white garments on which the symbol of their craft was embroidered. The aldermen wore furred scarlet cloaks. Foreigners dressed according to the customs of their countries. The mayor and aldermen rode out to meet the king, as the gildsmen in their white garments lined the way. The mayor magnanimously did not have his sword carried before him, as he ordinarily would have done, because the monarch had not traveled with his regalia. Perhaps the monarch and his advisers hoped for a quieter

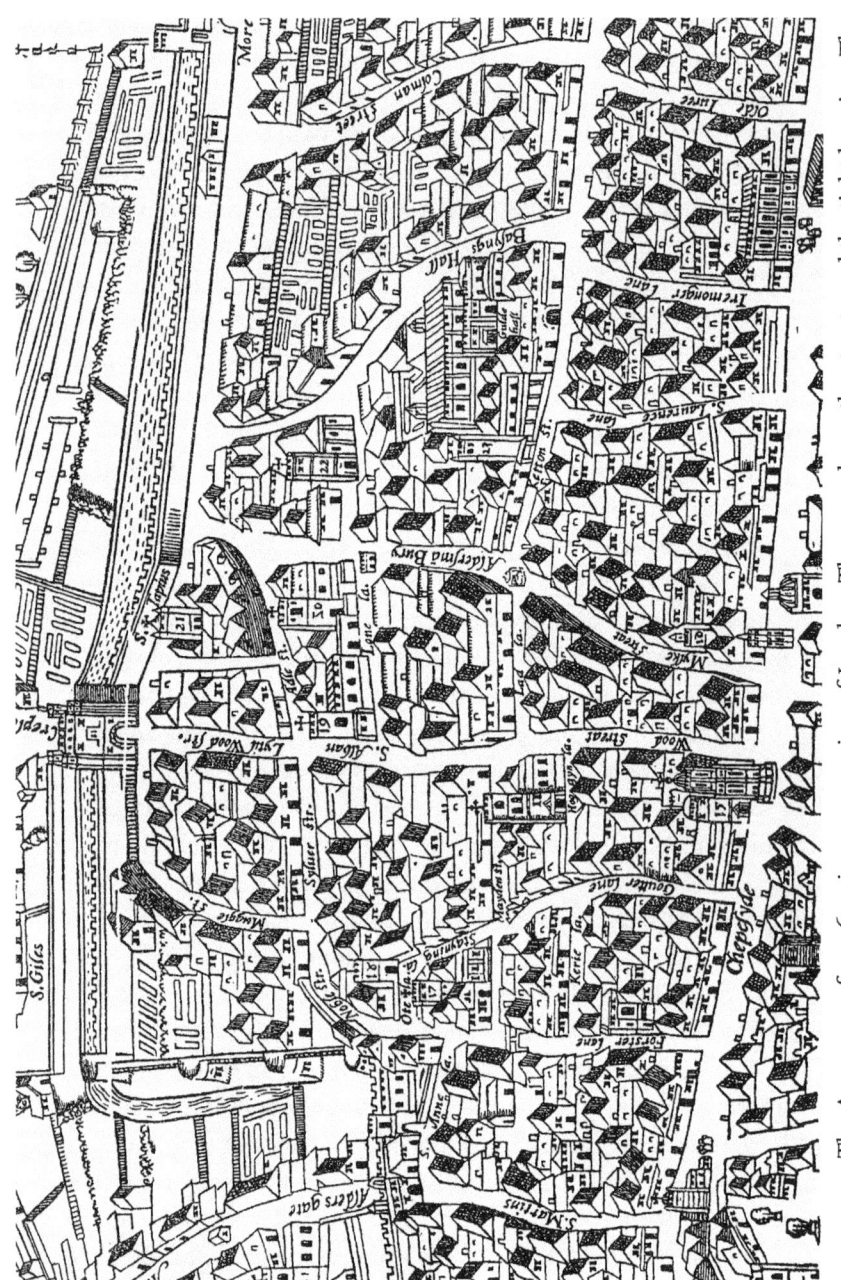

FIGURE 2.1 The Agas map of c. 1560 gives an overview of London. The map shows the streets and the tight housing. The lower part of the map shows the Great and Little Conduits in the middle of the Cheap where the processions took place. The Guildhall is the large building to the northeast. The city walls are clearly shown. Courtesy of the London Metropolitan Archives.

entry. The pageants that had been set up along the route through London demonstrated the importance of the mayor and the city to the monarchy, lecturing the king on the virtues of a good monarch. The city adorned Henry with a beautiful breastplate and other symbols of office. The message was that it was the mayor and aldermen of London who protected the realm, not the other way around.[55] (See Figure 1.2 for a map of royal entries)

By the fifteenth century, the city had come to have confidence that the mayor could negotiate with the monarch, whoever he might be. London had proved to be a formidable unit, with its own powerful government and ceremonies. After the reign of Richard II, the city no longer experienced the revocation of its charter. While it continued to provide money and gifts to the monarchs and staged magnificent and increasingly elaborate royal entries, it had proved to be responsible in keeping the peace in the city and managing its own affairs.

3
Civic Rituals and Elected Officials

IN 1378 THE mayor issued an order to the aldermen: "That you be properly mounted on the morrow of St. Simon and St Jude [October 28] next ensuing, to ride in honor of the City and the Mayor, from the Guildhall to Westminster, on which day he is to take his charge there; and that you be arrayed there in cloak and hood at least, that are particolored in red and scarlet, and white, the red on the right side."[1] The mayor was on his way to take the oath of office at the Exchequer, and this was the most solemn and most spectacular of the civic ceremonies. In a society in which hierarchical authority was most commonly determined by inheritance of title and office, as in the case of royalty and nobility, or sanctified by ordination, as in the case of clergy, elected civic officials had to establish rituals to cement their authority, power, and dominance. The mayors and sheriffs in London and elsewhere were in an anomalous situation of being elected for a one-year term. External symbols of office were as important as the power that they wielded as elected officials or the charters that guaranteed their power. The public processions, elaborate and colorful clothing, musical accompaniment, and rituals of seating at the table all showed the elevated status of the officials. These events were serious matters that indicated the power of office. They were not merely public theater, nor were they costume parties.

London's civic ceremonies grew out of two centuries of popular unrest. The desire for orderliness in the power relations within the city and with the crown is apparent in the *Liber Albus*. As the literary scholar Sheila Lindenbaum has observed, civic rituals are "efficacious by artfully acknowledging and restating [social] differences, presenting them as such a natural part of the total picture that they are not perceived as differences at all." Diverse viewers are thus led to accept the existing power structure.[2]

Civic ceremonies that emphasized the legitimacy of the mayor and the other civic officials were essential to establish recognition and respect for the officers. Although they were expensive affairs, not only for the immediate office holders but also for the gilds that participated in the processions and watches, they were not a form of conspicuous consumption. They were closer to what Bourdieu described as "production of social capital."[3] Rituals preserved the elite's social status and asserted their control of the city's physical space.

Thanks to the city record keepers—chamberlains, recorders, and common clerks—who wrote reflectively about current events and the city's history, we have an insight into the struggles for dominance over the commoners and the compromises and assertions of civic rights against the crown. These men bequeathed their writings to the city or incorporated their views in their compilations of the city's laws and governance practices. The official record, the *Liber Albus*, made in 1419 by John Carpenter, the common clerk, outlined the order of the city after the turmoil of the late fourteenth century. A member of the victorious elite, Carpenter described the election procedures, ceremonies, oaths of office, and the dignity of the mayor's position in the realm. The book contains the script for the mayoral ceremonies and became the stage directions for subsequent centuries.

Recording and Theorizing Civic Power

Although many literate Londoners kept chronicles and collections of documents, of particular interest to this study are the officials who not only kept the city records but also made collections of documents relevant to the city's liberties and governance and expressed their theories of good governance.[4] They were conservatives, wishing to preserve order in the city, promote prosperity, and retain power in the hands of the elite. Londoners were not always loyal to the monarch. Elites could fight bitterly among themselves, and the commoners were often restive, but ongoing disorder was bad for business and bad for relations with the crown. To the winners belonged the writing of history; a theorist for the rights of the commoners does not emerge among these civic authors. When the *Jubilee Book*, Northampton's attempt to reform the government of London, was promulgated in the late fourteenth century, the mayor had it burned on the excuse that it was causing dissentions in the city.[5]

Arnald Fitz Thedmar, who wrote during the reigns of Henry III and Edward I, was the presumed author of *Liber de Antiquis Legibus* and the earliest citizen and civic official to extol the virtue of order.[6] His account is both personal and semiofficial, telling something of his own participation in the events that he recounts. He also tells something of his own history, explaining that his father had come from Germany and had remained in England as a merchant. Fitz Thedmar, also a successful merchant, became an alderman and a participant in the events he recorded, including the struggle between the barons and Henry III. At considerable risk to himself, he took the royalist side. Perhaps because of his royalist support, he came to have an official position similar to that of the later chamberlain; a note at the end of *Liber de Antiquis Legibus* in 1270 says that he had in his custody "the chest of the citizens of London."[7] In addition to notable cases of contention over city law and rights, Fitz Thedmar included letters and writs from the king and others to the mayor and sheriffs, indicating his access to the city archives.[8]

Although Fitz Thedmar espoused the idea that the city's rich and poor should act together as a single body, he laments the disruptions caused by some civic leaders who were demagogues and rabble rousers seeking to fulfill personal ambitions by stirring up the poor. With a nostalgia for an imagined past, he wrote that in previous time "precept had been often given in the Guildhall, before all the people" on behalf of the king "that all persons of the City, rich as well as poor, should be as it were, one body and one man, faithfully and in fealty to maintain the peace of the king."[9] In 1271 a demagogue had raised the mobs against the "discreet men of the city" and had himself forcefully put into the mayor's seat instead of standing for an orderly election. Fitz Thedmar describes the breakdown of civic order under this mayor: bakers went unpunished for selling short-weight loaves; the stocks to punish the bakers fell into ruin; and the sheriffs were corrupt. Hervy, the mayor, suspended the court of common pleas because he had a case in the court. His supporters were "many who have neither lands, rents, nor dwellings in the city, being sons of divers mothers, some of them of servile station, and all of them caring little of nothing about the city's welfare." Some of the more serious men of the city said that "no man ought to hold an office who covets it; seeing that such people think nothing about the welfare of those subject to them, but only about their own promotion."[10] When Fitz Thedmar died, in 1274, the city elite was in control. His account not only emphasized a need for a limited franchise in the city, that is, one that excluded those who were not citizens, but also a strong sense of the virtues required in a mayor. He wanted a mayor who would see that the commoners were fed a legitimate loaf of bread, the staple of the medieval life, and one who valued the city's fortunes more than his own. He expressed a merchant's idea of good civic governance.

The city did not commission Fitz Thedmar's book, but his account of events, charters, notable cases, and civic unrest served as a reference for any official needing a chronology or a precedent. His will does not indicate that he bequeathed his book to the Guildhall, but it was there for one of the city's great chamberlains, Andrew Horn, to consult, and certainly John Carpenter used the book in compiling the *Liber Albus*.

Andrew Horn, who was chamberlain from 1320 to 1328, was both a financial and judicial officer, charged with keeping the city archives and defending the city's privileges as an expert on the the city's customs and liberties. Horn was far more erudite than Fitz Thedmar and more learned in the law, but there are similarities in their collection of original documents for inclusion in their books.[11] In addition to such matters as charters, the assizes of bread and ale, craft ordinances, and lists of civic officials are some unusual pieces, including the Festival of the Pui (a society of foreign merchants in which members competed for the title of "prince" by performing songs and poetry). Of most interest for this study is the inclusion of Brunetto Latini's *Li Livres dou trésor* (The Book of Treasure).[12]

Horn's inclusion of extracts from *Trésor* shows that he read it with care and shifted paragraphs around for greater emphasis. Latini wrote the *Trésor* as an encyclopedia of thirteenth-century knowledge. Its sections on politics were derived from classical authors, including Cicero, Seneca, and Aristotle. The part that Horn extracted was meant as a guide for a *podestá* (an outside administrator hired by some Italian cities to overcome factional strife and run the city). Horn does not mention Latini, and he changes the *podestá* to mayor or governor. He made a separate paragraph "on the discords and struggles which arise in towns through neglect of guardians" blaming the problems on wealth, retinues, and intrigues. No doubt, he spoke to contemporary problems of London and England, since he wrote during the troubled reign of Edward II, when London was involved in the revolt against the king. His insertion of a separate section on the difference between a king and a tyrant, suggests a reference to the reign of Edward II.[13]

What, then, did Horn feel were the important, practical guidelines for the mayor of London that could be derived from a thirteenth-century Italian political theorist? The three pillars of government are justice, reverence, and love. The mayor should be just and pursue the city's prosperity. If he does so, the "burgers and subjects" will reverence him. A good mayor must be in the prime of his life, have nobleness in his bearing rather than through kinship, a sense of justice, a good understanding and knowledge of people and politics, and he should not be quick to anger. Horn was concerned that if the mayors did not possess these traits, the city could slip into factional fighting. Only the more substantial men of the city, who know its laws, should elect the mayor; Horn also recommended that a mayor serve only one term.

Turning to the mayor's duties, Horn's adaptation of Latini recommended that small cases should be settled speedily in the mayor's court and that major offenses should be punished. Punishments made openly serve as examples and instill fear in the subjects, but cruelty in punishment for the sake of instilling fear may be a short-term gain. Officials working for the mayor should not be corrupt and those who advise him should be wise and know the city constitution. A number of platitudes for behavior follow, such as avoiding the seven deadly sins, not talking or laughing too much, and attending mass. Finally, when the mayor gives his speech on leaving office, he should remind his subjects of the good things accomplished and prosperity during his time in office and ask the chamberlain (Horn being one) to continue to judge cases fairly and in accordance with the law. The mayor should be magnanimous and forgive those who had offended against him or his office, provided they are not criminals.[14] London's mayors, if they were effective, seem to have followed the advice; very probably a number of them read Horn's adaptation.

The books that Horn made and bequeathed to the Guildhall were a source for the next great compiler of the laws and customs of London, John Carpenter. Carpenter was appointed common clerk of London in 1417 and served until 1438, but he had already had a career in the government before moving to that office. His praise of London appeared in a florid passage, written before his elevation, as the preamble to an ordinance concerning the sale of eels. "Of all the cities of the West, this city of London, the most ancient, is rendered praiseworthy and famous by the governors thereof, men known to be and to have been persons of experience, and refulgent by their discreetness" and by their diligent laboring for the city.[15] Carpenter was highly respected, serving as a representative to Parliament. At his death, he left his library to various friends and the Guildhall.[16] Although he used the writings and rolls in the city archives, he relied heavily on Fitz Thedmar and Horn for much of the *Liber Albus*.[17]

In his preface to the *Liber Albus*, Carpenter wrote that he had compiled the book because the "fallibility of human memory and the shortness of life do not allow us to gain an accurate knowledge of everything that deserves remembrance." He mentions that one of the threats to the preservation of tradition was that pestilence could carry off all the older men who knew the laws and practices "at the same instant," and that the younger men who replaced them would have limited knowledge, and their ignorance could cause strife. The lasting anxieties of recurrent plague affected Carpenter and probably many others of the elite as well as the poor. He also spoke of the disarray of the archives and the need for ordering the body of materials contained therein. The *Liber Albus* (so named for its white leather cover) was used so extensively over a century that it became dirty and was later called the *Liber Niger*. A fresh copy of the *Liber Albus* was made in the early 16th century. A poem in the fly leaf remarks, "The book that once was white is white no more / Made black with grease, and thumb'd its pages o'er."[18]

Like Fitz Thedmar and Horn before him, Carpenter felt the need to find order after a period of chaos in the city and the country. He wrote during the mayoralty of Richard Whittington, when London and the kingdom had been restored to peace after factional fights over mayoral policy and the meddling of Richard II and the Duke of Lancaster in London's politics. Under Whittington's guidance, London again experienced security. As Carpenter makes clear, the elaborate rituals for the election and installation of the mayor were essential to ensure peaceful succession, and also to keep the government in the hands of the elite.

Carpenter, like Horn, explored the city archives to find historical precedence for the dignity of the mayoralty. Carpenter wrote about the position of the mayor in the feudal hierarchy of the realm. "Ever since England was a kingdom, the honor due to an Earl, as well as in the King's presence as elsewhere, has belonged to the chief officer of London." During his mayoralty, he is treated as an earl— "the sword is borne before him, as before an earl, and not behind him."[19] The mayor's elevated position in the feudal hierarchy was often referred to by chroniclers writing about the mayor or even by the official himself, although the title of Lord Mayor did not come into use until 1535. Carpenter uses the term "chief officer" indicating an elected position, not a hereditary one.[20]

Carpenter's desire for order and elite domination begins with a familiar lament about the disorder of times past and of periods when the king took the governance of London into his hands.[21] Carpenter explains that "in ancient times a vast multitude used to resort to the Guildhall" for elections. Citing Ecclesiasticus, he observed that "a gathering together of the multitude is a thing to be feared, because in such cases riots and tumults may readily occur."[22] The city records give us the composition of these noisy groups: "An exceeding number of apprentices and serving-men, belonging to citizens of the said city, as well as of other men, strangers to the freedom of the city ... [were] so loud and so clamorous" in "their shouting that the Mayor and Alderman were unable to understand the reason for their noise."[23]

Carpenter reflected on the bad old days, or as he called them "ancient times," when the commoners, who were not summoned to the election, rushed to the eastern side of the Guildhall and put forward one candidate only for the mayoralty. The aldermen asserted that because they had to be responsible to the king, they should have a major voice in the election. Carpenter notes that after this tumult, the aldermen and commoners agreed to a procedure that would permit orderly elections.[24] Only the "discrete men" of the ward, selected by the aldermen, would be in the Guildhall to submit a limited number of names to the aldermen, who would actually elect the mayor.[25]

While the *Liber Albus* is chiefly a collection of the city's major royal charters, ordinances and laws, exemplary cases taken from the Letter Books, and a reference guide to them, it is significant that Carpenter began the volume with the election of the mayor, the origins of the aldermen, and the election of sheriffs. His view of government, not surprisingly, was a hierarchical one, and his metaphor for government was a body politic with the mayor as the head; the sheriffs, the eyes; and other officials, the limbs.[26] The script Carpenter recorded for the election of the mayor was not new in 1419; the same ceremony had been performed throughout most of the last half of the fourteenth century, but its inclusion at the beginning of the book demonstrated its importance for the elite.[27]

The elite's reaction to the political turbulence of the late fourteenth century, with its disputed elections, street fights, the execution of one mayor, and the deposition of Richard II, was to legitimate their control of the government by maintaining a written record of their claims. "London's governors needed to make their regime seem unquestionably legitimate, as if it were the inevitable order of things, and for this they needed the skills of literate professionals." The elite commissioned Carpenter to perform this written legitimization.[28] Carpenter performed the task of recording the practice of mayoral elections and writing the script for elections. He was one among many city officials in Europe who wished to have order in process and processions. The late Middle Ages was a time of recording ceremonial activities.[29]

Establishing Official Power through Regulation of Space

The ceremony surrounding mayoral elections as described in the *Liber Albus* illustrates the importance of official space and its uses in the legitimization of official power. The uses of space are similar to blocking a stage so that the principles in the drama occupy the foreground relative to the extras and the chorus. Costuming is also of great importance, and this part of the drama was not lost on the city officials, who had the whole regimen of color codes to fit particular occasions. Lavish dress, furs, bright colors, and gold chains separated officials from commoners. Next was the action across the stage with each actor in the correct position and the principle performers proceeding with ceremonial action and speech. Gestures added to the ceremony's significance; the city elites making the suitable bridge either between the city and a noble or between the city and the commoners (*communarios*). The ritual was theater, and in London, as in Florence, the ceremonies and rituals underscored power.[30]

Carpenter was careful to point out the establishment of precedence in the election. The space within the Guildhall would be limited to those invited to attend. As he wrote: "For which purpose, they [the mayor, sheriffs, and aldermen] nominated the more discreet and more sufficient citizens of each ward, in such number as to them seemed requisite, and had them summoned by name to be present at the election of the mayor."[31] Only citizens of substance could participate in the vote (*probi homines* was the word used). Clearly, this was a victory for the elite over the commoners, although it was cloaked in terms of ancient tradition and royal mandates.[32]

A candidate had to have been an alderman and a sheriff before he could be considered for the office of mayor. He also had to have sufficient wealth to support the office, since officials were not paid. By 1419, it was expensive to be mayor. The ceremony itself had come to involve a number of attendants, who along with the mayor and aldermen, had to have new liveries. In 1389 it had been agreed that noncitizen vendors would pay half of their brokerage fees to the Chamber of the Guildhall to defray the costs of livery for the mayor, aldermen, and recorder on the occasions of the oath taking at Westminster and the Pentecost procession.[33] Many of the expenses of office were paid out of the mayor's personal purse. In addition to the expense, the demands of the office in terms of time were great. The mayor held courts almost daily, and feast days on the Christian calendar brought additional ceremonial occasions. For a mayor who was a successful merchant, there was the added expense of neglecting his business for the term in office. The burden of office became extreme, and thus no one was asked to serve more than one year, although some mayors, including Richard Whittington, served more terms. Carpenter points out that it was well understood that a former mayor could refuse to serve another year, in which case the commons would have to come up with two other candidates.[34]

In 1424, an ordinance was passed that stated "in consideration of the great and increasing expenses incurred by the mayors of that time in comparison to former times," it was agreed that no one who had been mayor should be admitted to the office until a lapse of seven full years. Further ordinances excused men from being mayor more than twice.[35] When William Estfeld agreed to stand for another term, his petition was read and caused a small crisis. The mayor and aldermen adjourned to their chamber to consult. The city's ordinance was quite clear: since Estfeld had served previously, he was not eligible. They decided to take the matter to the Common Council. This body rejected the nomination saying that "the laws made by their ancestors ... should be upheld, lest a thing once done should become a pernicious precedent."[36]

The burdens of the office were so large that already in 1346, some aldermen who were potential candidates absented themselves from the Guildhall. To avoid this problem the mayor, aldermen, and commonalty agreed that the election would take place on October 13 so that the newly elected mayor had time to put his affairs in order before October 28 when he assumed office. An alderman who refused the office of mayor was to be fined 100 marks and an alderman who absented himself at time of the election and the swearing in would be fined £20 unless he had a valid excuse.[37] The ordinance was no idle threat: in 1368, a man who failed to come when elected was fined.[38] Aldermen, however, could be reluctant to serve, and one time-honored solution was to raise a mob to come to the Guildhall at election time and noisily demand another candidate instead. A further ordinance, of 1414, complained that some wealthy citizens who lived in the city and enjoyed its advantages refused to serve, which was contrary to the oath of citizenship that they had taken in the Guildhall. Instead, they "with secret malignity, do not fear at present to infringe upon the good peace and concord of the city" and round up citizens and other persons and prevail on them and their apprentices and serving men to come to the Guildhall. Collecting this crowd, they make an uproar and promote someone else for the office who might not be qualified. The crowding and division into parties resulted daily in "various dissensions and contumelies" and threatened the peace of those dwelling in the city. The mayor and "many of the more reputable and more sufficient men of the city" agreed that they would in future impose a fine of £200 on any man trying to avoid office by this ruse and would imprison any of the mob that accompanied him.[39]

By 1419, the elite had exerted their power over the office and succeeded in excluding the mob. On October 12, "according to custom," a proclamation was made throughout the city informing the commons and aldermen about the impending election and that the selected commons from the wards and aldermen were to go to the Guildhall on October 13. All others would be refused admission. The doors of Guildhall were closed for the election so that the access to electoral space was limited.[40] Mass was said, an innovation with the election of Richard Whittington in 1406.[41] To draw boundaries between the elite and the commoners, the ceremony for the selection of the mayor divided the physical space and power spheres of the Guildhall between the common area and the elite. The recorder announced the reason for their summons; the commoners were to nominate two aldermen who had been sheriffs and were "fit and proper person[s] for the office of mayor." The representatives of the commoners adjourned to the eastern side of the Guildhall, where the sheriffs held their courts. In other words, they met on the less prestigious end of the hall. After selecting two candidates, they instructed their common pleader, the serjeant-at-arms, to traverse the space between them and the current mayor and aldermen, who stood at the opposite end of the hall (the west end), where the mayor was accustomed to holding his court. The common pleader's office permitted him to move between the lower status to the higher status space to make nominations. The elite received the nominations and ascended into an even more restrictive and exalted space, the chamber above the main hall, where they held the actual election.

Descending back into the main hall, the current mayor took the newly elected one by the hand and led him down to the hall to announce his election and instruct the commons to hold themselves in readiness for his installation on the Feast of Apostles Simon and Jude (October 28). This handclasp, the first public, physical contact in the ceremonial process, indicated a passing on of power through the elite. When the mayor and aldermen took their seats, the recorder, who was present at the vote, conveyed the name of the mayor-elect to the commons at the other end of the hall. If the mayor-elect was not present, the mayor, aldermen, and sheriffs would go to his house to inform him of his election.[42] Fifteenth-century elections followed this procedure, and a detailed description of an early sixteenth-century mayoral election demonstrates that the election process still occurred.[43]

The outgoing mayor's act of leading the incoming mayor by the hand had two functions. It showed the continuity of the office and power of the mayor, and it informed the assembled representatives of the commoners about the elevation of a well-known figure as their leader. An analysis of gestures in the Middle Ages emphasized the symbolic efficacy of nonverbal actions, which bestowed meaning and power to political or sacramental rituals. Gestures and the use of space employed in the mayor's election and installation pertain to the efficacy, much of it nonverbal, of establishing his office. As is common in ritual practice, not just words but also gestures had to be executed accurately in the minute, scripted details that both law and custom had established; their strict performance contained a sacral element.[44]

At the installation of the new mayor (fifteen days after the election), the aldermen, city officials, and the commons met for the ceremony in the Guildhall. At ten o'clock in the morning the mayor and all the aldermen were arrayed in cloaks of violet. The common crier called for silence. The recorder, seated to the right of the mayor, announced that in conformity with the ancient usage of the city, a new mayor was to be installed. He spoke of the accomplishments of the outgoing mayor, to which the mayor could respond if he wished. Rather than follow Latini's prescription for the outgoing- mayor to give a speech highlighting his achievements in office, the recorder did it in his stead. Then the mayor vacated his seat to make way for the mayor elect and sat on his left. The traditional words and gestures of efficacy followed. The serjeant-at-arms (town crier) held "the book with the Kalendar, with the effigy of Him Crucified on the outside thereof" (probably the gospels with a martyrology) and the mayor elect placed his hand on the book. The common clerk read the oath that the mayor would take the next day at the Exchequer. Promising to uphold the oath, the new mayor kissed the book. Figure 3.1 is of a late fifteenth-century Bristol ceremony, but the picture represents the London ceremony as well. The former mayor then presented the mayor elect with the Seal

FIGURE 3.1 No illustrations of the mayoral election in London exist, *The Maire of Bristowe is Book* has an illustration of the passage of power between the old mayor and the new in Bristol. The new mayor is in the process of swearing on the gospels as the old mayor holds the book. The recorder reads out the oath. The man opposite the recorder holds the sword of state. The two sheriffs have their symbols of office in their hands. The aldermen array themselves on the right. The space is divided with the commons at the bottom of the picture behind a barrier. Since Bristol copied London's practice, this is an accurate representation.

Courtesy of the Bristol Archives.

of the Statute Merchant and the Seal of the Mayoralty. The mayor elect addressed the people and city officials about the needs of the city, asking the aldermen and sheriffs to aid him in the coming year. The sword of the city was born at the head of a procession in which the current mayor again took the mayor elect by the hand and led him to his home, followed by the aldermen, city officials, and the commons. The sword then preceded the outgoing mayor to his home, since he would carry out the duties of office until the next day when the oath was sworn at the Exchequer.[45]

Because the mayor held office at the sufferance of the crown—or as the *Liber Albus* put it, the mayor was the king's representative in the city—the oath was repeated the next day at the Exchequer and the king was usually present. The royal ceremony established the mayor's dependency and the city's freedoms on the king's pleasure, thereby confirming the mayor's position in the broader hierarchy of the realm. On October 29, the incoming mayor, the old mayor, and the aldermen met at the Guildhall at nine o'clock in the morning. For the oath taking at the Exchequer, they wore particolored cloaks and hoods of red, scarlet, and white, with the red on the right side.[46] The sheriffs were also present, and the guildsmen in the mayor's livery company and the other guildsmen of the city were arrayed in their livery. They processed on horseback through London (by 1453, they went by barge).[47] On the procession to Westminster and back to the city, the space around the mayor was established ritually in order to reinforce the status boundaries that separated the mayor from all others in the city. On the way down the Cheap, the sword was born before the mayor elect at the front of the procession, with the past mayor, aldermen, sheriffs, and those wearing the personal livery of the mayor coming next. Then came the livery companies in order of their prestige.

At the Exchequer, the mayor repeated his oath and the chancellor of the Exchequer admonished him to preserve peace and tranquility in the city and to keep prices reasonable for the city dwellers.[48] The mayor then agreed to be accountable. Special attorneys were appointed to answer challenges to the city's authority should this be needed in the Exchequer, the Common Bench, and the King's Bench.

The procession, in reverse order, then returned to London. The commons in their livery were first, then came the members of the mayor's livery and his livery company, and finally the mayor and aldermen. The very space around the mayor was set off and protected. Since he had no equal in the city, "No person . . . moved so close to the Mayor but that there was a marked space between." To insure and preserve the inviolability of the area around the mayor, the serjeants-at-arms, the mace-bearers with their silver gilt maces, and the mayor's sword-bearer went before him. The two sheriffs were on either side bearing white wands. The recorder and aldermen brought up the rear. They led the mayor to his house and then departed.[49] (See figure 1.2 for the map of the inaugural route.)

A festive dinner was held for a select group, at the new mayor's expense and often at his residence.[50] Following the repast, the mayor went to St. Thomas de Acon, where he was met by the aldermen and the men in his personal livery. The group proceeded to the nave of St. Paul's Cathedral for prayers of thanksgiving to Bishop William, who was credited with gaining recognition of the city's liberties from William the Conqueror. Moving into the churchyard to the tomb of the parents of St. Thomas of Canterbury, they prayed for all Christian souls. Figure 3.2 shows old St. Paul's Cathedral, which played such a prominent role in the city ceremonies. Finally, the procession, holding lighted torches, went through the market at Cheap to the church of St. Thomas, where the mayor and aldermen made an offering of one penny each. That concluded the ceremonial day.[51] The solemn words, orderly procession, and maintenance of the exalted spaces informed onlookers that the mayor was the dominant political figure in the city and that no one but the king had precedence over him. The ceremonies underscored the liberties of the city and the mayor's role as the person charged with maintaining these liberties.

By the sixteenth century, the mayor's procession had become more elaborate, featuring pageants along the way, but in the early fifteenth century the show was the resplendent garments, the stately procession on horseback or by barge, musical accompaniment, and numerous banners. Indeed, a move was made to limit some of the excesses of minstrelsy in the early fifteenth century because the gilds were competing for the number of minstrels they could have marching before their liverymen, which was causing dissension among the gilds. It was ordained that there would be only three bands of minstrels and that they would ride before the mayor and not before the companies.[52] The mayor's riding was a major civic festival in London, celebrated with some rowdiness by the population. Ordinances forbid "disguisings and pageants from the mayor's house to the water and from the water to the mayor's house."[53] The current Lord Mayor's Show is of a later date.[54]

As the mayor of London often declared, the city was a model for other cities in the kingdom, so that it is not a surprise that the election of the mayor in other cities resembled that of London. Norwich's borrowing of

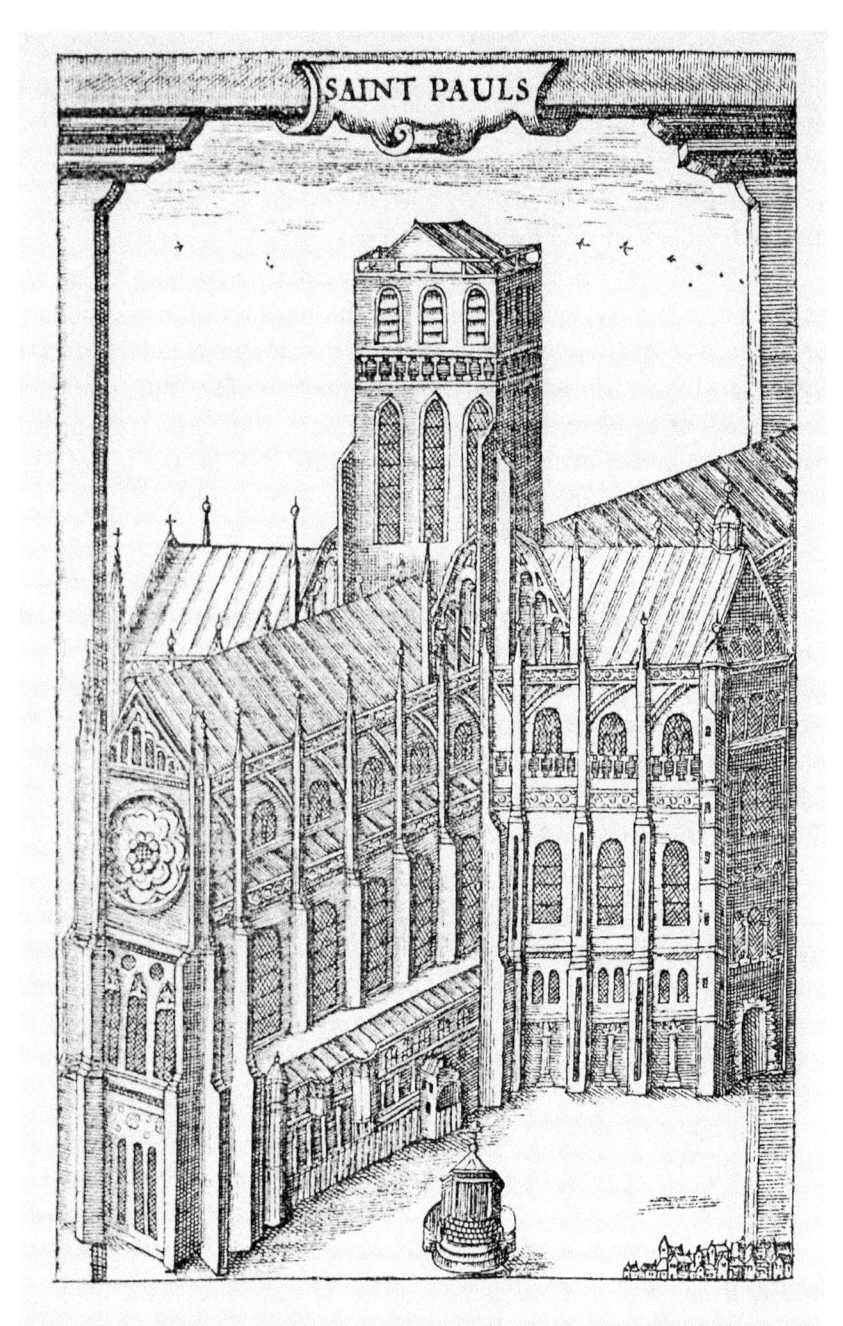

1. S. PAUL'S CATHEDRAL AND PAUL'S CROSS, FROM SPEED'S
MAP OF MIDDLESEX, 1610.

FIGURE 3.2 Old St. Paul's without its medieval steeple from John Speed's map of London.

Reprinted in W. Sparrow Simpson, *S. Paul's Cathedral and Old City Life: Illustrations of Civil and Cathedral Life from the Thirteenth to the Sixteenth Centuries*. London: F. Stock, 1894. Courtesy of the Newberry Library.

the city's election was so close to London's that when their Guildhall was completed in 1412, it had an upper room where the mayor, aldermen, and sheriffs could retreat to accept the nominations for the next mayor from the commoners gathered on the floor of the hall. The commoners sent up two names for the elite to select one as the next mayor. The outgoing mayor then seated the incoming mayor on his right hand in the Guildhall. In a disputed election, the outgoing mayor rejected the nominations from the floor and did not allow a vote, instead choosing his own candidate, led him by the hand to his house thus establishing him as mayor. Placing the emphasis on the ritual act of leading the new mayor to his home instead of voting led to a crisis in city governance that took years to mend.[55]

Bristol also borrowed its election format from London. *Ricart's Kalendar* gives a detailed description of the proceedings. The mayor and then the sheriffs first named a candidate and then the meeting was opened to the assembled group to voice their choices. The person with the most endorsements became the new mayor. The seating of the newly elected mayor next to the outgoing mayor and the leading of the newly elected mayor to his house completed the ritual. After the oath taking, banquets took place at the homes of both men, followed by a procession to the church.[56]

The close similarities of the ceremonies and rituals in these urban settings indicate the solemnity and efficacy of the scripted behavior. The importance of space in the Guildhalls, the words that were spoken, the gestures between the outgoing and incoming mayor, the procession to the home of the new mayor, the carrying of the sword, and the shared meals all contributed to the sense that power had passed from one mayor to the next.

Processions, Livery, and the Household

The mayor's use of ceremony and the demarcation of official space did not end with his inauguration. On November 1, All Saints' Day, not long after taking the oath at the Exchequer, the mayor, his livery company, the sheriffs, the aldermen, and some of the other substantial livery companies met after dinner at the Church of St. Thomas and proceeded to St. Paul's. Inside the cathedral the places assigned to the gilds, mayors, and aldermen again indicated the social status of public officials. The mayor was on the right- hand side of the altar. The aldermen distributed themselves on both sides of the altar according to rank. After the services, they again went on procession. On St. Stephen's Day (December 26), the Feast of the Innocents (December 28), Circumcision (January 1), the Feast of the Epiphany (January 6), the Feast of the Purification of the Virgin (February 2), and other holy days, the mayor and officials held church services and processions. Clothed in their livery robes, they went to St. Paul's, where they stood in their places of honor and heard the Vespers.[57]

Easter week was a major ceremonial time. Here the commoners, both men and women, joined the mayor, aldermen, and sheriffs and in the forenoon on Monday, Tuesday, Wednesday, and Thursday went to the Hospital of the Blessed Virgin Mary outside Bishopsgate to hear a sermon.[58] An early sixteenth-century account of the processions spelled out the required dress. On Good Friday the mayor and aldermen were to wear their pewk (good quality woolen in the fifteenth century) gowns "without chains and tippets." But on Monday and Tuesday of Easter week, the aldermen and sheriffs were to come in furred scarlet gowns with their cloaks and process on horses. At the hospital they were to remove the cloaks to hear the sermon. On Wednesday in Easter week, they were to wear violet gowns and suitable cloaks, but the ladies were to wear black.[59]

Pentecost (Whit Sunday in England) processions underscored the official space of London. In a sense, it was a perambulation of the city, much like beating of the bounds in villages. Before dinner (about nine or ten in the morning) on the Monday in Pentecost, the mayor, aldermen, and sheriffs in their new livery assembled at St. Peter upon Cornhill. Joining them were all those in the mayor's livery and in the sheriffs' livery. On this occasion the two rectors, those of St. Magnus and St. Nicholas, led the procession, followed by the sheriffs and their men in their livery followed by the mayor and the aldermen in their livery. The rector of St. Peter had pride of place at the end of the procession.

The presence of church officials is the only mention of an official clerical role in London's civic processions. In fact, Participation was regarded as a special privilege and the church officials paid the serjeants-at-arms and the mace bearers to protect the rectors from the press of the crowds. If they failed to pay the officials, they faced distraint (official seizure) of property until payment was made. Progressing through the Cheap, they entered the churchyard of St Paul's on the north side where the church officials met them. Together they processed out of the churchyard and entered by the close of Watling Street and so entered the cathedral by the great door on the west. Once in the nave they heard the hymn "Veni Creator" and made offerings on the altar.[60] The second day same group started at St. Bartholomew's in procession with the common people of Middlesex and again arrived at St. Paul's by the Augustine Gate. On the third day, the group met at St. Thomas de Acon and, joined by the commoners of Essex, processed to St. Paul's.[61] In these three days they traversed the city's main thoroughfares to impress the symbol of civic authority on the entire population and on those of the nearby counties.

The *Liber Albus* notes that "shortly before the feast of Pentecost, it was the usage for the mayor and aldermen to meet, and come to a full understanding as to the suits of vestments to be provided," because the suits were a status symbol that upheld the dignity of office. Another custom associated with Pentecost was that an ornamented rod topped with a red rose was to precede the mayor from the church of St. Peter upon Cornhill to the to St. Paul's Cathedral to be offered there "according to ancient custom of the city."[62]

The color schemes for official processions were more closely allied to heraldic colors than ecclesiastical ones.[63] The usual livery worn for the mayor's oath was a particolored outfit of red and white. Red indicated power and strength, and white indicated peace and sincerity. Perhaps the white worn by the gildsmen at the entry ceremony for Henry VI had been an indication of peace and loyalty. Scarlet, which symbolized the law, was also favored. Violet, worn on occasion, suggested justice and sovereignty. Other than the traditional red and white, there is no indication that the committee deciding on the livery thought about the significance of the colors. Being good merchants, they might have made the decision based on what was available or what pleased them. The livery changed at least twice a year, on the oath swearing at the Exchequer and on Pentecost, but Christmas might also bring new robes.[64] So important were robes as the symbol of office that, in 1358, it was ordained that none of the liveries be given or alienated within the year under a penalty of 100s. If a mayor or alderman died within the year, the executors could not alienate or give away his gown that year.[65] By the late fifteenth century, the gowns had gotten so long that the Common Council in 1486 had to limit their length because they were hindering the wearers' the performance of their offices. In the future gowns had to be at least a foot off the ground.[66]

The deliberations of the aldermanic committee to decide on the livery colors are preserved in the *Journals*. Favored colors were scarlet or deep red for Christmas and Pentecost in some years. But violet could be used for Christmas and Pentecost as well. On one occasion when the officials were to meet the Lord Cardinal of England, they wore crimson. The scene must have been a very colorful one since the Cardinal also dressed in a hue of red. But there was some consternation about color for one of Henry VI's arrivals because the men of Coventry, "it was said," would wear green, so the officers and serjeants of the aldermen had to wear motley, and the commoners had to wear light green to distinguish them from the men of Coventry. When the king next came to the city the officials wore scarlet and the serjeants were to wear russet. But the commons on this occasion (four hundred of them) were to wear a deep red.[67]

Clothes not only made the man; they also made the official for the specific occasion. In 1381 the mayor and aldermen had agreed by common consent "for the dignity of the said city" that they would be arrayed for the Feast of Pentecost "in cloaks of green lined with green taffeta." If they failed to do so, they would face punishment from the mayor. The alderman John Sely arrived at St. Peter upon Cornhill wearing a cloak that did not have the green taffeta lining. The mayor and aldermen determined that as a punishment, John should invite them all to his house for a feast. "And this judgment shall extend to all other aldermen hereafter."[68] The punishment for inappropriate dress was an occasion for both a ritual meal and the establishment of a general principle of retribution for the omission.

Two major holidays, those surrounding the winter and summer solstices, worried those who wished to preserve order in the city. The officials and elites had their processions at Christmas, but Christmas was also a traditional time of bacchanalia, including mumming and disguises. People dressed in costumes and wore masks over their faces so that they could not be recognized. The elite did not disapprove of this playacting, rowdiness, dancing, and dicing, since they participated in mumming, occasionally entertaining royalty.[69] But they feared that the London mob might turn to crime and rioting. Starting in the 1370s, city ordinances were issued that warned the aldermen about the Christmas disguisings and asked that watches be posted in the wards and that a curfew be strictly enforced. They forbade the wearing of visors and masks and imposed a curfew of eight o'clock in the evening.[70] The multitude of official processions surrounding the saturnalian period of Christmas might have served as a method of policing, as well as honoring, religious holidays.

The summer solstice was more threatening, perhaps because of the longer hours of daylight (consider the long summer days in England and the long winter nights). By tradition, the festivals of St. John the Baptist (June 24) and Sts. Peter and Paul (June 29) were celebrated by bonfires in the streets and also by popular revels.[71] The elites' fears were practical. Fires could burn down the city, as they had in the past, and the destabilizing effects of a week of misrule might lead to property damage and rebellion. Dissatisfied journeymen, servants, and apprentices could see the midsummer revels as an opportunity for great mischief.

The Midsummer Watch perhaps had its origins in military preparations in the event of invasion, but by the late Middle Ages it had become a time of revels in the streets in many towns.[72] It retained a military flavor in London because the mayor, sheriffs, aldermen and other officials turned out for it armed, so that it became a ceremonial way of controlling the mobs on these potentially riotous nights of celebrations. The antiquarian John Stowe, looking back with nostalgia at his early years, recounted the beauty and color of the Watch in the early sixteen century. He described how the householders spread tables with food to serve to friends and neighbors, invited passersby to participate, settled grievances with their neighbors, and decorated their houses with garlands and lanterns.[73] Perhaps these were the rosy recollections of an old man, because at the time Snow was writing, the Reformation had obliterated the Midsummer Watch.

We have an account of the medieval Midsummer Watch in *Letter Book H*. In 1378 the aldermen were instructed to prepare for the watch of the city on the eves of the festivals of St. John the Baptist and Sts. Peter and Paul. They were to appear with the good men of their ward "armed and arrayed in red and white, particolored (red on the right and white on the left), over armor, and to keep watch over the holidays." The aldermen and their retinue were to meet the mayor at Smithfield on the eve of the feast of St. John and then proceed through the wards of the city. A marching order was given, and different groups of wards gathered under particular signs, such as lances of white with red stars, lances of red, and so on. All were to carry cressets (grated pans containing a fire, mounted on a poll) to light the way. The procession was to make its way through the various wards of the city and to keep order.[74] By 1521, when more complete records permit an understanding of the ceremonial nature of the Midsummer Watch, a distinction was made between the marching watch, most of whom were gild members, and the standing watch, who would keep order within their wards. Although citizens were to keep lanterns going through the night and water buckets by their doors in case of fire, the real peacekeeping was in the hands of the standing watch in the wards and the progression of the mayor. One of the solutions for illuminating the streets and the watch was to have a cresset bearer, as shown in figure 3.3, illuminate the way. Misrule occurred under the surveillance of the elite. These liveried nighttime processions allowed the elite to keep control of the civic and ceremonial space of London when it was most likely to be challenged.[75]

The mayor's space was always filled with liveried officials who were in the pay of the city, whether he was in his house or on official business. The sword bearer was the chief household official and attended the mayor on all occasions. The mace bearers were present at all official functions. Two of them were serjeants of the mayor and four came to be known as serjeants of the chamber and also had functions in the mayor's court. Like all officials, they wanted their own livery, and in 1377 they successfully appealed to Common Council, arguing, "When your said serjeants at great assemblies ought to go before the Mayor, they are not arrayed all in the like suit, but are clad, each of them, differently from and disparagingly as compared with the other serjeants, so that they cannot be known for officers of the city, by reason of the diversity that there is in their vestments." They won their suit and the city paid for their livery.[76] A number of other officials, such as the common crier (serjeant-at-arms), master of the hunt, and so on, attended the mayor at official functions on a rotation, and many of them ate at his expense in his house.[77] The mayor was never without attendants, as would befit a noble of the realm.

Maintenance of the Mayor's Space and Dignity of Office

In his role as mayor he had to defend his status against those who challenged it. In Norwich and elsewhere, the person of the mayor, as well as his official position, carried the legal authority of the office.[78] It was the mayor's responsibility to defend his position in the name of the corporation that he represented. The challenges to mayor's authority from citizens and inhabitants are discussed in chapter 4; here we look at his position as one equal to that of an earl in the realm. Establishing this precedent in face of challenges from an earl required diplomacy.

The mayor of London's position was recognized in the hierarchy and the protocols of the realm. When Henry V announced his planned expedition to France in 1415, he instructed his brothers, John, Duke of Bedford, and Humphrey, Duke of Gloucester, and other powerful nobles, along

CRESSET, AND CRESSET BEARER WITH ATTENDANT

FIGURE 3.3 The Midsummer Watch on June 24 and 29 brought out the mayor, aldermen and sheriffs to patrol the streets. It was time for misrule in the city and the officials patrolled it throughout the night. To light the way cresset bearers carried their polls with blazing fire on top.

From an older illustration, reprinted in Robert Withington, *English* Pageantry: *An Historical Outline*, vol. 1, Cambridge: Harvard University Press, 1918. Courtesy of the Newberry Library.

with the Archbishop of Canterbury and the Bishop of Winchester to meet with the mayor and aldermen at the Guildhall. The question arose of the appropriate seating order for such a powerful company. The lords agreed among themselves that since the mayor was the king's representative in the city, the mayor should sit in the middle of the dais with the archbishop and bishop on his right and the princes on his left.[79] They recognized the mayor's position in the realm by ceding the prestigious space in the Guildhall to him. On a later occasion, the Duke of Gloucester, who was Protector of England by this time, stood to the right of the mayor in the Guildhall. The swords of both men were held before them.[80]

Not all meetings between the nobility and the mayor went as smoothly as these. What happened when an earl challenged the mayor's position within his own space of the city? A noble with an army or large retinue could easily overrun the city and threaten the mayor. A case involving the city of London and the Earl of Derby underscores the fine-tuned posturing that was characteristic of elites when they were dealing with boundaries of behavior. In the autumn of 1342, in the initial phases of the Hundred Years' War, the earl arrived in London with troops armed for war in France. Some members of the earl's retinue got into a skirmish with some Londoners during which a goldsmith was seriously wounded. The circumstances of the fight indicate the prickly relationship between Londoners and members of the nobility. An inquest reported that on the day after the Feast of the Decollation of Saint John (August 29), the goldsmith was in Friday Street when he was "struck lightly" by the hoof of a horse ridden by the Earl's groom. The goldsmith reacted angrily, calling the groom a "ribald" and striking him with his fist and then his knife. One of the groom's companions struck the goldsmith with a sword.

Fearing reprisal from the Earl's army, a delegation of the mayor, aldermen, and several commoners responded immediately and waited on the earl at his inn. The earl threatened not to take his troops to France unless he received satisfaction, but to "visit his enmity upon all citizens of London wherever he found them." Although such action against London was unlikely, a hothead on his way to war was capable of anything. The mayor called the commonality to consider what to do. This body was not very sympathetic with the Earl's complaint, but saw the wisdom of getting him and his army abroad in the service of Edward III. The only solution was to offer the earl a gift to mollify him The next day, several aldermen and commoners were chosen to make the effort to placate the earl. One would think that this would have been considered a most difficult assignment, but the record states that they went with "cheerful demeanor" (*vultu hillari*) and begged the earl not to blame the whole city for the actions of one person, offering him a gift of a thousand casks of wine. "Highly delighted" (*letus et jocundus*), the earl accepted the gift and "insisted on them dining with him, though they begged to be excused." This polite exchange ended after dinner, when the earl decided to meet with the mayor, aldermen, and commonality at Clerkenwell that evening. His honor assuaged, he thanked them for the gift, but released them from the obligation to give it, and immediately left for the continent.[81]

Common to the reconciliation cases among these closer social equals was the offer of propitiation and recompense, with wine as a ceremonial item. For the offended party, particularly if he was perceived as a social equal, as was an earl, the magnanimous response was to forgive or lessen the penalty. In the case of the offended Earl of Derby, the situation was delicate indeed. The mayor, since within the city he was considered to be above earls, could not go on bended knee to the earl. So, instead, some of the aldermen and commons undertook the task. Because of the official equality of the mayor and the earl, for the earl to accept the thousand casks of wine would be an insult to the mayor. The impasse was overcome with a good-humored offer, a jocular acceptance, the offer of a shared meal, and a magnificent gesture of release from both the promised gift and the threat of destruction. The earl, in the end, had traversed the space between his lodgings and the mayor's congregation in order to show how generous and truly noble he was. The rejoicing citizens accompanied the earl out of the city, thereby removing him from their space and preserving that of the mayor and citizens. The wounded goldsmith bore the brunt of the blame at an inquest a few days later. All faces were saved, save his.

The mayor was supposed to uphold his position, not only for himself, but also for the dignity of his office and for the welfare and honor of the whole city. Of major symbolic importance in delineating rank and dignity was the seating at a banquet table. In the city of London, the mayor's rank was "next unto the king in all manner of thing" and so his position relative to the king had precedence over an earl. John Russell, steward to the Duke of Gloucester, observed, in his courtesy book, that while an earl would be of higher status in ordinary circumstances and correctly assume the first place of honor over a mayor, who was listed below a baron, abbot, or chief justice, in London the mayor's rank superseded the ordinary seating rules.[82] But at a banquet given by the serjeants-at-law at the Bishop of Ely's hall in Holborn, in 1464 (Holborn was within the bars and under

London's jurisdiction), the Earl of Worcester came from the washing of hands before the banquet first and took the seat of state in the hall. When the mayor "seynge that hys place was occupyd hylde him contente, and went home a gagne with owt mete or drynke or any thonke, but rewarded hym he dyd as hys dygnyte requyryd of the citte." He took with him the aldermen and all the other city officials that he could find and served them a banquet as magnificent as the one they had just left. The menu included swan and other delicacies, and the table appointments of gold and silver plate were equally grand.

When the hosts discovered the mistake, they tried to make amends by sending meat, wine, bread, and "many dyvers sotelteys." But when their spokesman arrived to present these gifts to the mayor, "he was fulle sore a schamyd that shulde doo ye massage, for the present was not better thenn the servyse of metys was by fore the mayre, and thoroughe owte the hyghe tabylle." The mayor magnanimously thanked the messenger for his concern, but clearly indicated that a mere earl was not going to ruin his dignity by invading his official, ceremonial space. As the record notes, the offense against the mayor was against, not simply his personal dignity, but that of the city. His office required this show of "living well is the best revenge." The chronicler noted, with approval, that "thys the worshippe of the citte was kepte, and not loste for hym."[83]

Establishing precedent with the monarch was difficult, but the ceremonial space accorded to the mayor had to be maintained for the honor of the city. One of privileges that the mayor and city claimed was to serve the king and queen at their coronations. The privilege of being part of the ritual surrounding the coronations was carefully guarded by the feudality of England. The right to be butler, carver, and cup-bearer went to families who had a hereditary right to these roles. The mayor's privilege was to dine at the coronation banquet, where he and selected aldermen were seated at the first table on the left side of the hall, near the king's cupboard. The mayor's privilege was to aid the king's butler, who was a nobleman. After the dinner when the king went into the chamber devoted to spices, the mayor was to serve him a spiced wine. As a reward for this service, the mayor was given the golden cup with a cover from which the king had been served and the ewer as well.

This "ancient privilege" had to be defended, and when Edward IV's coronation was planned, a petition was made to the Duke of Clarence to ensure that the mayor had his place. Permission being granted, the mayor's place was entered into the city's records for future reference.

The petition said that it was the right and duty of the mayor to serve the king at his coronation banquet with a gold cup on a gold laver and that these items should be given to the mayor after the spiced wine was drunk. The cup could be a magnificent gift. Richard III gave the city a gold cup garnished with pearls and precious stones.[84]

The Aldermen and the Sheriffs

Both alderman and sheriff were ancient offices, older than that of the mayor. The aldermen formed an oligarchy of twenty-four men at the beginning of the fourteenth century (by the fifteenth century, Farringdon was divided and the number rose to twenty-five), representing their wards. Various rebellions tried to limit an alderman's term to one year or to have aldermen represent a gild rather than a geographically defined ward, but by the end of the fourteenth century, the office had become one held more or less for life. Indeed, an alderman could only be removed at the pleasure of the king and the mayor acting with other aldermen, but this seldom happened.[85] By the fifteenth century, it was the custom for the ward to present four names to the mayor and the current aldermen and they would then select the man they wanted. The *Liber Albus* instructed that the mayor was to go to the ward and meet with the assembled freemen who would present names of candidates. If this process failed to produce a viable candidate, the mayor and aldermen would intervene and "appoint some man who is honest, rich, and circumspect."[86] All candidates were from the merchant elite. In the terms of the day, they were *substantial* men (wealthy) and *discrete* (liveried members of a powerful gild.)[87] By the middle of the fifteenth century, it was directed that no person should be admitted as an alderman unless he had goods to the value of £1000.[88] It was sometimes hard to get aldermen to serve particular wards. Smaller wards with smaller populations were more desirable, and aldermen did move around to get to a smaller ward. Farringdon Without was considered a difficult ward because of the peacekeeping problems.[89]

The position of alderman could be an onerous one because it required daily administration in both the ward and in the city courts and councils, as well as personal expenditures in raising money either for loans to the crown or gifts to the king. The *Journals* document the reluctance of some Aldermen to serve and the possible punishments and persuasions that could be used to keep them in office. Richard Goslin wished to be discharged from the office, and the court thought that his arguments were reasonable, but it was decided that he would lose his freedom if he did not stay in office. Another alderman asked to be excused, but three other aldermen were deputed to exhort him to stay. It was possible, but costly, to be excused. When John Middleton was exonerated from the office, he had to pay 500 marks toward the conduit in the Cheap, "lest it should be taken as a precedent."[90] Some men did manage to retire when they were too old to carry out the duties of office. Nicholas Wooton retired for reasons of infirmity and an honorable testimony was recorded in praise of his service for forty and more years. Another alderman was allowed to retire because he was "infirm and broken down by old age." But others who wanted to retire were not allowed to do so and were fined.[91] Being an alderman conferred power and the glamor of fine livery, but to some it must have seemed like a life sentence. Nonetheless, it was a highly desirable office for the elite men of the city and one to which they strove to ascend. The position marked a true arrival among the oligarchy of the city and was a badge of financial and political success.

The new aldermen took an oath of office before the mayor and current aldermen at the Guildhall. No other ceremony is recorded, but the office played an essential part in all civic ceremonials. Aldermen wore the robes that the committee decided on and received from the city some supplement for the expense of their livery.[92] While they certainly wore the livery on all the major occasions on the civic calendar, they also wore these robes, or some modification of them, on a daily basis as they conducted business in their wards and at courts. The livery made them immediately recognizable as officers of the law and of the city government. Considering the price of cloth in the Middle Ages, it would seem unusual to wear robes only on specific occasions and to change them several times a year. The rule against selling the robes when an alderman died also points to their daily function of identifying the official. The city could not have someone impersonating an officer of the law.

When Alderman William Wootone went to the Shambles on the Eve of Pentecost in 1388, he looked at the meat that Richard Bole, a butcher, had for sale. He asked Richard the price (London had an official schedule of prices for victuals). The alderman said the price was too high and Richard foolishly responded, "I do verily believe that the meat is too dear for thee; who, I suppose, never bought as much meat as that for thine own use." Taking a closer look at William, Bole saw that he was wearing the hood of an alderman. Getting himself deeper in trouble he said, "Art thou an Alderman?" William answered, "Yea; why askest thou?" To which Richard responded, "It is good thing for thee and thy fellows, the Aldermen, to be so wise and wary, who make but light of riding on the pavement [a raised area in front of shops], as some among ye have been doing." The alderman complained to the mayor, who had Richard arrested. In lieu of spending half a year in Newgate, he was sentenced to leave prison with his head uncovered and his legs and feet bare. He was to carry a lighted wax torch weighing a pound and walk from Newgate through the Shambles, down the Cheap as far as St. Lawrence Land and to the Guildhall to offer the torch at the Chapel there.[93]

Sheriffs were elected yearly, on September 21. Only a select group was present at the election, as was the case with the mayor's election. The mayor selected one of the sheriffs and the Common Council selected the other. The sheriffs were, in the words of John Carpenter, to be "the eyes of the mayor" in keeping watch for him and reporting to him. The job, although it was for one year only, was an onerous one and usually filled by younger men. Each sheriff was responsible to the Exchequer for half the fee farm (a sum negotiated with the king for the amount of tallage due from the county of Middlesex (£300), for the prisons in London, and for holding their courts and keeping the records). They did the dirty work of the mayor. Because it was a difficult post, some candidates tried to avoid it. The *Liber Albus* covered such a contingency by stating that if the sheriff elect failed to appear for his swearing in at the Guildhall, he was to have £100 worth of property confiscated. In one case, the candidate was denied his freedom. For the most part, the candidates served their terms because it could be a step toward an aldermanship and, potentially, to the mayoralty.[94]

The sheriffs swore their oath at the Guildhall on September 28, and the next day, at the Exchequer, since the office was held at the royal pleasure and it was to the Exchequer that they were answerable for the fee farm. The celebrations surrounding the oath taking became increasingly elaborate, and in 1389, the riding of the sheriffs was limited because of the expense. It used to be that men of divers gilds were accustomed to be clothed in a new suit of clothing and to hire horses and incur other expenses at the presentation of the sheriffs on September 29 and to incur similar expenses shortly afterward when the mayor rode to Westminster on October 28. In future, the sheriffs should only give clothing to the city's officers and their own serjeants, and they should no longer ride but go by boat or on foot. Those accompanying them should go in their last clothing and not have new clothing given them, or risk a penalty of 100 marks.[95]

Literate officials, civic ceremonial, and court cases showing the triumph of the mayor's authority all revealed a desire for order and respect for the dignity of civic officers. Horn and Carpenter, lamenting the unrest and riots of the past brought on by rabble-rousers of the nonenfranchised, emphasized the ceremonial aspects of the office of mayor to elevate him above the commoners. Although Carpenter provided a script for the mayoral and shrieval elections and installations, in many respects he was only reporting on the practices at the time. These became more established as the elite consolidated their power in the fifteenth century. By then the elites enjoyed the control that they had gained over the rebellious inhabitants and had won respect from the citizens and from the kings and nobility.

The official rituals did not only advertise the elite's power; they also served to establish in practice the political theory that their position was part of the natural social order of the city. The mayors, aldermen, and sheriffs had a recognized place in the hierarchy of the kingdom, as well as in that of the city. The fifteenth-century elite controlled not only London's politics, but also the civic space and ritual performances. Although the city's official calendar called for processions and ceremonies on holy days, London's civic rituals were secular. The officials met for masses, prayers, and hymns, but the bishop of London and the clergy in general were not leaders of the occasions. Like the lay elite of the realm, the civic officers had their own rituals independent of the Church.

4
Rebellion and Submission

A CASE IN 1415 summed up the governing philosophy of London officials about the relationship between the governors and the governed: "Seeing that all true policy dictates that the more securely and more liberally any city is governed, the more are the rulers and governors thereof beloved and duly honored, their people with fitting obedience holding in dread their rule."[1] The record of the case, perhaps recorded by John Carpenter, practically quotes Horn's version of Datini. In establishing a civic culture that permitted the peaceful governing of late medieval London, the mayor and the gilds had to enforce codes of behavior for citizens, apprentices, strangers, and aliens. The expected behavior was already recorded in civic and gild ordinances, as well as in oaths that apprentices, gild members, and citizens took. Transgressions occurred, however, and then the authorities moved quickly to assert their power and punish the rebellious. Slanderers of authorities, people who resisted reprimands and arrests, unruly apprentices and journeymen, committers of frauds, and bawds and prostitutes all had to be punished publicly to serve as examples to the population.[2] The city ordinances and the language used in passing judgments expressed strong censure of obstreperous behavior.[3] The rebels were not the revolutionaries of 1381, nor are the major usurpers of the fifteenth century part of my story. The revolutionaries' stage was the national scene, not the local one of lessons in civics. The people considered here were often just individuals or groups of people who were, as we would now say, pushing the envelope. Their punishment and, perhaps, subsequent exoneration depended on their social status and the degree to which they threatened civic officials or the liberty and reputation of the city.

Punishments were made to fit the status of the offender. Elite offenders pledged large quantities of wine to be given if the offender should misbehave again, but monetary fines could also replace wine, prison, or public humiliation. Symbols that were widely known were common, such as the whetstone that was hung around the neck of a liar. A common punishment was removing some of the offender's clothing. To walk through the streets bareheaded, or without shoes, or to wear a shift in public identified and humiliated the offender. Public spaces in the city were part of the theater of punishment. The punishment of the hurdle dragged through the streets by a horse and accompanied by a tabor and musicians was reserved for the lower ranks, usually tradesmen producing fraudulent goods. The procession ended at the pillory on Cornhill. Distinctive dress or a shaved head might identify bawds and prostitutes. The more elite offenders appeared in the Guildhall in front of an assembly of their peers and the commonality. In addition to these spatial and visual signs, writing might also be used. Sometimes a written statement was attached to the pillory or to the clothing of the person and sometimes hung on the wall of the Guildhall. Oral proclamations of the offenses were common.

The words used to describe the offenses convey the urgency of upholding the city's common good. The king was often included among the victims of insults to the mayor and aldermen. Because the mayor was the king's official in London, those who imputed wrongdoing to the mayor were also attacking the king's authority. The whole of the community of London was endangered by spoiled foods not only because they caused sickness but also because the reputation of the city suffered. Nuisances caused discord and inconvenience in the city. Bawds and prostitutes endangered the city's moral cleanliness and were an abomination. The descriptive terms were part of the shared ethical assumptions of the market place. The language underlining the shock at the breaking of the ethical code was as much a part of the lesson as the punishment.[4] Records of court cases might underscore the moral lapses by saying that the offenders were "not fearing God" or that their offense was "displeasing to God." Because the words are important for understanding the official concepts of good civic behavior as opposed to bad, cases are quoted extensively in this chapter.

Protecting the Official Elite

City officers, by taking slander and insult to the mayor, sheriffs, and aldermen seriously ensured that their dignity was maintained. Words of insult and slander, particularly in public settings, were as serious as physical assaults. In a largely oral society, words were remembered and could undermine the authority of the city governors.[5] When, for instance, William Mayhew slandered the mayor by saying that he had rendered an unjust judgment, the grocer was brought into the full court at Guildhall "and because the aforesaid words had been spoken falsely, maliciously, and expressly redounded to the shame and dishonor of the mayor and other governors of this city, and in order that others might be prevented from speaking like words, it was considered and adjudge, as had previously been done in like cases according to the custom of the city on many other occasions, that the said William should have a year's imprisonment … and pay a fine."[6]

The tradition in the city was that anyone found guilty of striking a civic official would lose his hand, but this draconian measure appeared in only one case, as we saw in chapter 2. The worst punishment was removal of citizenship, because it meant that the offender could not trade in the city.[7] To receive a lighter sentence, the guilty parties had to abase themselves in the mayor's court.[8] In the case of a high-status offender who was of known good repute, the aldermen and mayor could forgive the fine or other punishment on the promise of future good behavior. Such acts of generosity showed the quality of mercy that an elite official could exercise, thereby strengthening his prestige in the city. The city officials had imbibed the lessons that Horn's Datini selection recommended.

The process of mercy can be seen in the actions of John Walcote, alderman of the Ward of Walbrok. In 1388 he summoned the reputable men of his ward to come and discuss various matters touching the king and the city. The bedel of the ward went to the house of Robert Staffertone to summon him, but Staffertone refused to come. When pressed again to attend, Robert told the bedel that the alderman could come to him "that he might then have kissed his buttocks (*culum*)." John Walcote, assuming that "he had used those words unadvisedly and without thought," again sent the bedel to summon Staffertone, and again he refused. John reported the matter to the mayor, who had Robert put in prison. The mayor and aldermen met to determine what should be done because the insult was not just to the particular alderman but also disparaged the king, the mayor, aldermen, and sheriffs "who represent the judicial status of the city, and also because every freeman swears an oath of obedience to the city officers when he is sworn as a citizen." As a result, Robert was to spend forty days in Newgate. On the same day, however, John Walcote "personally entreated" the mayor and aldermen to show mercy. Robert humbly begged forgiveness. He was returned to prison, but on the next day, Palm Sunday, he was taken to his house. His sentence was that "between the eighth and ninth hour, before dinner, with his head uncovered and attended by an officer of the city," he should carry a lighted wax candle, weighing two pounds, through Walbroke, Bokelersbury, and so by the Conduit and Cheap to St. Laurence Lane in the Old Jewry, and along that lane to the Chapel of the Guildhall. He completed this humiliation, presented the wax candle to the Chapel, and was released from his prison sentence.[9]

When Gerard Corpe made his protest and slanders at the Guildhall, he did so in public and at the city's most important civic occasion. Within the ceremonial space involving the solemn installation of the new mayor in 1339, Corpe intervened in the oath taking of the new mayor, Andrew Aubry, to complain about the laudation of the outgoing mayor, Henry Darci. The protest was dramatic. "Full of wrath," he jumped on the counter, the table at which accounts were taken and at which the city clerks sat, and "uttered words of contumely against Henry Darci, threatening him, and imputing to him that when he was mayor, he called him, Gerard, a malefactor and common rifler (plunderer)." The record in the *Letter Book F* seems to express the horror of this event because it goes on to say, in a rather shocked tone: "the same Gerard there with divers oaths affirmed, that no words had been uttered in the City for twenty years past at a dearer rate than those would prove to have been, by reason of his revenge." Gerard asserted that he could produce twenty men of his rank to testify that he was not a "rifler." A vindication of the character of someone such as Gerard could be done through the oaths of a number of honest citizens who avowed that he was of good repute. We have reason to believe that the account is accurate, for the record tells us that the threats and reproofs were heard by all present, including the mayor, aldermen, commonality, and, most importantly, the city clerk, who took it all down.

Gerard was sent to Newgate, the prison for felons. Gerard's rebellion lasted only four days. He went humbly before the mayor, aldermen, commonality, and Henry Darci on November 2, acknowledged his slander, and asked Darci for pardon. He also asked the others present for pardon. He agreed that he would bind himself and all his goods, moveable and immoveable, to the value of forty casks of wine to be paid to the commonality should he offend again. He then made an oath that he would keep the peace and found twelve men who would stand surety for his compliance.[10]

Gerard Corpe came from a distinguished family of the Pepperer's gild (Grocers). His father had served as an alderman and his brothers or close relations were also members of the gild. Perhaps Gerald had thought that Mayor Aubrey, a Pepperer, would take his side, but instead the mayor chose to uphold the dignity of the mayoral office by throwing Corpe into Newgate. The permitted reconciliation was consistent with someone of the rank of the Corpe family. But Gerald seems to have been a bad apple. In 1342, he was accused of assaulting an Italian and his servant was accused of being obstreperous with the night watch.[11]

The slander of officials took various forms. One man was accused of neighing like a horse as the mayor and aldermen rode by.[12] Another said of Mayor Hamo de Chigwell that he was "the worst worm (*pessimus vermis*) that had come to London for twenty years, that there would be no peace in the City so long as he was alive, and that it would be a good thing if his head was cut off."[13] Thomas Mayneld, a grocer, had been found guilty of "irregular and sinister doings and sayings" in his ward and compared the actions of William Sevenok, the alderman, to those of Mayor Nicholas Brembre. He pointed out that Brembre, "a man lately of as high dignity in the City, and even higher than he [Sevenok] ... was afterwards drawn and hanged." Mayneld was sentenced to a year and a day in prison, but Sevenok intervened on his behalf saying that a year imprisonment would "entail the utmost distress" and asked that he be released on a bond of £200 for his future good behavior.[14] Mayneld was a distinguished member of the Grocers Gild and a colleague of Sevenoak. Again, a compromise was the expedient solution to his slander.[15]

In 1355, on the feast of the Epiphany, Roger Torold, a vintner, who was sitting and probably drinking with "trustworthy men of the city" and "quite losing his senses, shamefully," reviled Thomas Leggy, the mayor "with abusive and horrible words." As his friends reported to the mayor the next day, he had said "I, Roger Torold, do defy the said mayor, the whole of this Feast-day and the whole of the year next to come, and, what is more, the whole of his life." He also said that if he caught the mayor outside the city, the mayor would never return to the city alive. The mayor, sheriffs, and aldermen met in Guildhall to discuss the matter. Torold was attached and appeared in court, where he admitted to his loose words and put himself on the mercy of those present. He was put in prison while the officials consulted about a "chastisement and punishment that might inspire others with dread of so offending in the future." A week later, he appeared before the officials, as well as an "immense multitude of the Commonalty," and offered of his own volition to pay a hundred tuns of wine. Of course, he was a vintner. This huge promise of wine was reduced to an agreement that he would enter into a bond for £40, to be paid if he offended again.[16] Richard Horn, however, was ordered to pay twenty casks of wine for trespass against the mayor and aldermen, but by special favor the fine was reduced to ten casks, nine of which would be payable if he were convicted of ill behavior again.[17]

Wine was of considerable importance in medieval culture. Gifts of wine could be persuasive with officials, and London did not hesitate to use it in this way.[18] A shared drink at a meal could also bind a peace between feuding gilds. Here the wine was used as expiation for a serious trespass against officials. The vast amounts of wine required for this latter purpose was usually reduced or was replaced by the pledge that it would be paid, or a money equivalent would be posted with a bond if the offender persisted in his behavior. The offender had to find suitable sureties who would guarantee his good behavior and were liable for the amount if he defaulted. This arrangement averted the prescribed year and a day in prison. But only those with an otherwise good reputation and known wealth could make amends in this way.

Other slanderers might serve their prison sentences or might be exposed to public humiliation. One offender, who called the late mayor Nicholas Wottone "Nicholas Wytteles [witless]," among other offenses, had to post a bond of 500 marks for his good behavior. Because he had made his insults and slanders in public, he had to undergo the public punishment of being led through the Cheap with his head uncovered.[19]

Although culprits performed most of their acts of submission in public, writing could be used as well. Serious transgressors' names were written on tablets that were placed in the Guildhall so that anyone who could read would know who they were. In 1354, King Edward III wrote to the mayor on the behalf of Robert of Thame, who was a citizen and a mercer, asking that his name be removed from the tablet because it was "to the everlasting scandal and undoing of his estate." He and four other men had been impeached in the city, fined, imprisoned, and stripped of their citizenship. The final humiliation was that their names were inscribed on a tablet in the Guildhall. Robert's offense is not known; however, in another case, four men who had been collecting taxes in one ward were convicted of extortion, fined, stripped of their citizenship, and had their names written on a tablet in the Guildhall. They said that they had made restitution, paid their fines, begged that their names be removed from the tablet "that was so prejudicial to them," and to be restored to citizenship. The tablet was taken down and destroyed.[20]

Mixing criticism of the mayor with the politics of the day was a very serious offense. William Mayhew, the grocer mentioned earlier, was an outspoken critic of the mayor and aldermen, claiming that the city was poorly governed and that John Constantin, a cordwainer who had been beheaded for starting an insurrection in February 1384 had been falsely executed. William appeared before the authorities and admitted that he had said those words. He was to receive the customary punishment of a year and a day in prison and a fine. Because he was a member of the Grocers' Gild, to which the mayor, Brembre, also belonged, he was allowed to post a bond of £40 for his future good behavior.[21] The city was understandably on edge at this time, for the horrors of the revolt of 1381, when the streets of London were scenes of murder and mayhem, had not been forgotten. Constantin's attempt to raise a riot also came at a time of internal unrest among the governing elites of London.[22]

Dabbling in religion could be as dangerous as commenting on politics. In 1416, John Russell, a woolpacker, mixed himself up with the suppression of Lollards. Lollardy, a heretical religion started by the followers of John Wycliff, had become a major problem in England by the beginning of the fifteenth century. The first statute against Lollards was passed in 1401, and a second one was passed in 1414. Sir John Oldcastle was the head of the sect and had been charged and put in the Tower. He escaped, but was caught and executed in 1417. Meanwhile, a Lollard was tried and executed in London in 1415. Russell, therefore, made his accusations against Thomas Fauconer, a mercer, alderman, and former mayor, in a highly charged atmosphere. He said, within the city and outside it, that Fauconer had been responsible for the burning of Richard Surmyn (or Gurmyn or Turmyn), a convicted Lollard, along with a Letter Patent from the king pardoning him. Richard had been condemned in ecclesiastical court and been turned over to the secular arm—that is, Mayor Fauconer—to be burned. Russell further said that the king was so incensed that his Letter Patent had been ignored that he had Fauconer put in the Tower of London and held until he had paid a fine of £1000. Fauconer was very anti-Lollard, but London on the whole was sympathetic to Lollardy.[23] Fauconer moved swiftly to have Russell condemned to stand at the pillory with a whetstone around his neck for spreading lies. Russell denied that he had said such slanders. Twelve men acted as surety for his appearance and agreed to pay £100 if he failed to come to court. He did not appear. The mayor and aldermen sentenced him in absentia to stand at the pillory in the city on three distinct market days for an hour each day with a whetstone around his neck. Russell, meanwhile, had taken sanctuary in Westminster. The men who stood surety for him were arrested until the sum was paid to the city. They were not wealthy men and implored John to appear before the mayor so that they could get their money back. Eight months later, he went and humbly bowed before the mayor and aldermen and presented a written confession in English. He confessed that he had slandered Fauconer and admitted that his words had also hurt the mayor, aldermen, and the "worshipful estates" of London.[24] After acknowledging his guilt, he no doubt did his time on the pillory with the whetstone.[25]

Many ordinary people who simply had private grievances against the mayor and aldermen had the misfortune or misjudgment to connect them with current politics. John Walpole, a tailor, had a prolonged confrontation with Mayor John Fressh on January 29, 1395. He had an ongoing complaint and bill of trespass against John Botlesham of Bury, who had been a serjeant of the city and keeper of prisoners in Ludgate, a debtor's prison. If the charges were correct—and Walpole was not the only one in the suit complaining of the terrible physical abuse of prisoners and the denial of customary charitable relief—he had reason to be aggrieved. Walpole had received a promise of a settlement of £30, but lost it due to a technicality of law.[26]

The political situation that January was the turbulent one that surrounded the last years of the reign of Richard II and internal struggles in London. According to the jurors' account, Walpole made a number of assaults on the mayor's dignity. First, as the mayor was entering the gate at St. Paul's, Walpole had invaded the mayor's space by approaching him and actually taking hold of his sleeve. Not only the gesture but also the accompanying words were offensive, which the jurors described as "derisive": "Oh mayor, do justice to me." The mayor told Walpole to put his problem in a bill and justice would be done. Walpole was not satisfied, but began to attract the attention of passersby with noisy insults. He shouted, "What use is it to make you a bill when all the magnates of England have made my plea and acknowledge my action?" He had, indeed, contacted the Duke of Lancaster about his case but received no remedy. Mayor Fressh was crossing the churchyard as Walpole shouted insults at him, when he met Sir John Busby and Sir William Bagot, intimates of Richard II. The shrill-voiced critic continued to badger him, calling the serjeant against whom he had a plea "a false ribald and harlot [a rogue or vagabond]" and saying that if he were not one he would make him one. He then accused the mayor again of playing at tables with his serjeant, "harlot as he is." The harassment continued as Walpole followed the mayor through St. Paul's, shouting and taking him by the sleeve. He finally shouted, "Mayor, do me justice, or I will bring such a mob about you that you will be glad to do justice," and at these words of insurrection, the mayor had him arrested and taken to Newgate. But he continued protesting the whole way, insulting six previous mayors as he raised the hue and cry. The jurors said that "a great part of the uproar and rancor in the city ... was spread by the ill-will of John Walpole." He was only released to his sureties after sealing a bond for £100 should he offend again.[27] John Walpole was not a major figure in the political battles to which he referred, but the jurors said that his rancor had been causing disturbances in the city since 1388.

Walpole's case underscores a number of points we have observed about the demands of citizenship, the use of oral accusations in a largely illiterate society, and the boundaries surrounding the mayor's space. Words, gestures, and the violation of the space surrounding the mayor were all significant attacks on the dignity of the office. Walpole had moved into the mayor's space and presumed the intimacy to pluck his sleeve as well as shout at him. The mayor is depicted in the records as maintaining his official dignity throughout by not shouting back at Walpole. Only when confronted with a threat of an insurrection did he have the offender thrown into Newgate prison.

Many people objected in one way or another to the judgments of the mayor's court and to the disciplinary actions of the city officials. Beatrice Bassett called an alderman a "thief" when she was reprimanded for putting refuse in the highway, and Beatrice Langourne called an alderman "a false thief and broken-down old yokel" when arrested for the same offense.[28] Men resorted to insults and even violence when they were facing arrest.[29] When the sheriff's serjeant came to bring William Gedyngton to prison, Gedyngton took the sergeant by the throat and tore his clothes. The record points out that this was an offense against the oath of obedience to city officers that Gedyngton had taken as a citizen.[30] When the mayor summoned Peter Thorndon, a beadle in Tower Ward, to inform him about charges made against his office, the messenger returned saying that the beadle refused to come since "Sunday was not a suitable day, because after dinner the senses are overcome by ale." For this derision of the mayor Thorndon was forced to come.[31]

The respect required for city officials extended to the city laws and institutions as well. Simon le Heaumer was charged with attacking people in the sheriff's court and spitting on the plaintiff. The plaintiff spat back once in Simon's face and then fled so that Simon lost his case by default. Simon was deprived of his citizenship until he paid 2 marks to the plaintiff.[32] Misbehavior in a city court could not be tolerated. Citing a statute that ordained that "no one shall presume to publish or spread false news, or to invent the same whereby dissension, or tendency to dissension or scandal, may be produced between the king and his people," the mayor and alderman committed John Topesfeld, a smith, to the pillory and the whetstone in 1371. Topesfeld had claimed to have overheard that strangers and citizens alike would be allowed to trade freely in London and that in the future all plaints would be taken to Westminster. Since these were lies and completely against London law, he had to be made a spectacle of.[33]

Repeating rumors about the mayor or aldermen also required investigation. William Asshewelle, bedel of the Ward of Cornhill repeated a rumor that John Chircheman and Hugh Fastolfe, both aldermen, had been arrested by the king's council and sent to the Tower on two horses with their hands tied behind their backs and a piece of parchment sewed to the shoulder of the same John explaining the reason for their arrest. And further, the Duke of Gloucester had hit Chircheman in the head. Asshewelle claimed he had heard this in various places in the city and that he had repeated it to other people. He was removed from office and told to report the people who had started the lies to the mayor.[34] The communication of rumors was dangerous in a still largely oral society.[35]

Offenders against the Common Good

City officials had broad concerns about the cleanliness and order of the city, as well as the food supply. Those who infringed on the rules had to be punished and made a spectacle of in order to educate the public about the city ordinances and the punishments for those who did not obey them. Although a comprehensive discussion of all the infractions of city ordinances is not suitable here, a few examples suffice to show how shaming rituals were used to enforce them.[36] The victualing trades, because they were of supreme importance to the reputation of the city and the welfare of the people, are prominent role in the records. Prostitution, pimping, and nuisances threatened the moral reputation of the city. The city officials tried to instill their concepts of civic behavior through the use of emotive and dramatic words to describe perpetrators' deceits and the harm to the city's reputation. Humiliating punishments were prescribed for the offenders. To draw attention to the punishments at the hurdle and stocks, the city paid minstrels to accompany the processions. A proclamation of the reason for the punishment was made at the stocks.[37] The visual, the written, and the oral all came together to impress the lessons on the city's denizens.

The *Liber Custumarum* and the *Liber Albus* set out the customs of the city that reflected the market morality expected of those trading in the city. A preamble to a series of regulations of the victualing trades and other trades in the city referred to them as of "ancient usage" that ought to be proclaimed throughout the city each year after the Feast of St. Michael (or Michaelmas, September 29) so "that the peace of God and the peace of our Lord the King shall be well kept and maintained among denizens and strangers; and that the places and the lanes of the City shall be kept clear of all manner of annoyance, such as dung, rubbish, pigsties, and other annoyances, under heavy penalties."[38] The emphasis on cleanness appears throughout the *Liber Albus* and it extended to moral cleanness, including regulation of prostitutes and bawds.[39] The mayor's oath of office concludes with "in all things which unto the mayor of the said city it pertaineth to do, as well in regulation of victuals as in all other things, well and lawfully you shall behave yourself."[40] An entry by John Carpenter, in *Letter Book I* concerning the importation of Dutch eels, praised the oversight of London's food supply pointing out that the mayor and aldermen "unweariedly labour to end what is for private advantage only, and to increase the public weal; nay even more than this, it is their object that, in these modern times, it may not be for anyone to rave about the supply of anything, and of victuals more especially."[41] Carpenter's reference to the possibility of a popular "rave" if victuals were not abundant was not an idle comment. Medieval urban governments knew that food shortages could give rise to unrest, and they shared in the dominant moral view of the time that the poor must be fed.

Nowhere were the moral assumptions about the market place more important and more often vocalized than in the provision of bread and other victuals for the population.[42] Bread, particularly that made from wheat, was the staple of the English diet providing most of the the population's caloric intake.[43] It was so important that a royal decree established the Assize of Bread (*Assisa Panis*), which was first issued in 1281 and repeated thereafter.[44] The *Liber Albus* contained more specific regulations regarding bread and its quality than for any other provision sold in the city. Control over the supply of bread began with the process of milling the grain. The opportunities for fraud were numerous so that careful scrutiny was essential. As the regulations were reiterated in 1419, "By virtue of the first writ the good men of the city had ordained the punishment of the hurdle for bakers offending against the Assize of Bread and for millers who stole corn." To catch dishonest millers, the city weighed all the corn sent out of the city to be milled and also weighed all the flour coming back into the city. This was to "prevent the practices of mixing chalk, white sand and bran with the flour." The city maintained weights, balances, and weighing houses and charged the millers one halfpenny for each quarter (8 bushels) weighed.[45] The city would impound the horses of millers who were guilty of stealing flour or other frauds. The owner of the mill had to pay to redeem the horse and also to make satisfaction for the stolen flour. The guilty miller was to be put to the hurdle. If both the owner and the miller showed contempt, "all persons shall be forbidden to go to his mill with corn for grinding until such satisfaction shall have been made."[46]

The assize was designed to control the price of a farthing loaf of bread because that was the smallest coin (a quarter of a penny) in circulation and ensure that bread was available to the poor. A farthing would buy a loaf of wastel, the most common wheat bread. Since the price of grain varied considerably from harvest to harvest, the weight of the loaf would vary as well. When the price of wheat went up, the weight of the farthing loaf went down, so that in times of a bad harvest the consumer would get less bread for his or her farthing. The assize made no attempt to control the price of grain but concentrated on regulating the supply of bread.[47]

To comply with the Assize of Bread, London appointed four assayers to determine the weight of bread each year. At the Guildhall, they took an oath before the mayor and aldermen to do the assay well and faithfully "for the profit of the common people of the city and for others coming there." At the feast of St. Michael, the men were "to buy three quarters of corn, one namely upon the Pavement of the Chepe, one at Greschirche or at Billyngesgate, and a third at Queen-Hythe." In other words, they were to buy grain from the year's harvest at the various grain markets. The assayers were not connected to baking or milling but came from a variety of trades. Assaying was such an important position that many of the assayers were aldermen or later became civic officials, such as chamberlains, sheriffs, and even mayors.[48] The prestige of their membership indicates the importance that the city put on the assay and suggests that some of the assayers were also responsible for the rhetoric of the court cases. The position carried both legal and moral authority.

After the feast of St. Michael, the assayers gave the grain to bakers to make "wastrel, light bread, and brown bread." After baking the bread, "with great diligence" they were to present the hot loaves to the mayor and aldermen, who were to weigh them while still hot. The weight of the loaves was used to calculate how many half-penny loaves could be baked from a quarter of grain, calculating the price of the grain in halfpennies. The weight of these loaves, then, became the standard weight for the sale of bread of these qualities in the city for the year. The price of the loaf was determined by the price of grain, taking into consideration the expenses involved in producing the bread.[49] The public nature of the assay offered a visible reassurance to consumers of the effectiveness of the civic government and gave transparency to the process.[50]

Suitable punishments for fraudulent bakers were outlined in the *Liber Custumarum*. A baker making bad or lightweight bread would be drawn on a hurdle through the city's widest streets from the Guildhall to the baker's house, with the faulty loaf hanging from his neck. For a second offense, he would be drawn on a hurdle through the great street of the Cheap to the pillory on Cornhill where he would stand for an hour. The third offense called for the forfeiture of the whole oven of bread to the king. The ovens were very large so to lose the whole of an oven of bread would be a considerable loss. The fourth offense led the loss of the oven of bread and expulsion from the trade of bakers.[51] Only the most egregious offenders and recidivists received the humiliating and economically devastating punishments; others were warned and fined.[52]

The use of space for these punishments is instructive. The Guildhall was where the baker was tried and convicted. The evidence presented against him was the fraudulent loaf, which was then suspended around his neck. He was confined to a hurdle and drawn through the paved and dirty main streets to his own home. Since most of his customers would be the people in his neighborhood, this exposure would be bad for his business. The additional offenses led to a parade on the hurdle, with musical accompaniment, to the stocks on Cornhill. Figure 4.1 shows William Abcot, a baker, on a hurdle behind a sprightly horse. Not only bakers, but also other offenders against city ordinances were treated to the same uncomfortable procession to the stocks. City streets became a location for shaming rituals.

The illustration at the beginning of the *Liber de Assisa Panis* shows a prosperous man at his oven, but in the next picture he is bareheaded and unshod; his hands and feet are bound; the offending dough hangs

FIGURE 4.1 The clerk taking down the case of the baker, John Abcock, drew a sketch of him being drawn on a hurdle in the *Journals of the Common Council*, COL/CC/01/01/05.
Photo by author, with permission from the London Metropolitan Archives.

from his neck, and he is being dragged on the hurdle. The exposure of his flesh—the bare head and feet—was typical of medieval humiliation rituals. The pillories are also illustrated and appear to be tall enough for people to easily see the offender. There are holes for both hands and the head and a board across the upright beam for the person to stand on. Women were allowed a seated pillory called a thew.[53]

John Bird, possibly the subject of the illustration, was one of the most notorious examples of a deceitful baker. The language of the case illustrates the terms used to describe fraud and the emotional implications for the community at large. On June 4, 1327, Bird was attached to answer "certain falsehood, malice and deceit, by him committed to the nuisance of the common people." His falsehood consisted of "skillfully and artfully" causing a certain hole to be made upon a table of his called a *moldingborde*." The board was designed like a mousetrap with a wicket that could be closed or opened. When his neighbors brought dough for making bread, John would hide one of his servants under the table. The servant would open the wicket and when John kneaded the bread, the servant would collect bits of dough until he had a great deal of dough. The loaves Bird baked would then be underweight. The record says that this caused "great loss to all his neighbors and persons living near" and to anyone who brought dough to him to make into loaves. The offense went beyond the harm to the immediate victims and involved the scandal and disgrace of the whole city and, especially, of the mayor and bailiffs, who were required to uphold the Assize of Bread. His deception was called a fraud (*fraude*). He and nine other bakers and two bakresses were accused of the "fraudulent and malicious" practice of making bread with a moldboard that had holes in it. The city said that John and the others had "falsely, maliciously, and deceptively" sold the underweight bread "to the great damage of the neighborhood and the scandal of the city." The mayor and aldermen concluded that the matter would be judged as a species of theft and that it was "neither consonant with right nor pleasing to God that such falsehood, deceit, and malice, shall go unpunished." The tables were to be "utterly destroyed" and the offenders would be drawn through the street on a hurdle with some of the dough hanging around their necks. They were to stand at the pillory for a day until Vespers at St. Paul's.[54]

The other offense in selling bread was adding filth to it that made it unwholesome or provided bulk. To avoid the introduction of foreign matter into bread, a London ordinance forbade bakers to start their fires with ferns, stubble, straw, or reeds.[55] But the potential impurities that might enter into bread from these practices pale in comparison to some of the charges that appear in the Assize of Bread. John de Strode was accused of making bread that contained filth and cobwebs, and Richard Heyne not only sold short-weight loaves, but also mixed sand into his bread. Both were forced to stand at the pillory. Heyne's had the offending bread was carried before him on a lance.[56]

Horse bread, loaves made with beans and peas and bran but no grain, could also be fraudulently sold.[57] Since horse bread was not covered by the assize, cheating was rampant among hostellers, who bought bread in Southwark or made it in their own ovens. A city ordinance directed them to buy horse bread from city bakers and to insure the quality by putting the maker's mark on it.[58] Richard le Young was accused of a number of fraudulent practices for which he was put to the hurdle. He had sold horse bread without the proper baker's mark and sold loaves of lightweight bread using a false peck (a quarter bushel) measure.[59] A baker who sold sixteen loaves of deficient horse bread was paraded on a hurdle with a loaf of the bread hanging from his neck in the front and a bundle of hay on his back.[60]

Bakers did not take punishment for their fraud passively. One baker, Richard Davy, who underwent the discomfort and humiliation of riding the hurdle accompanied by rough music, got off the hurdle at his home, went inside, and came out with a big bone, which he threw at the tabor (type of drum), breaking it through the middle.[61] Another baker called the mayor and aldermen liars for impugning the quality of his bread; he was forced to stand at the pillory with a whetstone around his neck.[62]

A trade allied to the bakers was that of the provisioners of cooked food and pies. The city relied on expert cooks to determine if prepared food was wholesome. When Robert de Pokebrokie, a chaplain, complained that Henry de Walmesford, a cook, had sold him veal that was "hashed up, stinking and abominable to the human race, to the scandal and opprobrium of the City and the manifest danger of the plaintiff and his friends," six cooks testified independently that the meat was good. The mayor and aldermen called for a further examination, and all the experts testified that the meat was "good and wholesome."[63] By contrast, Henry Pecche prosecuted Henry de Passelewe, a cook, in 1351, for selling him two putrid capons baked in pastry. Pecche and his guests, who were hungry, ate through almost the whole of the first pastry before they discovered that it was "putrid and stinking." Pecche opened the second one and found that it was, as well. Pecche protested that Henry de Passelewe had sold putrid and stinking capons that were "an abomination to mankind, to the scandal, contempt, and disgrace of all the city" and risked the life of the plaintiff and his friends. The cook said that they were good when he sold them. The court brought in "good and trusty men of the trade" of piebakers to examine the second capon. They concluded that the birds were rotten when they were sold. Henry de Passelewe was to be taken to the pillory with the capon carried before him; he was to stay there for the space of a one-league journey during the daytime, and a public announcement was to be made at the pillory about his offense.[64]

Cooks and piebakers were sworn to examine their trade practices periodically to make sure that prices were reasonable and the food healthy. They were to report offenses to the mayor and aldermen.[65] In 1379, a special ordinance was passed pointing out that the pastelers of the city have "baked in pasties rabbits, geese, and garbage (giblets) not befitting and sometimes stinking, in deceit of the people and have baked beef in pasties and sold the same for venison." A schedule of punishments was proclaimed for those who sold such pies.[66]

Given the lack of refrigeration, poultry, meat, and fish could quickly become unfit to eat. For those who sold putrid fowl, meat, and fish, the usual punishment was a public proclamation of the deficiency of the items, time standing at the pillory for the offender, and the additional punishment of having the spoiled birds or fish burned under their noses.[67] This was the fate of John Russelle, who was accused of trying to sell thirty-seven pigeons that were "putrid, rotten, stinking and abominable to the human race" as well as being a disgrace to the city. The poulterers who were called to testify found that the pigeons were rotten, and John was sentenced to stand at the pillory while the birds were burnt under his nose.[68]

Like cooks, piebakers, and poulterers, reliable butchers were also sworn to see that meat they sold was wholesome and at the right price. In 1349, butchers, selected from the parish of St. Nicholas Shambles, were charged with seeing to it that prices were not raised above what they had been prior to the Black Death. They recommended that flesh from bulls that had not been baited was more wholesome than that of those that had.[69] Sometimes the animals had died of disease, but a butcher tried to sell the "putrid and poisonous" carcasses.[70] Like other offenders who traded spoiled foods, butchers were condemned to stand at the pillory with the bad meat burned under their noses.[71]

An Assize of Ale regulated the quality and measures of ale, just as the Assize of Bread regulated bread. Ale tasters or ale conners were to taste the brews to be sure that they were of the right quality.[72] Most of the offenses, however, were over deficient measures of ale rather than the quality, and the punishment was a fine.[73]

Wine was a very expensive item in London, so it was carefully regulated. The use of wine as propitiation for insults to the mayor indicates that the offender was of a very high status. Since all wine was imported, and since so many foreigners undertook to transport and sell it, London early on appointed scrutineers of wine; these eventually became the master and distinguished members of the Vintner's Gild. Because of the product's high value, the techniques the swindlers used were much more complex than baking sawdust into bread or rotten pigeons into pies. The fines were very high and the offender could lose the right to trade in the city.

London was very concerned about bad wine, as a number of cases in the court books show. In 1419 the city passed an ordinance that virtually gave a recipe for making fraudulent wine. The ordinance complained, "For as much as now a days and long time heretofore, both Englishmen and aliens, in common harm of all the people, and great slander of this

City, naught charging there own untruth and deceit, daily using within this City their wine of Spain, Rochelle, and other remnants of broken, sodden, reboiled, and unthrifty wines of other countries, when they are feeble in color, and naught in value, to put in diverse butts and other vessels, that are here resined and gummed with pitch, and other horrible and unwholesome things, for to reduce and bring again, in deceit of the people, a pleasant color to the sight, and a likely manner drinking of Romney to the smell and taste." In this method, they "sophisticate" and "counterfeit" the wine so that it tastes and looks like a Romney. Any coopers who prepared the barrels for this purpose would be punished. The wine was confiscated and thrown in the gutter, the offender fined and taken to the pillory. Two years after this ordinance, William Horold followed the recipe and made false Romney. "Therefore the mayor and aldermen, willing that every man the rather should eschew such falseness and deceit in time coming, have after the form of the aforesaid Ordinance awarded, that he shall stand here on the pillory this day an hour."[74]

An inquest, in 1427, held before the mayor and aldermen put the Vintners under oath to tell the truth about Gerard Galganet, an alien, who had "sophisticated" his wine. He had six casks of old wine from La Rochelle. It was pale in color and bad tasting. To these he added new Spanish wine, and then he "colored, composed, and sophisticated them with wine cooked and colored to give them a pleasant appearance and delectable taste." These he put into thirteen butts "which had been smeared and lined with diverse gums and resins (*cum diversis gummis et Rasis ... uctis et linitis*)" with the result that it tasted like a good Romney wine. With recipes like this, he was able to sophisticate a number of other wines as well. The jurors condemned him for his "deception of the king's people and ... contempt of the good ordinances of the city.[75]

The punishment for selling bad wine, since the quantities were usually large, was a fine and sometimes imprisonment. In 1430, the mayor, alderman, and the Common Council forbade three foreign brokers to act as wine brokers because of the frauds they had committed. Were they to offend again they would be put in prison for a year, and they or anyone dealing with them would be fined 100s.[76]

In addition to investigating the wine sold by importers and brokers, the Vintners were to appraise wine sold by retail in taverns and to "place a distinctive mark on the vessels" assessing the value of wine they contained. They could ask to see the wine drawn, and the doors to the cellar were to be opened completely so that light came in when they were making their inspection. A local taverner who was guilty of selling unwholesome wine was condemned to the pillory, where he had to drink a draught of his own wine and have the rest poured over his head. He was not to sell wine in the future unless the king permitted him to do so.[77]

Taverners, who were supposed to sell wines at a regulated price, rebelled against the city regulations. The city officials "were given to understand that all the taverners of the city, making confederacy and alliance among them, had closed the doors of their taverns, and would not allow their wines to be sold in contempt of our Lord the King, and to the annulment of the ordinances aforesaid, and the common loss of all the people." This insurrection of the taverners forced the mayor and sheriffs to go through the middle of the Vintry and Cheap and other streets and lanes to find out the names of the miscreants. These taverners were then brought before juries at the Guildhall. The mayor and aldermen thus "put a check on their malignancy."[78]

People who bought goods outside London to sell before they could come to market were a continual problem to the city: "forestalling," as it was called. While many of the purchasers were small-time retailers, both women and men, the problem was so serious in 1423 that a general proclamation was read throughout London against the practice. It stated that the franchise to the citizens of London granted by the king and his predecessors and approved by Parliament ordained that no one should intercept goods and victuals coming by land or sea before they reached the markets of London on pain of imprisonment and confiscation of the merchandise. The mayor and aldermen had learned that many freemen, having no consideration for the said franchise, bought cloth, wool, wine, hides, and the like. in Southwark and other places outside London and took them back to the city to sell. City officials, desiring that no one should claim ignorance of the law, had the proclamation read in the streets of London.[79]

Although the people the proclamation addressed were freemen of London, it also applied to hucksters, women and men who hucked, or haggled, goods in the street as opposed to in shops. Sometimes they were called *regraters*. They bought such goods as grain, malt, salt fish, bread, beer, wine, and prepared foods and resold them in neighborhoods.[80] Sometimes they had stalls or shops, or they simply spread out their goods on the street. In the busy lives of Londoners, hucksters played an important role since they could supply quick meals and drink, making it unnecessary to go to a shop for prepared food.

A few examples clarify these petty economic misdemeanors. Alice, wife of Robert de Caustone was condemned to "la thew," the pillory for women, for thickening the bottom of a quart measure with pitch.[81] Alice le Strengere, who resided in New Temple, and other women who were widows or wives of chandlers were selling wax candles of false weight in December, not only a dark month of winter but also one in which candles played a large role in religious festivities. They were excused, provided that they did not offend again.[82] The methods of these petty hucksters were elucidated in one inquisition. "Elene Steer, Katherine Lylye, wife of Henry Racheford, Margarete Bury, Luce Clerk, Jonet Wodham, Katherine Wylde and all their fellows are forestallers of fish, eggs, chickens, and capons." According to the record, "they rise in the morning and wait in the evening, when such victual or butter or cheese come, and go into the boat and buy it up privily, thus making a dearth of such victuals and hindering common people of the city."[83]

For the city and its officials, a sense of civic values and civic pride assumed dominance in the language of their records. Being businessmen themselves, they subscribed to the ethos of the trading community. They were concerned about the reputation of their city and had some abstract ideas about purity of the body politic, as well as of the bodies of the citizenry. Bad bread, sophisticated wine, and poison pies were bad for the reputation of the city, bad for the health of inhabitants, and a disgrace to elected officials. It was horrible, abominable, foul, unhealthy, and fraudulent to produce bad products, and they did not hesitate to use such language.

In addition to the alimentary health of the population, the city was concerned about moral health. The city's attitude can be found in the preamble to a proclamation from 1439. Responding to sin in the city, the mayor and alderman resolved, "For as much as now of late days many persons in this Cite be found defiled in the detestable sin [of?] lechery ... and many diverse persones also ben common nourishers promoters and provokers of the same sins in displeasure of almighty God and against the laws of this Cite good customs and usages." Because the old ordinances were not being enforced, the misdoers had gown bold. Proclamation was to be made about the intention to enforce the law.[84]

The *Liber Albus* first signaled out male bawds (procurers of prostitutes), since the gender hierarchy of the city put men in first place as offenders to be dealt with in the law. A bawd convicted on the first offense was to have "his head and beard ... shaved, except a fringe on the head, two inches in breadth." He was to be taken to the pillory accompanied by minstrels and set thereon for a period determined by the mayor and aldermen. For a second offense, he was to undergo the same public rituals of humiliation but also ten days of imprisonment. A third conviction carried the same punishment, after which he was taken to a city gate, and "there let him forswear the city forever."[85]

Humiliation rituals were not simply the stuff of legal texts and customary civic recitations of laws. One particularly vivid example from 1517 jolts us into an understanding of how bodies and their articulation became part of the language of medieval rituals of punishment and marginalization. Joan Rawlins wanted to go to London to earn the higher wages as a servant that the city afforded. Her patroness had connections with a tailor, John Barton, and asked him to conduct Joan to London and find her "good and honest service." He took her to the city but left her at the house of a waterman (boater on the river) while he went across the Thames to a bawdy house in Southwark "where he proposed to put her." Realizing his designs, she "begged the waterman's wife on her knees" to be taken to the authorities, which the older woman did. John Barton was convicted, and since he had a previous record of "dishonorable transactions with women," he was imprisoned at Newgate. His punishment was to be paraded about town holding on to a horse's tail, with a paper on his head explaining his crime. The proclamation of his villainy was read at various public places, so that the illiterate, most probably young, serving women, would learn about the dangers of a man such as he. He was then pilloried for a time and conveyed out of the city.[86]

Women were also accused of being bawds and procuresses, but their punishments were in keeping with the gendered assumptions of the day. Any woman who is a "common receiver of courtesans or a bawd" and who has been attainted "let her openly be brought, with minstrels, from prison unto the thew and set there on" for a length of time specified by the mayor and aldermen. Her hair was to be cut but the length was not specified. For women, the cutting of the hair was a more obvious humiliation than for men. Women normally wore hoods or wimples that surrounded their heads, covering the hair and neck. Thus these keepers of bawdy houses were being exposed as no woman, honorable or not, would be and not with long hair but with cropped hair, a primitive symbol of the marginalization of morally offensive women. Imprisonment and exile completed the punishment for repeat offenders.[87]

Alice Boston was tried for selling her apprentice, "late a young damsels, innocent of sin," to various men. Boston was described as a woman "not dreading God nor shaming the world." Her behavior was to the great shame of good people, and her vicious governance should not pass unpunished. The mayor and aldermen ordained that she should be led from prison on three market days, accompanied by pipes and other minstrels, to the stocks and stand three days for an hour as her cause was proclaimed.[88] Elizabeth, wife of Henry Moring, was also accused of being a procuress for her apprentices, to whom she was to teach embroidery. The jury's verdict was that "because through such women and the like deeds and scandals had befallen the city" and "in order that other women might beware of doing like," she should be taken from the Guildhall to Cornhill and put on the thew and remain there for a hour with the cause proclaimed. She was then taken to a city gate and made to forswear the city forever. If she returned she would be imprisoned for three years.[89]

Prostitutes received somewhat different treatment than did bawds. Unlike pimping, procuring, or running a bawdy house, prostitution was acceptable in both civil and canon law. The Church found prostitutes' activities more acceptable than adultery or other forms of sexual sins in which men, including clergy, were likely to engage. The city fathers of late medieval Europe generally found that prostitutes contributed to the city coffers, and so they often ran brothels themselves. London officials did not engage in licensing or running brothels, although they did allow prostitutes to set themselves up in certain places in the city, particularly Cokkeslane, or encouraged them to ply their trade across the river in Southwark. Those practicing elsewhere were subject to arrest and punishment.[90]

The initial offense for prostitution did not require the removal of clothing or cutting of hair but, rather, the addition of clothing and symbols that both covered and identified the woman as a prostitute. The convicted offender was to be taken from prison to Aldgate "with a hood of ray [striped cloth], and a white wand in her hand." The "hood of ray" became a symbol of the blurred and mixed status of the prostitute, just as various items of clothing identified and shamed Jews in other cities at the time.[91] The public parade, accompanied by minstrels, preceded the offender to the thew, where the cause was read; then "she was led through Cheap and Newgate to Cokkeslane where she was to take up her abode." The city law was intent on labeling and signifying on the first offense; only on the third conviction was a prostitute to be rendered unattractive and unmarketable by being shorn, while sitting on the thew, and taken to a city gate and made to forswear the city.[92] Actual cases confirm that the public spectacle was performed.[93]

The preamble to the laws concerning bawds and prostitutes emphasized that the process of punishing them was intended to return the city to "cleanness and honesty."[94] But the ritual humiliations had an educational purpose as well. They indicated to the onlookers, particularly the great number of youths and foreigners who flocked to London each year, that the city would punish those who transgressed the laws. As a byproduct, of course, they also educated those who wished to procure sex for hire about where to go, and whom to look up.

Many of the moral offenses were noted at wardmotes, but these presentments leave no indication of the punishments, since the aldermen sent the complaints to the mayor for action. A wardmote was a meeting of all the male inhabitants of the ward, called together by the alderman for the purpose of reporting moral lapses, defaults, nuisances, and promoting the general well-being of the ward. It was an opportunity for neighbors to bring local irritants and violations to the alderman's attention. The articles that the wardmote addressed were comprehensive and included the identification of strangers not in frankpledge, courtesans and procuresses, rebellious persons, and violators of curfew; the economic offenses of hucksters, bakers, and brewers; building violations, and provisions against fires; obstruction of the right of way; and control of swine, cows, dogs, and ducks.[95]

The most complete picture that we have of deviant behavior comes from the Portsoken Wardmote of 1465 to 1483.[96] Men were accused of being strumpet mongers and barrators (making false charges and maintaining false suits); breaking the peace; acting as free of the city in trade when they were not citizens; and being beggars, night walkers, eavesdroppers, extortionists, or just "suspicious." Married people were often involved in mutual activities of deceit: strumpet monger / strumpet, bawd, scolds, false claimers of free status in order to trade in the city, maintaining servants, and suspicious behavior. Women were accused of being strumpets, bawds, and scolds. The breakdown is similar to that the historian Marjorie McIntosh found in her study of England as a whole.[97]

If the accusations were not prosecuted, what was the use of the exercise in the wardmote? The historian Frank Rexroth has argued that the labeling of those people was punishment enough. They would be shamed in their neighborhoods. If it did not reform their behavior, it at least let everyone know that they were of ill repute. In themselves, the wardmote presentments performed a shaming function.[98]

A more pressing issue than rounding up and shaming bawds and prostitutes was the physical cleanliness of the city. Because of the close living quarters, all sorts of problems arose in connection with obstructed streets, houses encroaching on a neighbor's property, privacy invaded because of wrongly placed windows, noxious fumes, offensive latrines, and runoff rainwater. These were serious issues because they threatened the health of the citizens, and caused tensions in neighborhoods that could disrupt the peace. By tradition, the *Assisa de Edificiis* (building ordinances) was part of London law from an early time and was recopied in all the major compilations, including the *Liber Albus*.[99] The great fires of London in the twelfth and thirteenth centuries prompted the assize of buildings, but the preamble states that it was "for the allying of the contentions that at times arise between neighbors in the city touching boundaries." and other matters of argument.[100] The assize provided guidelines for building and also provisions for bringing private disputes before the mayor and twelve aldermen, who would visit the site to observe the alleged nuisance.[101] To aid them in their deliberations, they might call carpenters and masons to offer expert opinions. The complaints could be about shared walls that encroached on a neighboring building or were dilapidated, gutters that flooded the neighbor's property, broken pavements, cesspits and latrines that were too close to a neighbor's house. One of the most sensitive subjects for medieval Londoners was privacy. Windows and doors that permitted neighbors to overlook their property and see their business were most offensive.

A typical complaint was that of Robert Asshecombe, a citizen, who complained against Robert Accon, also a citizen, and his wife, Mazera. Robert stated that his neighbors had diverse lights, windows, broken down walls and openings to latrines in the tenement adjoining his through which they, their tenants and lessees, and household could see and hear the private business of his tenants, lessees, and household. Moreover, they threw filth and rubbish onto his property and the stench of their latrines was unacceptable. He won his case, and Accon and his wife were forced to repair their building.[102]

London's intricate rituals of exclusion and inclusion into the body politic showed a shrewd awareness of boundaries of the exercise of power, the need for compromise, and the strict enforcement of law. The governing of London required a balanced approach to social status that would permit the wayward citizens to be reintegrated for the promise of future good behavior. The method worked, since many of the offenders and slanderers among the elite went on to become worthy citizens after their affronts. On the other hand, the lower-class slanderers, the bawds and whores, and the offending victualers were subjected to an open, public punishment. The public humiliations were explicit warnings to possible future offenders to avoid these offenses or to the populace not to buy goods from those vendors. The public nature of punishment was didactic. In the process of explaining the reasons for the punishments, the city officials explained their philosophy of governing and the reasons they administered certain punishments.

5

Gilds as Incubators for Citizenship

AT THE INDUCTION ceremony for a new gild member, the candidate had to swear "to keep all the good ordinances of the same craft that have not been repealed, both present and future" and "not disclose the secrets and skills of the said craft but always behave as a good and true man towards your wardens and your company." A further injunction was "to keep the peace of the city to the utmost of your power."[1] By the fourteenth century the gilds were increasingly an extension of the civic government, assuming many of its roles of regulation, dispute settlement, and entrance into the freedom of the city. Gild ordinances existed alongside those of the city, though the city ordinances had precedence. If the gilds failed to manage their members, the miscreants were turned over to the mayor and aldermen for discipline. Gild membership, therefore, already presumed a knowledge of and acceptance of the laws, customs, and governance of the city. The leading members of the most powerful gilds provided the pools of candidates for positions in city governance. The relationship of the gilds to the city government has been described as a "community within a community."[2]

Within each gild a distinction was made between those who wore the livery (the gowns and hoods of the gild) and those who did not. Below these were the apprentices and the journeymen, or bachelors, who had finished their apprenticeships but did not become masters. As apprentices moved through the graduated ranks of membership, they assimilated the desired codes of behavior through their residence with masters, oaths, cultivation of civility, and the discipline in the gild courts. Some scholars have identified the ceremonials surrounding oath taking for membership, the gild common meals, and processions as fundamental to gild identity.[3]

Early fraternities of merchants and crafts were associated with religious and social practices and licensed by the Church rather than by the municipal government. Throughout the Middle Ages, gilds or misteries retained something of their early identification as religious fraternities through their patron saints and religious processions. By the 1320s the associations of craftsmen and merchants had begun procuring charters from the city or from the crown, and the fraternities and associations of like crafts became melded into the more secular misteries or gilds.[4] Royal charters, many granted in the fourteenth and fifteenth centuries, made gilds into corporations and with that development, a gild began the transition to becoming a company.[5] The adoption of livery brought the title of "livery company."

One would think that identifying the gilds would be an easy task, but there was no comprehensive list of them, and some gilds may have existed informally but were not registered anywhere. In 1422, the Brewers' Company clerk listed 111 organized crafts, but his list left out some of the most important crafts.[6] The most prestigious companies in the fifteenth century were the Mercers, Grocers, Drapers, Fishmongers, Goldsmiths, Skinners, Merchant Taylors, Haberdashers, Salters, Ironmongers, and Vintners. The fortunes of the companies rose and fell. The Fishmongers Gild, for instance, was very powerful in the fourteenth century, but suffered some decline in the fifteenth century. The shifting prestige of the different companies accounted for the rivalries over position in civic ceremonials. Most of the gild records did not survive the Great Fire of the seventeenth century, but a scattering of them did, including of the Mercers, Goldsmiths, Brewers, and Grocers, and they give us insights into the internal dynamics of gilds.

Gild Governance

If the gilds were to take over some of the functions of the civic government, they needed cohesive internal governance. As it developed in the late fourteenth century, the gild organization was oligarchic, as was the civic government. Masters and wardens were selected from among the wealthiest members and had considerable control over the gild membership. They served as the intermediaries between the civic and gild organizations, coordinating their enforcement of consumer protection and discipline of members with the mayor and aldermen.

Acquisition of a royal charter from the king fixed the gild's governance.[7] In 1390 the Taylors sought a charter that would permit them to elect a master and four wardens annually, have a livery for the men and women, and hold a feast on St. John the Baptist's day. The Goldsmiths' royal charter followed in 1393 and granted the right "yearly to elect out of themselves four wardens to oversee, rule, and duly govern the said craft and community and all and every member there of." The Skinners and the Mercers followed suit, although the Skinners had a master in addition to the wardens.[8]

Gilds were very similar in the power they gave to the masters and wardens. These officials had a range of gild governance matters to oversee: apprenticeships, the admission of new members, ensuring the quality of the goods produced, and adherence to trade practices; handling gild finances, including managing rental properties; charities; reconciling disputes among members; disciplining wayward members; cooperating with the mayor and aldermen; choosing the livery for the year; and ceremonies, including feasts, processions, and funerals. The position was one requiring good managerial skills and was so demanding that it took up much of the time of the four wardens.

The election of the wardens was a closed system; former wardens appointed their successors. The most prosperous members of the company became wardens, in part because they had the most at stake, but also because they had to have enough wealth to take up the financial burden of the office. Although minor variations existed among the different gilds, most of the elections were closed to the general membership and only announced on the gild feast day. All gilds had elaborate ceremonies for the installation of the new wardens. A feast, paid for in part by the wardens, was held on the saint's day of the gild. The ceremony required all members to be present, wearing in their best livery. Malingerers were fined for nonattendance. After a procession into the gild's hall, the retiring warden passed a garland to the new warden as a symbol of his office. These were then placed on the banquet table. Figure 5.1 shows the garland that pewterers wore at their election as wardens. The ceremony was a way to invoke the members' loyalty to the gild and its wardens and create a sense of camaraderie, cemented with a shared meal. For the master and wardens themselves, it was an assertion of power and recognition of achievement.

The Goldsmiths elected their wardens at the general assembly in April and they took up office in May, on St. Dunstan's Day (May 19), the day of their patron saint. The four incumbent wardens, four ex-wardens, and any alderman who was a gild member elected the new wardens. The election breakfast was a generous one in which all the members participated, even

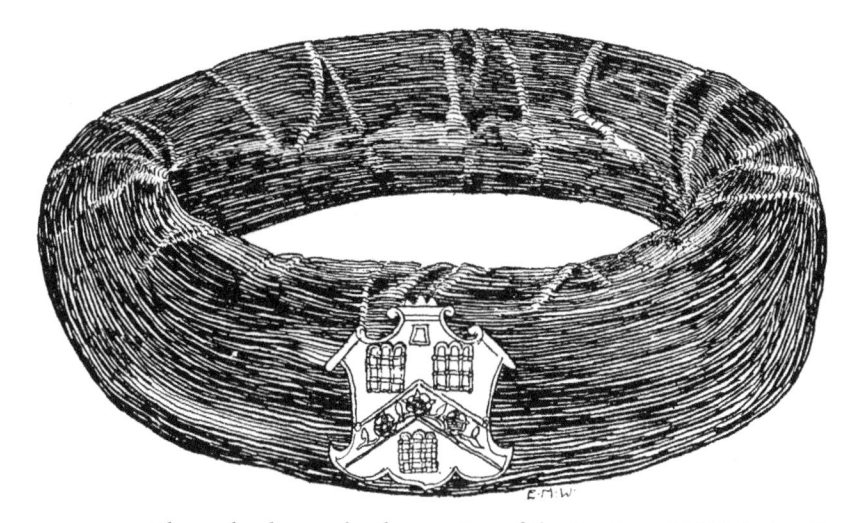

FIGURE 5.1 The garland worn by the masters of the Pewterers' Gild during the election ceremony. The garland shows the workmanship of the Pewterers. Some of the garlands were open wire structures into which seasonal flowers such as roses, lavender and pinks could be inserted.

From Charles Welch, *History of the Worshipful Company of Pewterers of the City of London, Based Upon Their Own Records*. London: Blades, East and Blades, 1902, with permission from the Newberry Library.

if they had little voice in naming the wardens. They had forty gallons of red wine, two barrels of ale, spice cakes and buns, two hundred eggs, and the necessary spices and flour. The installation dinner was more elaborate; ceremonies involved a gild "loving cup," garlands, and tables set with the best company products.[9]

The Mercers followed a similar election procedure, although they imitated the election of the mayor in that the retiring wardens retreated to an upper room and elected the new wardens by a ballot, in which they pricked their choices on a piece of paper listing the candidates. A feast, which all members were required to attend in livery, followed. Since the Mercers' saint's day was that of John the Baptist (June 24), the garlands usually had roses and perhaps lavender and pinks (in season in June) and were worn on the heads of the new incumbents.[10]

Since serving as warden was expensive and aggravating, many of the more substantial members tried to avoid election. The Grocers provided that anyone chosen who did not agree to serve within eight days would be required to pay 10 marks toward the salary of the priest. In extreme cases, they were to be put out of the gild "for all days." But because it was understood that the position was burdensome, gild rules provided that no one who had served would have to serve again for seven years.[11]

As the gilds became more established, they acquired property in the form of bequests, built halls, administered quarterly dues and extra taxes and fees, and had oversight of the alms houses for indigent members. By the fifteenth century, the administration of the gilds had become so complex that it was necessary to have accountants, collectors of rents, chaplains, and scribes. In addition, committees regulated specific issues, such as liveries and who should wear them, music and musicians for particular occasions, and other outstanding matters. Many of the gilds established a court of assistants drawn from among the established members to aid the wardens in deliberations. The Mercers had twelve assistants selected by the wardens. The Grocers had six, and the Taylors had twenty-four. The use of assistants did not broaden representation in governing, but rather eliminated the general assembly from the decision-making process. Oligarchic control was reinforced.[12]

Membership through Apprenticeship

Membership in a gild brought with it citizenship. As we have described, one could become a citizen of London by completing an apprenticeship, through patrimony, or by buying it (redemption) or acquiring it through favor. In any case, a gild had to accept the person as a member in order for him to become a citizen. Few lists of gild members survive. Some of the most complete information that we do have is for the Mercers' Company. Of the 1,047 members recorded in their account book between 1391 and 1464, only sixty-eight were admitted by redemption, compared to 979 who were admitted through the completion of apprenticeship. Between 1465 and 1528, 699 of the admissions were by apprenticeship, ninety by redemption, and fifty-five through patrimony.[13] Although there was concern in the early fifteenth century that too many people were obtaining citizenship through redemption because of the lack of apprentices, by the later fifteenth century apprentices were again filling the membership lists. At least for the Mercers, and for the Goldsmiths and Grocers, for which some membership lists also survive, education in civic behavior would be done primarily during apprenticeship.[14]

Women were not barred from apprenticeship or from gild membership, but the roles open to them were limited. Women mostly entered into apprenticeships that involved working with a master's wife on a related craft, such as silk weaving. London did not have exclusively female gilds, as did Paris. Few girls completed apprenticeships, perhaps simply using the skills they acquired to make them more desirable marriage partners. Wives of gildsmen could attend gild feasts and widows could continue their husband's trade, including training apprentices, but most widows remarried members of the same gild.[15] Only the Brewers' Gild had a number of female members who wore the livery. But these women never held gild office.[16] Women, therefore, do not appear frequently in gild accounts or court rolls, except as participants in the feasts, as almswomen, and as major donors to their former husband's gild. The generous bequests that widows made indicate their personal identification with the gild.

Since successfully completing an apprenticeship was the most common way to become a gild member, this important training not only educated youth in a trade but also in citizenship. The education began with an apprenticeship to a member of one of the gilds. Selecting of an apprentice was a serious decision, because the apprentice moved into the master's house and essentially became part of his family. He might also become heir to the business or marry into the family.[17] For the apprentice and his parents or sponsors the selection of the master was of equal importance because they wanted assurance that their child would be well treated and trained. In both cases it was not the experience of learning the craft alone that dictated the choice, but also the close relationship of trust between the mentor and apprentice.

The qualifications for an apprentice, which included both good character and a financial commitment, indicate that the candidate was already promising material for gild membership and citizenship. A master's network of family, friends, and business associates recommended candidates so that the master would already know the character of the young man. Since most apprentices were from the country, their acculturation to London and the behavior required of a gild member were learned in their master's household.[18]

At the age of fourteen or older, the young man and his sponsors negotiated a an apprenticeship contract with the master. The candidate could not be of servile peasant stock, but had to be freeborn. Entry into one of the prestigious gilds was usually reserved for the sons of London citizens and for those from the gentry class in the country. These were the young men who might move into the city oligarchy in due course. Entry fees could be very high. Apprentices for a goldsmith, for instance, could expect to pay 10 marks for seven years and £5 for ten years of training.[19] In practice, however, contracts were individually negotiated and payment varied.

The contracts establishing an apprenticeship contained not only the financial arrangements and expectations of time needed to acquire expertise in a craft, but also the type of behavior that would be required of both the apprentice and master. The master agreed to teach the apprentice all the secrets of the craft and to provide him with food, clothing, shoes, and a bed. The apprentice swore not to marry and not to fornicate. Included in the latter was the wise precaution that the apprentice was to have no sexual relations with anyone in his master's household. He was not to engage in the temptations of the city, such as drinking, gaming, and going to theaters. Especially, he was not to gossip about his master's affairs but to remain loyal to the master's interests and not waste the master's money. He agreed to accept discipline if it was not too severe and not to go to another master or run away. In the event that he did not live up to these commitments he could expect punishment or, in extremes, the termination of his contract. Both parties sealed the contract and posted bonds for compliance with the agreement. The contract was then filed with the gild and the city.[20]

Late medieval society honored the public and performative celebration of major transitions, and thus the written word was not adequate for as important a step as becoming an initiate into the mysteries of a craft. The rite of entering into apprenticeship, moving from one liminal stage to another, required solemn ceremonies and many witnesses to impress on the mind of the youth and those around him that he was undertaking obligations that had implications for his life for the next seven to ten or more years and into adulthood. One remembered the obligations better when rituals reinforced them. The two powerful authorities in the apprentice's life, the gild and the city government, both had initiation rituals.[21] The rituals must have been awe inspiring to a youth of fourteen to eighteen, especially if he had come from the country. Since many gilds had adopted colorful liveries by the end of the fourteenth century, the oath taking was a display of future power and the colorful gowns he would someday wear himself.

The oath emphasized conventional loyalties to the king and his heirs and appealed to God, the saints, and the gospels to bind it. The heart of the oath, however, involved the master and the gild. "And well and trewly ye shall serve your master for the terms of your apprenticeshood." In addition the apprentice swore to be obedient to the wardens. "In reverence to the secrets of the said fellowship ye shall keep and give no information to no man but of the said fellowship." The secrets involved not only trade secrets, but also information on the internal governance of the gild itself. To underline the sacred nature of the oath, the master might first take the apprentice to the church associated with the gild. Thus the Mercers required that every master taking an apprentice first to enroll and swear him at St. Thomas Church. On the first Monday after the beginning of Lent, at an assigned hour, the wardens were to read to the assembled apprentices the terms of their contracts so that they could not claim ignorance of them. To insure attendance, the gild would impose a fine of 12d. on absentees.[22]

The city was concerned about apprenticeship because it was preliminary to citizenship and because the contract was an official, legal arrangement that the city monitored through the wards and the mayor's court. Registration of the contract with London's chamberlain could be delayed, but was supposed to be done within a year and a day after it was signed. Again, the occasion was an impressive one, for it was intended to show the apprentice the power of civic authority. In the early fourteenth century, the apprentice and his master met with the chamberlain in Guildhall, who examined the candidate and his indenture. William Bothe, an apprentice, described the ceremony when he appealed against his master for a broken contract. He said that he and the man who was to be his surety "went before Robert Colwythe, Chamberlain of London, as was customary and the Chamberlain reviewed the articles of apprenticeship and examined William Bothe." His apprenticeship was approved and entered in the papers.[23] The ward kept the record of enrollment, which is always referred to as the "paper." One apprentice said, in 1443, that his contract was enrolled in "the register marked D of apprentices."[24]

Feeling the competition from foreigners after the Black Death, the Commons of London asked that one day in the month be set aside for "gildedaies" to distinguish the importance of the apprenticeship examination and enrollment as opposed to gaining citizenship by redemption. Apprentices would pay 60s. for the ceremony. The enrollment was to be further dignified by having not only the master and apprentice appear, but also six other men who were full members of the mistery to testify to the apprentice's fitness. If the apprentice were found acceptable, he would be received in the presence of three alderman and the chamberlain.[25] The recommendation for this impressive and expensive ceremony was never carried out.

Enrollment, however, was difficult to enforce, even though a fine of £20 could be levied against a master for not doing so. The city tried to embarrass masters by ordaining that the names of apprentices not "entered on the paper" in the first year be announced in the Guildhall. But both masters and apprentices had their reasons for not hastening to proceed with enrollment. First, the enrollment fees paid to both the gild and the city could cost from £1 to £5 for apprentices and £1 for masters. Apprenticeship cost enough without this extra burden, and in the period after the plague it was hard to find qualified apprentices in any case. From the apprentices' point of view, enrollment was expensive and could limit their flexibility to leave once they had an adequate knowledge of the craft. Others left because the arrangement did not work out and neither party pressed charges for honoring the contract. If an apprentice did not want to become a citizen and set up a shop, he had little reason to enroll in the gild. Therefore a number of apprentices never enrolled. Other apprentices enrolled near the ends of their terms if they did plan to become citizens and full gild members.[26] The Mercer's Company records show that between 1391 and 1464, 958 apprentices never completed their terms. In the fifteenth century the gild made a new attempt to encourage apprentices to enroll, perhaps because recurring plagues had depleted the numbers of young men wanting apprenticeships.[27]

What happened to apprentices who were not enrolled after completing their apprenticeships? Some may have left after having achieved a sufficient skill to return to their provincial towns and set up in trade. Others may have run out of money to pay for the issue fee, 2s. to 3s.4d. for the Mercers or more for other companies.[28] Some may have died while they were apprentices or switched to a different trade. London was notoriously unhealthy for anyone in the population and perhaps more so for apprentices, who often slept on the shop floor and were certainly not always adequately fed and clothed. And there were industrial accidents as well, particularly for those working with forges. Some may have acquired sufficient skills to work for wages as journeymen (skilled workers), but lacked the money to become masters. Given these factors, the high attrition rate among apprentices is not surprising.

After completing an apprenticeship and perhaps spending several years as a journeyman, a man, no longer so young, could become a member of his gild and a freeman of the city. Again, oaths and ritual ceremonies marked the transition to the new status. Those entering by redemption also went through the ceremonies.

The candidate for gild membership or his sponsors paid a fee to the gild and the city for the right to swear the oaths. As with apprenticeship oaths, the ceremony required the presence of the liveried members of the gild and civic officials. It would have been an impressive gathering. Most of the surviving gild books inscribed both the oath to the gild and the one to become a freeman. The Goldsmiths' oath was typical. Loyalty to the king and his heirs was emphasized, but, appropriate to one entering into the freedom of the city, the initiate swore: "to keep the peace of the city to the utmost of [his] power." Next came the duty owed to the gild itself: "And you shall work and cause to be worked good and true gold and silver without any deceit; and you shall not set glass or counterfeit stones in gold contrary to the good rule and reputation of the fellowship; and you shall warn the wardens straightaway of any deceit which shall come to your knowledge for amendment of the same." Next the candidate swore loyalty to the gild and its ordinances, both present and future and made a promise not to disclose the secrets and skill of the craft. The new member had to come when summoned by the gild wardens, unless he had a reasonable excuse not to, pay the yearly quarterage fees and all other charges, and not take an apprentice without the full supervision and assent of the wardens. The oath was sworn on the gospels and before the whole of the gild, dressed in full livery.[29] The Pewterers added a few more specifications. They emphasized conserving the "wellbeing of the Fellowship." Anything said to the prejudice of the fellowship should be reported to the master and wardens. The Pewterers swore not to work "privily nor apart with any person except he be free of the craft." In addition to the usual stipulations about paying gild dues, the Pewterers were to "aid and succor poor brethren."[30]

The oath to become a freeman of the city emphasized loyalty to the king and his heirs and added loyalty to the mayor and city officials. The franchises and customs of the city had to be maintained. The oath taker swore to pay all taxes and tallages and to report to the chamberlain any "foreigns" who were selling merchandise in the city. He also swore not to bring charges against any freeman outside the city courts. Then followed oaths regarding apprentices and their qualifications including the requirement to register them in the first year and make them free of the city on completion of their term. "You shall also keep the peace in you own person and you shall know no gatherings, conventicals [secret meetings] no conspiracies made against the peace but you warn the mayor." Again the emphasis was on the responsibility to "well and truly keep according to the laws of this city to you power so help you god."[31] The oath underlined loyalty to civic officials, obedience to the laws, paying taxes, keeping disputes and lawsuits within the city, and behaving in a peaceful manner.

Conspicuous Consumption and Gild Precedence

Of those who did set up shops after completing an apprenticeship, distinctions of rank among the gild the membership indicated a range of wealth and privilege. The highest status group were those who wore the full livery, hence the name of Livery Companies. Full livery consisted of a gown with a hood. To take up the livery meant paying an entrance fee that varied with the gild. The Saddlers required an ounce of silver or a spoon of silver valued at 3s. 4d. Members of the full livery, or those of the "clothing," served as officers of the gild and participated in civic elections and offices.[32] Below those of the clothing were the householders with their own shops, who were eligible to have a hood. Their entrance fee was somewhat lower. A Mercers' shop holder took an oath to the gild, ran his own shop, paid dues to the gild, attended the gild court, and kept weapons for the defense of the city. By 1456–57, a fee of £2 was charged to become a shopkeeper. Between 1456 and 1464 about thirty men paid the fee.[33] Some of the gilds also had householders who did not even have hoods. In 1420, the Grocers had fifty-five members in livery, seventeen in hoods, and forty-two householders not in hoods.[34]

Liveries were expensive and carefully regulated. In this respect the London livery companies were participating in a general explosion of interest in fashion, because of the greater availability of fine fabrics and the international exchange of ideas of dress. Outward appearances measured a man's and a gild's status, setting them apart in the streets and showing where they stood on the social ladder in a very hierarchical society. Gild regulations required conformity but also frequent changes of livery. Choosing the colors, as in the dress for civic ceremonials, was of major importance and part of the committee work of the members.[35] In the wealthy gilds, the gowns and hoods changed every year. In more modest ones, they changed every two or three years. But the wealthy gilds required that a given year's livery be kept for two years so that there would be an everyday livery in the older color and the livery in the new color to be worn on ceremonial occasions. The livery was not to pass outside the membership for the obvious reason that it identified the wearer with the gild. The gilds were concerned about the resale trade in their livery. In fact, the gowns were resalable in the used-clothing market, but they would be taken apart and the fabric used for other garments.[36]

Gild officials bought the cloth for the liveries. Those who were eligible to wear the cloth had to make an application and pay for the cost of the material. Members who disliked the cloth could take a pattern of it and have other cloth made, but it had to be the same color. At the beginning of the fifteenth century, a gown cost about 15s. to 16s. and a hood cost 2s. 6d. The Brewers, who had a very large membership, spent £185 in 1417. The Grocers, a wealthy gild, changed their colors frequently. In 1414 they wore scarlet and green; in 1418 scarlet and black were favored; in 1428 it was scarlet and deep blue; and in 1450 it was violet and crimson. The gild liveries were always particolored.[37]

Liveries proclaimed a strong sense of fellowship. The emotional importance is found in the *French Chronicle*, in which the author notes, in 1319–1320, "At this time many of the people of the trades of London were arrayed in livery, and a good time was about to begin."[38] He was referring to the charter of Edward II that gave the gilds control over citizenship by having the gilds admit members to both the gild and the city. The good times really came into their own in the fifteenth century, when liveries became more elaborate.[39] Members wore the livery to the gild assembly meetings, feasts and processions, funerals of members, and civic ceremonies. Because liveries were a public sign of the gild's strength, it is not surprising that failure to show up in the gild garments was considered a finable offense.[40]

Those who became "honorary members" of the cloth may not have planned to trade in the city, but wearing a gild livery became a symbol of prestige in London and the realm. Having "honorary members" contributed to a gild's status. Nobles and royal officials commonly joined gilds as honorary members. Edward III joined the Linen Armorers, as did Richard II.[41] Likewise, some foreign merchants belonged to gilds. Honorary and foreign members did not take apprentices or pay city taxes, but they might be involved in the convivial aspects of the gild or find the network of merchants and craftsmen useful.

City officials were adamant that gilds conform to the order to wear matched livery when meeting a king or queen. Thus in 1382, when the city rode to meet Anne of Bohemia, the new queen, all the gilds were to wear red and black. The distinctions among the different gilds was only embroidered on the sleeves. But the Goldsmiths on this occasion embellished their gowns with bars of silver work and trefoils of silver on the red part and five knots of gold and silk on the black side. Their red hats were sprinkled with silver trefoils. They must have been a sparkling presence. Special gowns and hoods were expensive. In 1401, the Grocers spent £67 on their own livery, an additional £6 for the livery of members who were riding with the sheriffs, and £43 on the cloth for the livery worn at the welcoming of Queen Johanna to England.[42]

The Brewer's Gild book tells us that when Henry V's body was bought to London for burial, all the aldermen and gildsmen were required to wear black, and every householder had to wear a black or russet gown with a black hood and to be present along the route through London. Certain crafts were to provide two hundred torches, of which the Brewers provided eight weighing a total of 138 pounds. The torchbearers wore white gowns, and the Brewers paid a share of the expense. The Brewers stood in St. Margaret's churchyard until the procession passed, and then they followed it on to St. Paul's. Many bishops and others sang masses. After eating, they proceeded to Westminster. The Brewers got back 112 pounds of wax, which they sold for 28s.[43]

The livery was such a symbol of prestige, that gifts of livery were a mark of distinction. Companies made gifts of their livery to the mayor, sheriffs, and other officials. Since such gifts made it appear that the civic officials were unduly loyal to one gild or another, ordinances in 1415 and again in 1423 forbade the mayor, aldermen, and sheriffs from taking the livery of any company except the one to which they belonged. As the ordinance explained, it was an old tradition, but had caused considerable outcry and "the custom is hardly able now to get a good word even said on its behalf."[44]

In the various civic processions, including that of the oath taking of the mayor and the sheriffs and the progresses of the mayor on major holidays, the gildsmen turned out in their livery.[45] If the mayor or sheriff was a member of their gild, they made special arrangements for livery, banners, musicians, and feasts. Since on these occasions disputes often erupted over who had precedence in the procession or in the standing in St. Paul, the livery companies wanted their members to turn out in their best livery as a symbol of their power and prestige.

As noted earlier, the fights between the Fishmongers and the Goldsmiths and the Fishmongers and the Skinners in the early fourteenth century probably arose over precedence in civic ceremonial. In 1477, the Mercers and the Grocers, two of the most prestigious and wealthy companies dealing in long-distance trade argued over the place they would stand on ceremonial occasions in St. Paul's Cathedral. The Mercers were then gaining in status, and the Grocers had gone into a decline. The Mercers complained that the Grocers had "unlovingly and unkindly" taken their place on All Hallows (All Saints' Day, November 1) and that this has caused "rancor and great malice, especially by means of uncourteous language on their part."[46] The feast of All Saints was a major day of celebration for the city. The *Liber Albus*, the city's book of precedents and governance, directed that on this day "the Mayor was wont, together with his household, to proceed after dinner to the church of Saint [Thomas], as also the Aldermen and the people of the Mayor's livery, who met together there, with the substantial men of the several mysteries, arrayed in their respective suits." They then processed to St. Paul's church to hear vespers and processed back again.[47] In other words, the All Saints' Day procession was one of those civic spectacles that provided occasion for a display of precedence, power, and male sartorial splendor. Such occasions indicated to the populace watching the solemn parade which gilds were the most powerful. The Mercers had every reason to feel that the Grocers had ill-used them.

The Mercers' solution was to go to an alderman who was a gild member and ask him to approach the mayor about meeting with delegations from both gilds. The meeting was not an official one at the Guildhall; instead the parties met at the southwest end of the Cloister of St. Paul's between eight o'clock and nine o'clock in the morning on December 24. After much discussion, the mayor pointed out that the Mercers had always stood in that spot and should continue to do so and to be first in municipal processions. The Grocers then requested that they be given a desirable place to stand, and the mayor agreed that they could stand on the steps going up to the choir.[48] Several factors went into the mayor's compromise. He appealed to precedent of long standing—an argument that held particular weight in medieval social constructs—and he settled the dispute during the holy season, when messages of peace would be most appropriate. But the matter had to be resolved that day. On December 25, the Nativity, and December 26, St. Stephen's Day, an even more magnificent procession of the mayor, aldermen, sheriffs, and worthies of the city proceeded to St. Paul's, where they met the Dean and Chapter. All took their arranged places.[49] A brawl over where these two powerful gilds stood for mass would have been out of place on such a public and solemn occasion. By taking advantage of the solemnity of the season, the mayor's negotiated settlement was much more likely to succeed because it invoked a divine element in its solution. Having been sealed by practice on Christmas Day, it was binding thereafter.

When the Skinners and Taylors (a newly powerful gild) had an argument over their position in processions, the mayor arranged, in 1483, that they should alternate places every other year. If one of their number should become mayor, then the gild he came from would have precedence for that year. To secure the agreement and "to set aside all manner of strife and debate," the Skinners were to invite the master and wardens of the Taylors to dine with them once a year, on their gild feast day, and the Taylors would then reciprocate on their own feast day.[50] The shared meal was a time-honored ritual of securing an agreement. It had been used more than a hundred years earlier in the agreement between the Fishmongers and the Skinners.

Gildhalls and Feasts

The conspicuous consumption of clothing was matched by the amount spent by the gilds on company halls and the feasts that were held in them. The halls were not simply meeting places, but emulated the London establishments of the feudal lords. Indeed, many of the halls were converted from either a lord's London residence or from a former religious house. In addition to a large assembly hall, there were a kitchen, pantry, storehouse, garden, account and treasury rooms, a chapel, reception room, a house or chambers for a chaplain, a treasurer, and a gardener, and perhaps a row of almshouses for decayed members. Figure 5.2 shows the Leathersellers' Hall with the center section showing most of the medieval building. The Taylors and the Goldsmiths built halls in the fourteenth century. The Goldsmiths acquired property in 1357 and began building in earnest in 1364, spending £136 pounds on a hall, kitchen, pantry, buttery, and two chambers with two beds. They kept adding to the hall and rebuilding portions of it through subscriptions of the membership and specific gifts. The interior was lavishly decorated with tapestries and a silver-gilt statue of St. Dunstan, their patron saint. The Grocers occupied their hall in 1431 and held a feast that the mayor and "many a worshipful person attended, beside the whole craft." They consumed two pipes (half a tun) of wine and nine barrels (one-eighth of a tun) of ale. They also maintained a garden with grape vines, stipulating that the grapes be allowed to ripen so that members could take home a few bunches. While the Grocers allowed only gild members to use the hall and to play tennis in the garden, the Brewers defrayed the costs of their hall by renting it out to other gilds that did not have halls, and even to a football team. The Taylors acquired the property

FIGURE 5.2 The Leathersellers' Hall as it appeared in the 18th century. The main building had been added onto in the 16th, 17th, and 18th centuries.

From the *History and Antiquities of the Worshipful Company of Leathersellers, of the City of London: with Fac-similes of Charters and Other Illustrations. London History of the Leathersellers of London*. London: E. J. Francis, 1871, with permission of the Leathersellers' Gild and the Newberry Library.

for their hall in 1331, but did not expand until the fifteenth century. By the end of the fifteenth century, the major companies and even lesser ones had gildhalls.[51]

Although feasts were a feature of gild life long before the advent of the gild halls, they became more elaborate and probably more satisfying when the gild had its own hall, buttery, pantry, and kitchen. Feasts were held on a variety of occasions, but most particularly on the gild's patron saint day. The saint's day was the major occasion for procession and a company repast. Feasts were also held on the occasion of the election of the wardens or, especially, when one of the members became a sheriff or mayor. The banquets gave the gilds a chance to renew the feeling of fellowship and to show their success in the city and the country. It was common to invite as many prestigious guests as possible, including members of the royal family and nobility, as well as leading churchmen. The outlay for the feasts was lovingly recorded in the account books and even favorite recipes were written down for such things as Christmas pudding. Not only were the gildsmen present, but their wives were also included in these events. One imagines that the whole city paid attention to the parade of members and their wives as they arrived at the hall for the banquet. And we must not forget the delicious smells that emanated from the gildhall kitchens. The Brewers' Gild was partial to fowl, particularly swan. In 1425, the gild paid £38 for twenty-one swans, two geese, forty capons, forty conies, forty-eight partridges, and a number of little birds. The cook was paid 23s. Then there was the rent of pewter vessels, rushes for the hall, lavender for the tablecloth, and minstrels. Apparently, at least so the Brewers thought, the quality of their feast made Mayor Whittington jealous, and he harassed the gild about the high cost of beer in the city. the Brewers denied themselves a feast the next year until he was out of office.[52]

The halls and the feasts were a signal of the gild's success and, like the livery, created a strong bond of collegiality and pride. The halls contained the poor box, whose monies were used to aid impoverished members, and a display case for the gild's collection of gild plate. The pieces of plate were symbolic of the gild's status in the city. The hall was where apprentices were sworn before the liveried members and where the successful apprentices took their oaths of gild membership and citizenship. Gild administration took place there including election of wardens, production of accounts, and reprimands to wayward members. Those who did not pay the required amount for the livery, produced substandard goods, and fought with fellow members, or worse yet, with the wardens, stood before the wardens and the whole assembly to be fined, perhaps expelled, returning on bended knee to do their penance.

The use of space in the gildhalls both indicated the gild's inclusivity of its members but could also become a powerful reinforcement of hierarchy. The space was divided so that, after the election of wardens and the ensuing feast, the officers sat at a head table, away from the rest of the members. The gild court also separated the wardens and other officers from those called before the court. Space was used to elevate authority, both physically and symbolically.

Journeymen or Bachelors

Known variously as journeymen, *lowys*, bachelors, yeomen or "young men," this group included a variety of men, some of whom were even citizens. Upon completion of their terms, they remained as servants to their master or with another member of the gild and were paid for their work. In some cases, the initial contract might have specified a term of a few years work for the master after the completion of apprenticeship. Other bachelors were former apprentices who did not complete their term but nonetheless had a good knowledge of the trade or who were aliens from the continent well versed in the trade from the training they had received in their own cities. All of these journeymen would receive a wage, but they could not set up their own shops or trade on their own. Although journeymen were associated with a gild, their position in it was limited. They could not attend the gild court and vote for gild officers, nor could they wear the gild livery. They were a restive group, prone to make "covins" and demand higher pay or the right to organize. The gilds faced the challenge of repressing them or integrating them into the gild system.[53]

When the journeymen had lived with their masters, in pre-plague London, it was possible to control their activities and keep them unmarried and dependent, but following the depletion of population in the second half of the fourteenth century and the consequent increased availability of housing, many moved out or lived in group housing, and some married. Despite the Statute of Laborers, they earned better wages than had the generations before the plagues. They formed a large group that could not be controlled in the traditional way, although the city and gilds suppressed these covins. The Saddlers' Gild complained, in 1369, that "there had arisen no small dissension and strife between the masters . . . and the serving men called yeomen . . . because that the serving men aforesaid, against the consent, and without leave, of their masters, were wont to array themselves all in a new and like suit once in the year, and oftimes held divers meetings, at Stratford and elsewhere without the liberty of the said city, as well as in divers places within the City."[54] The Saddlers, concerned about inconvenience and losses they might sustain, urged the mayor to intervene. As an indication of how well organized the yeomen were, when the mayor asked for their "governors" to appear, they did so and argued that "time out of mind the serving men of the said trade had had a certain fraternity among themselves." They arrayed themselves in like clothing and met at Stratford on the Feast of the Assumption of the Blessed Virgin Mary (August 15) and processed to the Church of St. Vedast in London to hear mass. The masters responded that they had only been doing this for thirteen years (all post-plague) and that "under a certain feigned color of sanctity," they were influencing journeymen to join their covin and in an attempt to raise wages. The masters said that wages had gone up from

5 marks yearly to 12 marks or more; and further, the yeomen were asking their fellows to attend the funerals of dead members and the yeomen were walking off work for this purpose without the masters' permission. The mayor and aldermen sided with the masters and forbade the serving men to form covins, suggesting that they could get justice from the city courts if they were having a problem with the masters.[55]

The Taylors' yeomen were in the mayor's court in 1415 because "some serving men and journeymen of the tailors, called *yeomen tailours*, dwelling with one another in companies by themselves, did hold and inhabit divers dwelling-houses in the City, against the will or their superiors in the said city, and of the masters of that trade." The inhabitants of the houses had been "unruly and insolent men without head or governance, oftentimes assembled in great numbers, and had held divers assemblies and conventicles." They had wounded one of the masters of the Taylors Gild. The city called the master and wardens of the Taylors to explain why they were allowing the serving men to live together without supervision and to commit such acts of violence. The gildsmen said that they had tried to control the men, but to no avail. They suggested that the mayor and aldermen summon David Brekenhok and John Stanbury, who were living in a house in Garlykhythe, to appear before them. Although the city records described the yeoman as "like a race at once youthful and unstable," it seems that they were more organized than the Taylors had admitted. The city officials forbade them to adopt livery, hold assemblies, and live together without supervision. The directive failed, however, and two years later they asked the mayor and aldermen to recognize them as the Fraternity of Yeoman Taylors so that they could assemble once a year in the Church of St. John of Jerusalem and make an offering for departed brethren and sisters.[56]

In the fifteenth century, some of the gilds, notably the Taylors and the Goldsmiths, gradually managed to integrate their associations into the larger gild structure. In both cases, the group included journeymen and bachelors. The Taylors granted journeymen permission to meet, and by 1437 they celebrated their saint's day in the church next to the Taylors' Hall and held their election feast in the hall itself. The purpose of the "junior" fraternity was mostly religious, but the group elected wardens just as the parent organization did. Other gilds gradually reach similar accommodations with their bachelor fraternities, thus integrating them with the more powerful gild. The Skinners, for instance, distinguished between the artisan workers and the importers of furs. The latter were, of course, the more prestigious and participated in civic government. By the end of the fifteenth century, most gilds had some version of a dual gild structure.[57]

Although they had started out as rebels seeking higher wages and independence, the yeomen's mode of organization was a conservative one structured in imitation of the gilds in which they had served as journeymen. They elected wardens, wore liveries, provided funeral services for departed members, had religious affiliations and held feasts, and had a common treasury. Not all of the members were citizens, but they were integrated into the city through their organizational model. It was a wise move on the part of the livery companies to co-opt the movement by granting the yeomen's groups recognition and inclusion, albeit with a lower status.

Aliens and Strangers

Another labor problem that gilds faced was the status of aliens and strangers. The desire to keep a monopoly over trade and commerce within the city made the citizens and gilds suspicious of immigrants. In some cases, these outsiders came with great skills that competed with the local masters or they had connections with the crown that bypassed the gilds. An additional problem was the less-skilled laborers who descended on London from the continent. The city and some employers argued that they were undercutting the wages of London's trained laborers. Furthermore, they were not acculturated to London, nor did they pay tallages or undertake the responsibilities of governing that the local men did. The aliens came largely from Germany or the Low Countries and were known by the general term *Doche* (Dutchmen), while the strangers or "foreigns" were English from outside the city itself.[58] As the gilds began to feel the squeeze of these outsiders, they complained to the city and to the king about poor craftsmanship, the counterfeiting of makers' marks, and unfair competition.[59] However, though the gilds requested the mayor and the king to regulate the aliens, the real problem lay with their own members, who very willingly hired alien journeymen.

The Goldsmiths in particular relied on alien and foreign workers; but in the fifteenth century the numbers of these workers increased and the gild felt it had to take measures to protect its monopoly. The gild already had the power to inspect all the gold and silver objects produced in England, though policing infractions was difficult. Many immigrants settled in Southwark, making daily observation of them impossible. Using their connections at court, some of the immigrants successfully set up shop and bought from the crown and from the gild the right to keep chambers in London. Licenses to work cost between 4s. and 20s. Some also bought entry into the gild and freedom of the city through redemption. By 1434, however, the Goldsmiths felt that they had to take stronger measures. In the "Ordinance of Dutchmen," they complained that many were making untrue gold and silver "unto the great common harm of all the king's people, shame and slander of all freemen goldsmiths" and that the immigrants would not obey the gild's rules and governance. To this end, the gild was to levy a fine 100s. on anyone of the craft, men or women, who used alien servants, but there is no evidence of enforcement.[60] The Taylors, likewise, wanted to regulate the journeymen who came from across the Channel, but found that their members cheerfully employed these men, who charged less for labor than those who had gone through an apprenticeship.[61]

By the 1450s the Taylors and Cordwainers had complained about alien workers taking jobs from natives and lowering the quality of their products. The Glaziers, Bladesmiths, Fruiters, and Bakers complained of the "foreigns." London journeymen said that the "foreigns" were undercutting their wages and prayed the city for redress. Among the other complaints was that foreigns and aliens did not pay "scot nor lot" (that is, they were not liable for the various tallages and special subscriptions that gild members had to pay) and that they did not serve on inquests of other aliens as they were required to do by statute. Although Edward IV tried to remedy the situation by writing statutes to protect native industry, some of the smaller gilds were forced to amalgamate to survive.[62]

Although the city acted on the requests, they could not stem the flow of immigrants. The Goldsmiths increasingly issued them licenses for several-year terms or for the life of the alien. The life terms cost £3 to 20 marks and were purchased by respected alien goldsmiths, who set up shops, employed journeymen, and sometimes even joined the gild, becoming respected members. Realizing that they profited from the skills that the aliens brought, the Goldsmiths agreed that competent goldsmiths would be accepted, provided they swore allegiance to the king and the company and promised not to reveal its secrets. The alien goldsmiths had to pay an annual fine and provide adequate sureties for their good behavior. Those Dutch with chambers were to have only one journeyman from their countries and were to hire English journeymen for the rest of their workshop. Their existing journeymen were to serve English goldsmiths for four years in exchange for meat, drink, and clothing, and then work for wages as hired men. The idea was to level the playing field for the English apprentices. Again, the plan was not enforceable. The licensing of alien goldsmiths continued, however, indicating that the company continued to assimilate the "Dutch."[63]

The Taylors were lax enough in the early fifteenth century to allow foreigners to be "botchers," that is, a worker who refurbished old garments. But by the end of the fifteenth century, as the population of London began to recover from a century of demographic slough, the Taylors found that they had many apprentices and native trained journeymen and wanted an intervention to protect them.[64]

Resentment against the "Dutch" in London did not disappear, and it could flare up into murderous attacks on their members. But within the ranks of the aliens, divisions also appeared between the "Flemish" and the "Brabanter" weavers. Like the English journeymen, the aliens sought to form gilds of workers to increase their wages and create a recognized association. Although the more elite aliens often gained acceptance, the journeymen did not enjoy the same tolerance. They all bore the brunt of anti-alien opinion in attacks.[65]

Gild Rebels and Respect for the Gilds

If the gilds had failed to control the aliens who infiltrated their trade, they had, by the late fourteenth century, become powerful enough to assume much of the responsibility for disciplining their own members. The gild courts punished members for showing disrespect to the wardens, making fraudulent goods, bringing legal actions against each other, breaking apprenticeship contracts, taking false oaths, and fighting publicly with other members. As an indication of court business, between 1334 and 1399 the minute books of the Goldsmiths' Gild showed twenty-two cases of faulty workmanship, nine of internal disputes, twenty cases of disrespect of wardens, and fourteen cases involving apprentices.[66] All gilds had ordinances requiring members to submit to the gild masters if they offended against gild rules and to take their disputes with each other to the gild rather than pursuing legal means.[67] The ordinance of Cutlers' gild is typical: "If any contention or injury be stirred up or begun among any folk of the said Fraternity, he who feels himself aggrieved shall come to the two good men elected and shall inform them of his complaint ... the good men shall endeavor an accord between those who are so at variance."[68]

Gilds set up arbitrations for members who had disputes. The Pewterers, for instance, employed arbiters to resolve disputes between members; to cover the expense of providing this service, the losing party paid part of the award to the company.[69]

If the gild's arbitration did not work, the gild took the matter to the mayor's court for legal punishment. Disobedience, insulting the gild master, and breaking gild rules were similar to rebelling against city officials and city laws. In 1364, a city ordinance proclaimed that "all the misteries of the City be lawfully ruled and governed, each in its kind, so that no deceit or false work be found therein by good men elected and sworn from each mistery. And if any be rebellious against them let him be fined and imprisoned."[70]

In a particularly difficult confrontation in the Taylors' Gild, one of the parties to the dispute, Heed, had been a master himself in 1483–84. The case was dramatic enough that the clerk recorded some of it verbatim. Heed and a man named Darby had argued over an apprentice and were allowed to cross-examine each other before the court of assistants and the wardens. Heed accused Darby of lying "lyke a false harlot." Darby got his chance to reply. "Sir, I note and remember in what place and whose presence I am in. And if I were in another place ... I wold speke as playne Englissh unto you as ye have don unto me." Heed ignored the arbiters the master had appointed and, when the master tried to mediate the dispute, Heed insulted him. The only recourse was to turn the matter over to the mayor. Heed was put into Newgate for four days, after which he apologized for his outbursts and agreed to submit to the arbitration.[71]

Gilds formed monopolies over their craft or trade, regulating the products they produced, where the products would be sold, and the behavior of members.[72] The Goldsmiths are a the primary example of a gild monopoly, and are thus featured here because their records are particularly full. But what was true of the Goldsmiths was true of other gilds as well.[73] When John De Barton engaged in a dispute with the Goldsmiths Gild "on account of evil outrageous deeds which were not good, suitable nor faithful," he was stripped of his livery and his membership in the gild. Essentially, that meant that he could no longer practice the craft of goldsmith in the city of London. He repented and in a meeting with the gild at the church of St. Peter in Cheap "bowed down with a humble head and begged mercy of the whole Company, and offered them 10 tuns of wine" by way of reconciliation. The "good men" of the gild took counsel and agreed that he should pay a pipe of wine [475 liters] and that he should fund support for a poor man of the gild at 12d. a week for a year. The ten tuns of wine were placed under his obligation should he offend again.[74] John Chapler, accused of selling silver objects on Cornhill rather than in the Cheap, was defiant toward the wardens and spoke "evil and malicious words to them and was disobedient and rebellious." They had him put in Newgate prison, where he stayed for four days before he found sureties for his good behavior and signed a bond, preserved in the accounts, requiring him to pay 40s. if he offended again.[75]

The usual reason gild disciplined members was that the product the member had produced did not meet gild standards. The gild, by its charters, had the power to inspect for faulty workmanship, not only in London and its suburb, but also at fairs and, eventually, throughout the realm. The usual offenses were mixing base metals with gold and silver, putting silver plate over copper, placing lead or tin in the bottom of chalices or cups, or putting glass instead of real gems into rings and broaches. Most of the business documented in the wardens' accounts, aside from the registering of apprentices and the usual recording of income and expenditures, concerned faulty workmanship, illegal trading, and the regulation of apprenticeships. The punishments for offenses were usually fines, but they could also lead to expulsion from the gild.[76]

In 1365, John de Bruges was found guilty of two frauds. He had produced silver metal work for a girdle, and it had been weighed in the presence of the purchasers, but then he substituted another one of lesser weight "to his own great shame and to the great disgrace of the said mistery." He had also mixed sand with silver filings and sold it for silver. He was stripped of his livery for these frauds and was not to have a stall on the Cheap for a year. He had to wait out his year; and then went before the masters with two men who stood surety for him. They undertook to pay the company a pipe of wine if he offended again.[77]

Multiple offenses were not uncommon, and the same names could appear over a number of years. Thomas Wood's offenses were so numerous that they took up a page and a half of the account book. In 1470, the wardens had discovered, on their search and assaying of the goldsmiths in London, that two of Wood's drinking cups were "deceivably painted and wrought in deceit of the king's people, and the silver of the said nuts [coconut shells] was right bad." They fined him 13s. 4d. Another search showed that a pair of gilt salt cellars and a girdle harness were grossly deficient in silver, an infraction for which he was fined 30s. A later search of his premises showed that he had "divers men working girdles, chalices, altar candle sticks, salts and other plate" that were defective in silver. The wardens took some of the offending items and ordered Wood to bring the rest to the Hall. He brought only three girdles, even though the wardens declared that they had seen fourteen in his shop. "As for the plate wrought, he said and affirmed right largely that it was gilded and delivered and was forty miles out of London," but the wardens knew that it was in his house and not sold. He eventually cooperated and brought all the items required, and they were all deficient in silver. He was rebuked, fined £10, and took an oath that he would not follow such practices in the future. To avoid the public humiliation of being brought before the whole company, he agreed to have an entire record of his frauds entered into the wardens' accounts. The frauds did not impede his success, however, and he went on to be a warden himself five years later and served as an alderman in the city for eight years.[78]

Since gild members swore to bring all disputes with each other to the gild wardens, these officials were engaged in conciliation among members. Some cases were matters of settling disagreements over the sale of objects or the use of the services of other members; some involved slander and name calling; some were over abuses of apprentice contracts. The wardens used persuasion, the possibility of a bond for good behavior, and fines to keep disputes within the gild. A feud between two gild brothers in which personal animosities, not broken contracts, were involved, placed the gild wardens in the position of mediators trying to get to the cause of the tensions. Their objective in mediation was to achieve equilibrium between two parties who had entered into an intractable disagreement. Not only did the disputants have to find harmony but the whole of the community had to return to a feeling of amity as well. Fighting between two gild brothers could create factions that caused fissures among the gild membership.

The mechanism of mediation can be seen in the case of Edward of Bowdon versus Davy Panter. Edward of Bowdon was an ongoing problem for the Goldsmiths, who had punished him when he was an apprentice for trying to strangle his mistress and had to put him out of the livery when he was a master because he committed fraud. Only the intervention of the queen persuaded the gild to take him back. His contentious nature appeared again in 1468 when "diverse matters of controversy and debate by the subtle suggestion of the ancient enemy of mankind, stirrer and chief mover of strife and contention, were moved and hanging between Edward of Bowdon and David Panter—which matters grew of forward and uncourteous language spoken and uttered by either of them to the other to their rebuke, troubling their neighbors about them and all the fellowship." The wardens initially tried to stop the fight by the time-honored solution of having them each post £40 to be given to the gild poor box by the one that first started to fight again.

"Against all humanity, not dreading offense to God," they fell out again "with outrageous, heinous and malicious language and also in assaults and making affrays." Indeed, their fighting was so notorious that it came to the attention of the king, and the Goldsmiths had to bribe someone at court to get the case back into their jurisdiction. The two bound themselves, for £100 each this time, and agreed to allow the wardens to settle the contentions between them. The wardens and six former wardens listened to "their complaints and the cause of the matter of their grief, with the answers and replications to the same put in by them ... in writing." They also examined witnesses. "And after ripe communication and due examination of both the parties with their proofs and witnesses," the wardens concluded that the dispute had started because Bowdon had called Panter a "whoreson, banished Scot," and Panter had called Bowdon "false traitor and false whoreson traitor." Various annoyances followed, since one party lived above the other and they shared a common entrance. After investigation, the wardens assured them that both charges were false. Panter was English by birth, despite his north-country accent, and Bowdon was not a traitor.

The wardens proposed a series of solutions to alleviate the animosity between them. In the future, neither should stop up the other's gutters or drains, nor cause their wives or servants to do so. "And because the house of the said Davy is over the shop of the said Edward ... the said Davy shall not willfully of malice, he or his servants cast or pour on his floor any water or other liquor to run or drop down into the said Edward's shop, nor make a dunning [loud noise] with hewing wood. Nor cast down water or dust out of the window upon the said Edward's stall." Each was to have a key to the front door, and "the door shall not be bolted against the other household." Furthermore, the gild would install in each dwelling a bell, hanging in a convenient place, so that they could summon the members of the gild if one or the other started the affray again. If a dispute broke out again, the one injured was "to suffer and keep silence, whatever be said or done, except bodily hurt" and report the incident to the wardens.

Finally, Edward of Bowden and Davy Panter had to perform the words and symbols of reconciliation. They were to shake hands and desire of each other "good love and brotherhood." Since they had put the wardens and others to expense and trouble, they were to pay £12 each into the common box, and each should "submit himself lowly upon [his] knees to the wardens before all the livery and ask pardon and forgiveness." Apparently, the mediation worked, for they did not reappear before the wardens. But Davy's north-country accent continued to invite harassment, and a few years later, a man was fined for calling him "a false knave and a rough-footed Scot" and throwing a weight at him.[79]

The language the gilds used to describe their unease with disputes indicates the seriousness of the infractions. The words of anxiety and outrage also affirmed the shared morality of the medieval market place.[80] The feuds are set in a context of eternity, history, and religion: "from the beginning of the world"; "against all humanity, not dreading offense to God"; moved "by the subtle suggestion of the ancient enemy of mankind." Their rhetoric lends gravity to what seem to us amusing stories of trade fights, name-calling, and nasty pranks. At the base of the warden's concerns were the maintenance of shared values, gild unity, and the need to keep infractions out of the king's courts. It was in the interest of this sense of community that the wardens were seldom vindictive, even against those who had attacked them personally. Fines were lowered, tuns of wine reduced to a single pipe, offenders released from prison, oaths of good behavior taken, and livery returned. Many of the offenders went on to be wardens themselves and respected members of the community. Gild wardens, many of whom became mayors and aldermen, had already learned the manner in which civic officials handled disputes in the wider community of the city.

Gilds were instrumental in the development of London's civic culture through apprenticeships, oaths, ceremonial dress, the election of wardens and gild governance, and reprimands in the gild courts for poor products and behavior unbecoming of a gild member and a citizen. Gild banquets and etiquette in the gild halls groomed men for participation in London's government and made them acceptable among nobles and representatives of the court. The processions, be they civic or gild, conveyed a sense of solidarity and indicated the gild's status within the city. A case in 1493, in the Taylors' records expresses the gild's anxiety over breaches of proper behavior. The gild feared that "the great infamy that of likelihood might have grown in time to come to the whole body of the fellowship ... if the said matter should be published and come to light before the Chamberlain of this city and further ... before the mayor and aldermen." The culprit was "openly shamed with a paper over his head" referring to him as an "untrue citizen."[81] The ceremony to return wholeness to the gild and the city was a ceremony involving written, oral, and visual performance of repentance on the part of the offender.

6

Civic Lessons for the Masses

AS EARLY AS 1312, the mayor, aldermen, and good men of the commonalty expressed their concern about the uninformed masses in the city and suggested ways to make the laws and customs more available so that "peace and concord be nourished and preserved throughout the city by neighborly unity." Recognizing that many recent inhabitants, owing to their youth, were not familiar with the "ancient laws, franchises, and customs of the city," the established citizens had the ordinances and statutes of the city enrolled in a register, so that they would be available to all who desired to see them and, further, that they be read in public assembly once or twice a year. The public reading would help to indoctrinate those who were not citizens and those who could not read.[1] The records at this time were kept in Latin so that the oral reading had to be in English to be understood by the masses. A reference in one of the chronicles, in 1327, refers to the new charter that Edward III had granted to London. It was "read and made public and translated into English by Andrew Horn, chamberlain of the Guildhall."[2] Horn wrote that Mayor Richer de Refham "caused the ancient customs and liberties in the books and rolls of the chamber of the city to be searched, and with the wiser and more powerful men assembled, together with the aldermen, in their presence he had them read and made public." Horn comments that in this and other actions the mayor "thus seemed to preserve and reform the king's city in its former glory."[3]

London had institutions, both formal and informal, that helped to settle the newly arrived and manage the people already resident. First and foremost was the oath of frankpledge administered in the wards. The parish church was also important because it was an institution that everyone knew whether they were from a city, the country, or the Continent. The parish was the center of life and cut across lines of citizenship and status. The parish churches also had religious gilds that drew both men and women from the community into their membership. Like the trade gilds, the parish gilds became educational tools for living in the big city. As well, the first institution that many new arrivals to the city might encounter was an inn or tavern. Innkeepers and taverners were required to also instruct their patrons on the city's rules.

Taverns

London was replete with taverns and inns. Residence in an inn cost as little as 1½d. a day. In the fifteenth century, a woman paid 6d. a week for room and board.[4] The presence of transient guests, however, created a fear of disorder that permeated all the official ranks. The king's chief concern was that taverns were places where people could meet to form "congregations, unions (*alligaciones*), and covins." In 1368 a group of skinners was attached to stand trial because they had met in a tavern and other places and formed a covin.[5] The Church condemned taverns as places to talk heresy, slander the church, and commit sexual offenses.[6] The mayor and aldermen, ever worried about keeping order in the city, continually prodded the taverners and innkeepers to take legal responsibility for their clients and enforce curfew and other city ordinances.

The peacekeeping role assigned to taverners and innkeepers turned them into officers of the peace. In medieval England, many people played such semiofficial roles but received no payment for executing them. The official stature of London's purveyors of drink and lodging came from statute law and London ordinances. A royal statute in 1285, recorded in the *Liber Albus,* echoed the Anglo-Saxon custom of regarding newcomers as the first night a stranger, the second night a guest, and the third night a member of the household. "No one shall be resident in the ward of an Alderman beyond a day and a night, if he be not in view of frankpledge." The host had to produce a guest who did not join a frankpledge for trial if necessary.[7]

A fourteenth-century statute sought to solve the problem of nightwalkers and plotters by closing the taverns after curfew. For the first offense, the taverner would have to pledge his drinking cup and be amerced 40d. The fines went up with repeated offenses.[8] Penalties were gradual but severe, and presumed that the proprietors were both well informed and answerable to the king for their tavern hours and their clientele.[9]

Control over aliens was a second concern of the statute. The language has a modern ring. "Some from parts beyond the sea, and others of this land ... do there [in London] seek shelter and refuge, by reason of banishment out of their own country, or who for great offense or other misdeed have fled from their own country." The complaint continued, "Some nothing do but run up and down through the streets, more by night than by day and are well attired in clothing and array, and have their food of delicate meats and costly." The solution that the statute offered was to allow only citizens or those who had become citizens and sworn their oaths to the mayor and aldermen to become innkeepers.[10]

The *Liber Albus*, in repeating the 1285 statute, added that no alien could have an inn or lodging-house on the waterside of the Thames because of the fear that aliens lodging with alien hosts were likely to form covins.[11] Zenobius Martyn, for instance, was indicted as a common bawd and an associate of prostitutes. He admitted to this charge and also confessed that he ran a "lodging-house for aliens and had acted as a broker against the ordinances of the City." He suffered the prescribed penalty and was put into prison.[12]

The repeated appeals made to innkeepers indicate that scandals had not stopped and were ongoing. In 1384, Mayor Nicholas Brembre again appealed for order, complaining that "larcenies and diverse evil deeds" were being committed openly because innkeepers were not careful about whom they harbored or how long they allowed them to stay. Innkeepers were to abide by the statute and not allow strangers at their tables on pain of paying a £100 fine. At that time, Brembre had 197 innkeepers swear to obey the law and to report innkeepers who did not do so.[13]

Further ordinances made taverners and innkeepers responsible for informing guests about the laws regarding bearing arms, keeping curfew, holding guests' goods for safekeeping, and so on. Aldermen and wardmotes were to keep a close watch on guests to see that they complied with the laws.[14] The officials and citizens duly carried out their responsibilities so that in 1372, for instance, Adam Grymmesby was committed to prison for not warning his lodger to leave his knife indoors after curfew. The watch confiscated the knife, and Adam was instructed to redeem it for his guest.[15]

Innkeepers were also responsible for protecting the property of their guests. William Beaubek of Kent claimed remedy against John de Waltham, innkeeper, on these grounds in 1345; and John Sappy, knight, did so against Thomas Hostiller of Le Swerd in 1380. Beaubek stated that he had rented a room for 1½ d. a week and that the innkeeper had given him a key to the room and an assurance that Beaubek's goods would be secure. William relied on the innkeeper's help to collect a debt and then deposited the money in a box in his room. Later, not only was the money missing but, so too, were gold and silver ornaments and plate that had been in the box. The innkeeper claimed that his brewer had entered the chamber by a garden door and committed the theft, but William held the innkeeper responsible for recovery of the value of the goods stolen. The court upheld him and the law. Sir John Sappy was also successful in his suit.[16]

On the whole, innkeepers and taverners appear in court records more often as breakers of the law than as enforcers. But that is a fairly typical problem with interpreting behavior from court records. Perhaps most did fulfill their peacekeeping obligations. By far the most common complaint was that they did not use the correct measures for their beer and ale, mixed bad wine with good, and did not let customers see the wine drawn.[17] In addition to charges of prostitution, charges of assault by taverners and innkeepers were also brought.[18] Despite the official doubts about innkeepers and taverners, they were often the first contact for people coming into London, and, as such, they were charged with the initial education of the newcomers.

The Wards

As we have seen, the ancient law specified that by the third night after entering the city, a guest was to participate in peacekeeping in the community by becoming a member of the frankpledge of a ward. The twenty-five wards formed the basic governmental units in London and each was administered by an alderman and the wardmote. The wards, however, wanted only those residents who were of good fame. In 1431, an ordinance required ward officials to make inquiries of new residents about where they came from and whether they had been charged with bad conduct or were unwilling to give sureties for their good behavior. Those who failed to meet these requirements were to quit the ward in four days.[19] It is difficult to imagine that all the wanderers in London could be tracked down to a fixed address in another ward or find sufficient references as to their good character.

Among the duties of the alderman was to take frankpledges. At the wardmote those who were not free of the city or had recently moved into the ward were to pay a penny and take an oath. The wardmote was sometimes held in the alderman's house, but could also be held in one of the gildhalls. Some people were exempt. Women of any age and male children under the age of fifteen were presumed to be under the control and correction of their husbands, masters, or fathers. Knights, esquires, clergy, and apprentices-at-law were also exempt. The oath was recorded in French, but must have been administered in English to be comprehensible to the majority of the immigrants. The oath required the usual allegiance to the king and obedience to the officers of the city. The peace of the city and the king's peace must be kept at all times. In addition, members of the frankpledge swore to attend wardmotes, participate in the watches as the constables required, and report any "evil covin" to the alderman.[20] Two rolls of frankpledge were kept, one for those free of the city and one for nonfree and hired servants.[21]

The wards offered the basic lessons in civic responsibility along with the obligation to participate in ward governance. Initially, the wardmote, a gathering of free and unfree residents as well as hired servants, advised the alderman. By the late fourteenth century, however, the *probi homines* (the established and respectable men of the ward) made up the ward's twelve-man jury. Once a year they made presentments of misdemeanors of ward residents, infractions of ordinances, and election of ward officials. The *Jubilee Book* of 1378, which was destroyed in London but a copy is preserved in Cambridge, had instructions for the wards. A primary function was to elect a beadle and select constables to patrol the streets. The beadle and ward jurors reported moral lapses, infractions of city ordinances, and disturbances of the peace. The *Liber Albus*, written forty years later, firmly placed the responsibility of keeping the peace on the beadle and the *probi homines*, indicating the increasing reliance on the established men of the community.[22] Significantly, the wardmote was a place where the ordinances applying to the ward and the city were read once a year. Newcomers and those already resident would have no excuse to misunderstand the import of the rules. In the 1378 version, the rules were to be read in English. John Carpenter's 1419 version does not specify what the language is to be, but they were probably read in English.[23]

For the heavy responsibilities placed on the beadle, he received some compensation from the ward.[24] The constables had the more dangerous jobs, however. They patrolled the streets, often breaking up fights or making arrests to take people to the sheriff's prison. There was an understandable reluctance to serve in the office because of the dangers involved. Fines were imposed on those who refused.[25]

Few wardmote records survive, so that it is impossible to assess the extent to which the swearing of frankpledge did occur, but those that exist suggest that neighbors were conscientious about reporting fellow neighbors and their infractions. Fewer "evil covins" were reported than were more routine neighborhood irritants such as noise, prostitution, and run down houses. The wardmotes were so important that Thomas Cromwell served as a ward juror in Broad Street ward in 1521. He heavily annotated the ward inquest himself.[26]

The Parish and Parish Gilds

Wenceslaus Hollar's panoramic map of London before the Great Fire shows the city bristling with church steeples belonging to the ninety-nine parish churches within the walls and an additional nine within the bars. (See Figure 1.1 for a sense of the density of parishes.) With so many parishes, it is easy to understand that the church and its activities were the center of a tightly knit community. Parishes were central to everyday life. Their bells marked the liturgical hours of the day and the passing of a parishioner. Their halls and churchyards provided not just services, but also entertainment and singing, communal meals, and sometimes even ward meetings. Stalls next to the church walls were rented out to small businesses and to beggars. The church marked the beginning of life with baptism, marriages were done at the church door, and burial masses and processions occurred at the church. Parish processions for Rogation Day were a type of "beating the bounds" around its borders and done with banners, singing, and music. That celebration and the feasts and drinkings were affirmation of communal identity.[27] While participation in services was open to all, the hierarchy of governance mirrored that within London with the wealthy men and their wives controlling the finances. Through its ceremonies and community activities the parishes taught and reinforced civility among its members.

The churchwardens' accounts (kept by laymen who administered the parish funds and paid for the upkeep of the church) from St. Mary at Hill, supplemented by the wills of wealthy parishioners, provide some of the best evidence of how a well-endowed parish functioned. The parish was one of five in the Billingsgate ward. St. Mary had a number of wealthy fishmongers, since it was near Billingsgate docks. It had, in the mid-sixteenth century about four hundred communicants, and probably the same number as in the late fifteenth century. Supplementing the support for the parish church were seven perpetual chantries that were bequeathed by wealthy parishioners to have a priest pray for their souls in perpetuity.[28] These major gifts and more modest *post obit* (after death) provisions by individuals provided money for the parish and also encouraged elaborate liturgy. St. Mary's hired chaplains for the chantries who could sing and perhaps also play the organ. The parish bought books of polyphony and hired singers for special occasions.

Rents collected from properties that donors left to the chantries and the parish church were a source of wealth. The accumulation of real estate and the number of disbursements to honor the donors' wishes required considerable administrative skill and the churchwardens' accounts indicate that it was done conscientiously. The parson along with the churchwardens and some of the more established men of the parish administered the finances, repaired the tenements, collected rent, and dispersed the payments. These men evolved an organization that had two churchwardens serving two-year terms. The terms were staggered so that one became a junior warden, moving on to become senior warden in the next year. Apparently, the wardens selected the men who would succeed them. One warden even made up a chart indicating the social hierarchy of the parishioners and consequently their ability to pay and participate in church governance. Aldermen, mayors, wealthy merchants all appeared on his list and on the lists of donors to the newly expanded church. They and no others are termed "the goodmen," although sometimes their wives shared the title. Service to the parish as churchwardens and as donors to the church fabric was all part of a spiritual bargain that reduced time in Purgatory. Support of the parish was among the good works that the church encouraged.[29]

Not only the wealthy raised money for parishes. Women who laundered and mended the altar cloths and vestments could offer their services for free rather than a wage. Women donated elaborate clothing for saints' statues and kept them clean. Especially popular were the female saints, who were supposed to aid in childbirth. Door-to-door collections, usually undertaken by a married couple, brought in money from those who would not be making big donations. Parishes also turned to fundraisers in the fifteenth century. Popular ones were Mayday and Hocktide, which was the second Monday and Tuesday after Easter. The tradition was for the women to tie up the men on Monday and for the men to bind the women on Tuesday. Release was procured through a donation to the parish church. The practice drew the attention of the mayors and aldermen as early as 1406 and remained a subject of condemnation through 1438. The injunctions are formulaic and probably do not refer to a parish activity but a general period of misrule: "No person of this city, or within the suburbs thereof, of whatsoever estate or condition such person maybe, whether man or woman, shall, in any street or lane thereof, take hold of or constrain, any person of whatsoever estate or condition he may be, within house or without." Apparently, the holiday was a general time of fun and rowdiness, and in 1446, before Queen Margaret was to arrive, the mayor again made an effort to ban the Hocktide celebrations.[30]

The adoption of the holiday for parish fundraising appears in the London churchwardens' accounts in the late fifteenth century. The historian of parishes, Katherine French, found that the parish churches encouraged women to organize the event and sometimes even provided a dinner from them afterward. The women did much better than the men at raising money, probably because their victims had more money to give away. At St. Mary at Hill the women gathered at least 22s. whereas the men collected about 6s. On one occasion the women raised £4.[31] Hocking and other women's services integrated them into the parish community in a more substantial way than doing laundry. In doing so, the women created all female groups that aided the parish, but also provided the women with a sense of governance.[32]

Other groups were brought into the parish fundraising activities. May Day cerebrations are less well documented in London than they were in the rural parishes, where it was a holiday for youths. John Stow speaks of the May Day celebrations, in particular, the large Maypole that was put up on Cornhill at St. Andrew Undershaft. It was a time for bonfires and shows of martial arts. In one parish, it seems to have been a children's fundraiser.[33]

If the parish organization was hierarchical, did the wealth of the parish trickle down to the poorer members? Spiritual benefits accrued to those who provided alms for the poor of the parish, who clothed the poor men who followed the hearse to the church, and who distributed food or money at funerals. All these charitable acts benefited the poorer parishioners. Bequests to the parish poor were often administered through the churchwardens. John Bedeham left money to three poor men at 4d. a week for 111 weeks and charged the parish to administer it. They duly did so, dispersing 111s. Other men provided for a bread and ale on the anniversary of their death. John Causton asked that on the first and second day of August the priests, clerks, children, and poor folks enjoy the repast. Goodman Cambridge did likewise.[34] The parish paid the expenses of two children including education, shoes, gowns and hose, and sometimes board. The children were educated, sang in the choir, and assisted with services.[35] The parish or wealthy parishioners provided burial for strangers who died within their borders. Sir John Plommer provided a bell that could be rung at the funeral of poor people at the charge of 1d.[36] Reciprocity was expected in that the poor would pray for the souls of the departed benefactors. Medieval Londoners felt that the very maintenance of the church, the parson, the chantry priests, the liturgy, and the fine music benefited the spiritual welfare of all parishioners and the city as a whole.

All parishioners participated in liturgical holidays that were both fun and edifying. The Boy Bishop was a power inversion festival that took place either on St. Nicholas Day (December 6) or Holy Innocents' Day (December 28). The choirboys dressed up as bishops and took the place of the clergy. The custom started in cathedrals and monasteries, but spread to parishes. The parish accounts contain references to miters, copes, and mantles. Some of these were very costly, being made of cloth of gold and velvet. About half of the London parishes celebrated this festival and perhaps even more did although there is not a record of them. The celebration was part of the general Christmas time festivities. Palm Sunday brought more serious entertainment. Men and boys played and sang parts of the Old Testament prophets. These celebrations got more elaborate in the sixteenth century, featuring platforms, painted cloth backdrops, and costumes.[37]

Parishioners' wills give a sense of the emotional ties that the parish fostered among its members. Testators often used fellow parishioners to act as executors for their wills, made bequests to friends in the parish, and left charitable gifts not simply to the church but also the parish poor. The wills suggest a close-knit neighborhood centered on the parish church. The elite relied on each other for service to the church and social interactions, but the poor were also part of their community of neighbors.[38] The selection of almsmen, sometimes individually named, and the inclusion of the poor in bread and ale events indicates a willingness to break bread with the less fortunate. Even poor women could be part of the parish landscape. The accounts of St. Andrew Hubbard show that the wardens received 6d. from Margaret Fruiterer for standing at the church door, and the beggar, Margaret Kene, paid a like amount to sit there. Kene must have done well collecting alms because she was able to pay 3s. for occupying a bench under the church wall for three years, and she duly paid that amount. During that time, she made 2d. for making two holy-water sticks (brushes used to sprinkle holy water).[39] She was as much a part of the parish as the elite and benefited from the generosity of the parishioners.

Parish gilds, voluntary associations connected with the parish church, also served as instructors in governance and civility for its members. They attracted some of the elite, but mostly the middling sorts, including couples and adult single men and women. Among other services, they provided a collective alternative to the chantries for smoothing the passage through Purgatory with prayers for dead members.[40] They were not in competition with the parish, but existed alongside and in cooperation with it, often contributing funds. Parish gilds became common in the fourteenth century in all the parishes of London and, indeed, throughout England. Historians have referred to them as "social-religious" gilds to distinguish them from the craft and merchant gilds and also because they provided social networks for members. London's 108 parish churches all had these associations of lay men and women. At least 150 such gilds existed in London.[41] They were often ephemeral groups that ran out of funds, but others came into being to take their place. In Italy, the confraternities were limited to men and were neighborhood and familial associations. Northern European socio-religious gilds were more like those of England.

Unlike craft or merchant gilds, the parish gilds were open to the residents of the parish or those outside it who were over fifteen years of age, but in practice, membership was limited to those who could pay the entry fees and quarterage (quarterly payments). The gild of St. Katherine at St. Mary Coleman St. charged new members 13s. 8d., whereas the gild of Garlekhith charged 6s. 4d. The gild of Sts. Fabian and Sebastian charged 13s. 4d. for new members and 4d. quarterage. A man did not have to pay an entrance fee for his wife, but she did have to pay the quarterage. That meant two shillings a year. Single women would pay the same as male brethren.[42] The gild of St. Magnus claimed to have a graduated scale with that some members paying 5 marks, some 40s., some 20s., and some nothing.[43] In other words, one had to have some disposable income to join a parish gild in London.

Gilds required moral rectitude as well as an entrance fee and quarterage. The Garlekhith gild stipulated that the aspirant be "of good loos (reputation), conditions, and bearing," loving Holy Church and his neighbors.

While the gild of the Assumption wanted entrants to be "of good conversation and fame."[44] The consent of the members was necessary for admission to the gild of St. Katherine. The newcomers were to swear on the book of the brotherhood to uphold the gild's articles. Each brother and sister, in token of love, charity, and peace should exchange a kiss of peace with all those present.[45] Good behavior had to continue among the membership. As one gild put it, if any of the brethren were of ill-repute, thieves, quarrelsome, or otherwise of wicked fame, he would be put out of the brotherhood without any delay.[46] St. Stephen's gild specified the offenses such as brawling, quarreling, wandering at night, playing at dice, and frequenting brothels as reasons for expulsion. Such a brother was given three warnings before being expelled.[47] To promote harmony in the gild, Garlekhith and others stipulated that members who had disagreements with each other were to seek arbitration by the gild masters. The party who did not abide by the agreement would be put out of the gild.[48] One London gild insisted that gambling was not permitted when the member was wearing the gild livery. Presumably, if he or she went home to change, gambling might be acceptable.[49]

Gild members could look very much like the haberdasher, carpenter, webber, dyer, and tapiser who turned up in their gild liveries to join Chaucer's pilgrims. The Trinity Gild and Sts. Fabian and Sebastian in the parish of St. Botolph without Aldergate have preserved accounts and membership records so that an analysis of members is possible. The registers cover the period of 1377 to 1463 and listed 667 members. Of these, 124 trades or occupations can be readily identified. The most common were brewers, with 25 members, followed by tailors, carpenters, butchers, dyers, grocers, maltmen, smiths, and goldsmiths. Only seventeen of the tradesmen were masters in their craft gilds. In addition to the tradesmen were 119 members who were clergy, government officials, and a few members of the nobility. Only one gild member became an alderman, but sixteen were common councilmen.[50] Of the nonclerical members admitted to the fellowship from 1377 to 1415, 69 percent were married couples, 26 percent were single men, and 5 percent were single women.[51] The London parish gilds were not the stepping-stones to power or the de facto town council that was true of Coventry, Westminster, and Norwich.[52] Wealthier merchants mostly found their religious and convivial association through their trade gilds instead of joining a parish gild.[53]

Lessons in civil and civic behavior were learned through gild service and attending the annual election meeting. The gilds had two wardens or masters and two men who kept the accounts and treasure. The Trinity Gild of Aldergate selected their new wardens on the feast of the Trinity with the outgoing wardens choosing the new wardens from those members living in the parish. St. Mary at All Hallows, London Wall, had four assistant masters in addition to four masters.[54]

Gild membership brought with it substantial benefits to members through social networks, identity with the fellowship, mutual religious services, and help if misfortune befell. The numerous bequests to gilds indicates their importance to people's lives. Gild identity was consolidated with an annual feast on the patron saint's day and, for those gilds that required them, liveries. Garlekhith and a few others had a livery and also a rule that the clothing was not to be sold within the year.[55] Fines for nonattendance indicate the seriousness of this convivial occasion. The London ordinances did not contain the explicit rules for behavior at feasts that those of Lynn did. In Lynn, the members were instructed not to hold on to the drinking bowl, to spit at the table, or nod off at the banquet.[56] Londoners must have assumed that their members knew their table manners.

Religious celebration was at the heart of parish gilds. Some were founded to add onto the parish church or repair it. Almost all provided candles for altars or before the image of their patron saint. Those who could afford to do so employed a gild chaplain and built a separate chapel connected to the church.[57] All the gilds were concerned with securing a decent burial for members and easing their passage through Purgatory by paying to have prayers said for the souls of the dead. The gilds provided torches, candles, and a hersecloth for the procession to the church. All members turned out in their livery for the occasion. Failure to attend incurred a fine of a pound of wax. If one of the brethren died ten miles or less outside London, the gild would arrange to have the body brought back. Members too poor to afford interment were buried at gild expense. The gilds paid for the service on the day of the funeral and mass the following day. In addition, they paid for thirty masses.[58] The collective burden of prayers was a type of mutual insurance for the afterlife.[59]

In addition to the spiritual comfort, many of the gilds offered some support for the sick and aged who had, not of their own doing, fallen into poverty or suffered misfortune. The Gild of the Holy Trinity of Coleman Street, not a wealthy gild, offered 14d. a week in charity. To prevent people from joining only when they were in need, gilds specified that one had to be a paid-up member for seven years. One gild specified that if a member received alms, he was not to beg in another parish.[60] Money for the aid came from the payments of quarterage, as well as from bequests and money put in the poor box. A few gilds added payment for a brother or sister who suffered poverty owing to robbery, accident, or fire and did not have the means to recover. Another offered aid to those who were falsely imprisoned. This last provision could have been welcome since prisoners or their family and friends had to provide the imprisoned's food, drink, and bedding. Some gilds were also prepared to offer loans to members if they could find people to stand surety for repayment. Another brotherhood encouraged brothers and sisters to offer employment to those young members who were out of work.[61] To know whether gilds actually acted on their provisions for charity, one would need to have the gild account rolls. Evidence for the dispersal of such charity for London does not survive, but the Trinity Gild in Lynn and the St. George Gild in Norwich, did make payments to members who fell into misfortune not of their own doing and also gave smaller amounts to the community poor.[62]

Parish gilds offered neighborhood social and pious networks for both citizens and noncitizens. They integrated into the community those who could afford the entrance fees and quarterly dues. Like parishes, they provided experience with governance. Their emphasis on seemly behavior, good will among members, and conservative religious practices reinforced the bourgeois values of tradesmen and women. Their openness to noncitizens and to women made them a valuable part of the larger body politic of the city and to the civil society of medieval England. Gilds connected the living and the dead through their rituals; they provided convivial gatherings; their liveries and identities advertised their cohesion and power as a social group.[63]

Lessons in the Streets

The streets of London were full of noise. In addition to the horses, carts, various industries, people talking, criers of goods for sale, and parish, funeral, and gild processions, there were the official proclamations. The serjeant-at-arms was a common crier, and he was a busy man. Public reading of charges against false bakers, liars, bawds, and prostitutes at the pillory have already been mentioned, but a number of proclamations on behalf of the king and the mayor were also made. Already mentioned is the recitation of city ordinances, but the common crier announced each will in Hustings and each plea terminated. He was also the city's mace-bearer. For his extensive duties, he was compensated with a robe or cloak when he was sworn in, a dwelling, a horse that was respectable enough that it would not disgrace the city when he carried out his duties, and he received payments for the various announcements he made. He was a recognizable figure in livery and on horseback and was well known to the population.[64]

As the editor of *Letter Book G* comments, it was not unusual for a new mayor to have the common crier recite the basic ordinances of the city as was done on St. Martin's Day, on November 11, 1354. The message prohibited wandering after curfew, having arms in the city except for the King's serjeants-at-arms; it required hostellers to warn their guests to lay aside their arms, and allowed anyone in the king's peace to arrest felons and deliver them to the sheriffs; no one was to join or maintain outlaws. Victualers, and others were to follow their trade; no taverner was to mix bad wine with good; brewers were to sell ale at specified prices; cornmongers had to abide by rules of city with no forestalling; filth was to be removed before houses; pigs were to be kept from wandering, and no forestalling of poultry or victuals, and so on.[65] It was a lot of instruction to take in at once and one wonders how many times and in what places these lengthy ordinances were proclaimed. But at least no one could plead ignorance of the law, and perhaps that was the purpose of the recitations.

Annual proclamations concerned keeping the peace on major holidays. They were rather formulaic: "That no manner [of] man nor child, of what estate or condition that he be, be so hardy to wrestle, or make ony wrestling within the sanctuary nor the bounds of St. Paul's, nor in none other open place within the City of London, upon pain of imprisonment of forty days, and making fine unto the chamber at the discretion of the Mayor and Aldermen." Similar proclamations were made against mumming plays and wearing of disguises in the streets over the Christmas period.[66] Other proclamations concerned lighting for the Christmas holidays, having a barrel of water ready in case of fire, and the keeping of curfew.[67] The inhabitants were continually kept informed, directed, and threatened by the common crier's public announcements.

Among the lessons in the street were bills of political propaganda posted on gates, walls, and church doors, but we have little record of their content. Certainly, they were read and repeated to those who could not read. The king was sufficiently concerned that he had proclamations made against them. One proclamation, in 1387, promises forfeiture of the goods of anyone who was "so hardy to speak, nor moan, nor publish . . . anything that might sound in evil or dishonest of our liege lord the king; nor of our lady the queen, or any lords.[68] Lollards' heretical manifestos appeared on church doors in the early fifteenth century and various political poems are mentioned in chronicles.[69] One of these was a piece of Lancastrian propaganda in 1456 to discredit Richard, Duke of York, featuring severed dogs' heads set on the standard in Fleet Street. Each head had a verse in its mouth complaining about how it had been sacrificed to the Duke's ambition.[70]

We know from the coroners' inquests that people in the street offered reprimands to those they perceived guilty of misbehavior. When two men attempted to cheat a man selling costard apples in the street, he raised the hue and cry. They tried to carry off five apples against his will. A passerby reprimanded the two men, who then followed the Good Samaritan and threatened him until he turned around and hit one of them with a staff. In another case, an esquire of the Earl of Arundel was riding fast enough through the street that he threw to the ground a woman carrying a child in her arms. John de Harwe, a porter, "begged him to ride more carefully," but the esquire struck him with a sword. In another case, two men reprimanded the prince's groom for urinating in a public lane. They claimed that they had informed him that there were public privies in the city and he should go there if he had to relieve himself. He claimed that they assaulted him with a knife, but he did not press charges and was fined.[71]

"Gregory's Chronicle" (1461–1469) has much to say about events in the London streets that provided lessons in behavior. He recounts the murder of a widow by a Breton who fled to a church to abjure the realm. But the women of the parish were waiting for him to appear after his forty days in sanctuary and pelted him with stones and dung and so killed him, even though the constables protected him. A frequent ending to Gregory's regular entries was a description of public procession of traitors from the Tower to Tyburn for hanging, drawing, and quartering, or the procession of Lollards to Smithfield for burning.[72] The heads of the traitors were placed on London Bridge and the quarters were distributed around the country. At one point the chronicler says that there were twenty-three heads on London Bridge.[73] The fate of more ordinary felons also drew comment. A man caught in a robbery after a royal proclamation that promised swift punishment when the king was in London was put to death at the stone cross in the Cheap.[74] The roundup of strumpets and forcing them to wear rayed hoods and carry white wands caught his attention, as well as the calls to keep the watch.[75] Occurrences on the streets of London did not escape this former mayor, and one can assume that the population of the city also observed and took lessons from what went on in the street. It is not surprising that Gregory and other chroniclers would have had some observations on the fate of Eleanor of Cobham, wife of Duke Humphrey of Gloucester.[76]

All London followed Eleanor Cobham's case and the one ballad that survives about her is a moral lesson that one should not presume to rise above one's social rank. The ballad, "The Lament of the Duchess of Gloucester," is a London one and must have been well known in streets and elsewhere long after she died.[77] The ballad story is intertwined with London's public spaces and reiterates its lessons on hierarchy. Eleanor Cobham married Duke Humphrey of Gloucester, who was in line for the throne should his nephew, Henry VI, die. Eleanor was from a gentry family and had married the Duke after his first marriage was annulled in 1428.[78] Londoners actively opposed Eleanor from the beginning. On March 8, 1428, a deputation of London women appeared before Parliament with a letter of complaint about Gloucester's desertion of his first wife.[79]

Eleanor's triumphant rise to power, riches, and social prominence ended abruptly in 1441 when she and several people close to her were charged with witchcraft, sorcery, and treason. According to the London chronicles, Eleanor received a message that her co-conspirators had been arrested while she was dining in luxury at the King's Head, a hotel that Edward III had built for royalty to watch the city pageants.[80] Eleanor was charged with forming a conspiracy with four other people, and the charges included necromancy, witchcraft, and sorcery.[81] Her trial took place before leading ecclesiastical authorities, London civic officials, and perhaps Henry VI himself. She admitted to some of the charges, but not all. She was convicted of sorcery. Her punishment was an ecclesiastical penance and her marriage to Humphrey was dissolved.[82]

Eleanor was to proceed in her chemise, holding a burning taper in her hand, to designated London churches (St. Paul's, Christ's Church, and St. Michael in Cornhill) on three market days, which she did on November 13, 15, and 17. It was not an easy penance. Scantily clothed for November, she went barefoot along the dirty, rough pavement, as a true penitent. It is the sort of punishment involving pain and public humiliation we have seen before in London. Because she was considered a political threat, she ended her life in exile on the Isle of Man, where she died in 1457, seven years after Humphrey's death.[83]

The moral lesson that Londoners were to take from the "The Lament" was that those who rose too high on the "wheel of fortune" were sure to fall off. The ballad is told as if she were the speaker instructing other women, with the words put into her mouth that "I was so high upon my whele / Myne owne estate I cowld not know...."[84]

> Alle women that in this world be wrowght,   angry
> By me they may insaumpulle take,   example
> As I that was browght up from nowght,
> A prince had chosyn me to his mate;
> My soffern lorde so to forsake,
> Yt is dulfull destenye.
> Alas! For to sorrow now shuld I slake:
> Alle women may be ware by me.
>
> I was so hygh upon the whele,
> My own estate I cowd not know;
> The gospell accordeth there-to ful well:
> Who wyll be hygh, he shall be lowe.[85]

The poem speaks of her punishment and her remorse. She says she "went bare fote and on my ffette ... and even suggests that she had to "ride the raille [hurdle]" or at least follow the traditional route that civic rituals of humiliation took. She concludes with a confession of wrongdoing and her "mysgovernaunce."[86]

Because so little popular poetry directly connected to London survives, it is hard to know what was sung in taverns, whistled in the streets, or enjoyed a general popularity.[87] Although a number of fifteenth-century poems have been preserved and are available in print,[88] there is no way of knowing whether the poems of Lydgate, Hoccleve, and Gower were known in the streets of London. Of the more popular poetry and carols, again, it is impossible to know what Londoners in general sang or recited. Much of the poetry is political comment and many poems lamented the evil of the times, but did any of these form a context for London's civic culture? The watermen of the Thames wrote a song about John Norman in 1453 for his innovation of taking a barge to Westminster for his oath taking as mayor, but only snatches of it survive.[89]

In addition to the deficiency of surviving popular ballads and carols, the plays of London are also absent. The chronicles mention plays at Clerkenwell/Skinners' Well, but no text survives. Apparently, the city contributed nothing to the plays, which were probably supported by parishes or clergy. Perhaps the civic processions and royal entries diverted revenue and talent in London.[90]

If oral lessons of morality in songs do not survive, some of the visual lessons are recorded. London's symbolic program on its buildings was predominately secular and related to rulers and to civic virtues. The gates of the city featured rulers. Ludgate had the images of Lud and other kings. As part of the reconciliation between Richard II and London in 1392, the king demanded that the citizens place painted stone statues of himself and his queen, Anne, above the stone gate of London Bridge. The royal arms of both, along with those of Edward the Confessor, were carved on the canopies. The project cost London £30. On Bishopgate, rebuilt in 1479 by the Hanse merchants, was a statue of the Norman bishop William, flanked by King Alfred and the ealdorman Aehelraed of Mercia. These were the men responsible for restoring London after the Viking raids and Bishop William negotiated the freedom of London with William the Conqueror. Erkenwald, the Anglo-Saxon bishop of London, appeared on the inner side of the gate. The presence of the bishops indicated that the bishop of London contributed to maintaining that gate. When Ludgate and Cripplegate were rebuilt in the late fifteenth century the coats of arms of the wealthy donors appeared on the gates. The city gates, therefore, presented a secular message and the largess of donors.[91]

The sculptural program on the front of the Guildhall perpetuated the secular message of London's civic buildings. The Guildhall, which had been in existence since the late twelfth century, was completely secular; a chapel was adjacent to it. In the early fifteenth century, a major renovation was undertaken and the façade facing the Guildhall yard was highly decorated. Figure 6.1 shows the placement of the statues at the fifteenth-century entrance to the Guildhall. The hierarchical statues in the niches included, at the apex, Christ in majesty, and below him were male figures representing Law and Learning, as seen in figure 6.2. An elaborate porch ran above the wide doorway and flanking the gate on either side were four female statues representing the four cardinal virtues of Discipline (Prudence), Justice, Fortitude and Temperance each trampling under foot a vice, as seen in figure 6.3. Such images were popular representations in the advice to princes' literature and in art at the time, but they must also have been a visual reminder of the civic virtues to those who passed the Guildhall or entered it to appear before the mayor's court.[92] These lessons in stone gave passersby a visual acquaintance with desirable civic virtues.

FIGURE 6.1 The 18th century drawing of the Guildhall shows the 15th century entry with the placement of its statuary. The Georgian windows above were a later addition.

From John Carter, watercolor, 1788,. with permission of the London Metropolitan Archives.

FIGURE 6.2 The two male figures from the 15th century entry to the Guildhall said to represent Law and Learning.
From illustration from John Carter. *Specimens of Ancient Sculpture and Painting Now Remaining in England for the Earliest Period to the Reign of Henry VIII*. London: Bohn, 1887.

London had many ways of inculcating lessons of civic behavior to both citizens and those who were newly arrived in the metropolis. First contact could be in a tavern where the taverners and innkeepers, acting as an extension of the peacekeeping, instructed their patrons in the civic rules and confiscated their weapons if necessary. Wards were the official arm of the city, requiring each newcomer to register in the ward and take an oath to obey the laws and officials of London. Parishes and parish gilds also integrated newcomers and long residents into the community. In terms

FIGURE 6.3 The four female figures from the 15th century entry to the Guildhall represent the four cardinal virtues of Discipline, Justice, Fortitude, and Temperance, each trampling a vice underfoot.

From John Carter. *Specimens of Ancient Sculpture and Painting Now Remaining in England for the Earliest Period to the Reign of Henry VIII*. London: Bohn, 1887.

of civic behavior, none of these institutions suggested anything other than respect for hierarchy. Even the parish governance and the parish gilds emphasized respect for the existing social order.

Lessons about responsible, civic behavior were everywhere. The very iconography of the city statuary reflected the civic virtues that were desirable. The parishes had performances, of which we know little, that taught generalized Christian virtues. Sermons, likewise, spoke of the wealthy offering succor to the poor, but the poor keeping their place. Londoners followed the morality taught by the parish priest and did provide for their own poor. But despite the general Christian overlay, London was a very secular city. The city crier was a familiar figure, telling people about correct behavior on the saturnalia of the Christmas holidays or the long summer revels of St. John the Baptist and Sts. Peter and Paul. Punishments for failing to obey the ordinances were spelled out by the city crier and those convicted were paraded through the streets. Finally, the streets, homes, and taverns must have been places to recite moral tales, but we only have one of these, "The Lament of Eleanor of Cobham." In a city that prided itself on its openness to upward mobility, the repeated refrain of maintaining the social and governmental hierarchy seems contradictory. But that hierarchy was one of achievement, not one of birth, and in this way it was very different from the nobility. In order to successfully move up in the hierarchy, one had to learn the correct civic behavior.

Conclusion

CONSIDER THE RUSH of activity in London as the city prepared for the annual inaugural procession of the mayor to Westminster to take his oath of office before the king and the Exchequer. The main route of the procession had to be cleaned. Prior arrangements had been made about the clothing of the officials (usually red and white) and the new hoods and cloaks tailored. Gilds had to have their representatives appropriately clothed in their colors, and they had to hire horn players and get out their banners. It was two weeks between the election of the new mayor and his oath taking. The city must have been very busy. And on the morning of the procession, the whole group had to be in readiness to march according the script that was formalized in the *Liber Albus*. Fortunately, since this was an annual event, the planning was somewhat routine. Royal entries must have been even more of a production because they involved getting out the structures that sat on the conduits, planning the tableaux, and new livery for officials and gilds. The conduits that normally ran with water had to be converted to run with wine. But the many ceremonials of London, ranging from the inauguration of the mayor to the humiliating ones of those who offended against the common good, were meant to convey messages beyond show. They established power relationships, and they taught lessons in civility and expected civic behavior.

London, like all premodern cities, drew much of its population from the hinterland and from abroad. Those who had citizenship made up a small portion of the population. The number of elites who served as gild wardens, aldermen, sheriffs, and mayors made up an even smaller part. The city's many immigrants had to be informed about the laws and ordinances of London, its customs and its officialdom, and the behavior expected of those who lived in the city. Ceremonies and rituals were an essential part of the process of assimilation. In a period when portraiture was uncommon, the annual event of the mayor's oath taking was a vivid tableau of those in power and the liveries they wore that identified them with their office. The political rituals of the mayor's and the sheriffs' oath taking established the power structure in London and showed the population, who were drawn to the show, who held the legitimate authority in the city.

A newly arrived man was integrated into the city through the requirement that he take an oath of frankpledge before the alderman of his ward when he established residence. He swore to uphold the laws of the city and to be obedient to the officials. In the ward, he participated in the ward governance. An apprentice arrived with a contract for his term, but he swore an oath to uphold his gild's rules and honor the king and the city government. The oath was taken before the whole gild, wearing their livery. When he completed his apprenticeship, he again swore an oath of gild loyalty and took his oath of citizenship. The oral component was an essential part of the public recognition of a new role for these initiates and impressed upon them the hierarchy that they were entering and the responsibilities that went with it.

Common to the ceremonies and rituals was an emphasis on establishing and maintaining hierarchy. English preachers repeatedly reminded people that the two basic tenants of Christian society were that it was organic and hierarchical. It was organic in the sense that it was frequently referred to with metaphors of the body, emphasizing the necessity of harmonious interaction of all parts to form a whole. Within that organic whole a hierarchy existed. The king was the head and, as one London preacher put it, the burgesses of London were the heart.[1] The London institutions all emphasized hierarchy, making the status of people in the their ranks clear. Within the city government, the mayor was the head of the body politic, assisted by two sheriffs and the twenty-five aldermen. These officials controlled the type of men who would serve on the Common Council and the appointment of city employees. A small group of elite merchant gilds, from the most powerful livery companies, provided the pool from which the mayor, aldermen, and sheriffs were selected. Within the gilds, hierarchy was strictly enforced. The wardens, selected from the most wealthy and prestigious members, who wore the full livery, regulated the gild products and practices, apprenticeships, and behavior of the members, including the yeomen. Masters controlled apprentices. The tavern keeper was responsible for his guests and referred to in the records as *pater familias*; the aldermen of each ward were responsible for frankpledge and wardmotes and the general cleanliness and peace of their wards. Even the parish church had a hierarchy; the lay churchwardens, "the good men" of the parish were drawn from the elite parishioners. Parish gilds required obedience to their wardens, set standards for behavior, and required an entrance fee and dues.

Challenges to the hierarchical order were inevitable. The mayor of London held the rank equivalent to that of an earl in the realm. Occasionally, an earl or duke would infringe on the mayor's status. The mayors were adroit at handling these clashes. The king was by far the most serious threat to the mayor and to the status of London in the realm. London's right to self-government came through a charter from the king, and a king could revoke it and take the city into his own hands, appointing a warden to govern the city. While London frequently lost its charter in the thirteenth century, only once more, at the end of the fourteenth century, did this happen. But London was always wary of the possibility that unrest in the city could bring the intervention of the crown. London officials and elites plied monarchs with gifts or made large loans to the crown. They provided lavish royal entry celebrations for the monarchs on their coronations, the arrival of their queens, and on return from foreign victories. They also acted swiftly to stop riots among gilds that could bring the wrath of the king on the city. These squabbles were sometimes settled with a ceremonial shared meal between the wardens of the rival gilds.

Many smaller challenges to the authority of the mayor and aldermen arose. Members of the elite had private grievances with the mayor or disagreed with his policies. They voiced their anger in person against a mayor or alderman or people who heard their derogatory words and reported them to the mayor. The mayor had a very persuasive weapon against such people. He could revoke their citizenship, thereby removing their right to trade in the city. For a businessman, this would be ruinous. They would be arrested and put Newgate prison, the prison for felons. Within a couple days they appeared before the mayor and aldermen on bended knee offering tuns of wine. The mayor and aldermen invariably showed mercy. To use a violent punishment on a fellow elite might start a factional dispute. Instead of the vast quantity of wine, the miscreant was either fined or posted a bond that he would pay the wine or a monetary amount if he transgressed again. Gild masters behaved in a similar fashion to those who broke the gild rules. The solutions worked well, and often offenders went on to become gild wardens themselves or to hold public office.

Those of lower rank in the hierarchy who insulted the mayor or aldermen or who broke the city ordinances could expect harsher punishment. London depended on victualers to supply the city with wholesome food and drink, and these trades were heavily regulated. Those committing fraud were punished. The moral cleanness of the city was also important, so bawds and prostitutes were punished. Offenders against the city ordinances would face imprisonment and humiliating punishments that involved stripping of some garments, penitential walks with a candle, perhaps a ride on a hurdle drawn behind a horse, and time on the pillory at Cornhill. Symbols played a part in these parades, with whetstones for liars, fraudulent products for cheats, and white wands for prostitutes as part of the show. The parades were very public, and there was music and a proclamation announcing the offense. The offender might even be escorted to a city gate and evicted forever. As the records of the cases state, the purpose of public punishment at all levels of the hierarchy was to teach others not to be so bold as to offend in this manner.

The city regarded itself as part of the larger Christian society. Its leaders assumed that the denizens shared these moral values. They expected moral rectitude from the inhabitants, and when it was lacking, their records show the dismay that they experienced, with such phrases as "not fearing God," acts "abhorrent to God," or "to the deception of the king's people" and "to the scandal and disgrace of the whole city." The pursuit of the common good was everyone's duty. This view was repeated in sermons, exemplified in parishes, underscored in the behavior expected from members of all types of gilds. In business, it was assumed that everyone who participated in trade would work within the laws and ordinances, but also with internalized constraints on their dealings. Shared norms were presumed, but they also had to be reinforced with good government and with continual lessons in proper civic values.

Londoners were masters of the symbols of power and their ritual use. Their symbols were secular rather than religious. The mayor had the sword of the city carried before him in processions. In contrast to other boroughs, in London only macebearers could carry a gilded mace like that of the earls. But what would have caught the eye of everyone in the street were the liveries. They were brightly colored with contrasting silk linings or they were particolored with red on one side of the body and white on the other. The sartorial splendor was a serious affair. A committee of aldermen selected the color and cloth of the new outfits. Gild wardens and the liveried members determined the cloth they would wear each year. Even the parish gilds had their liveries. Liveries were a corporate identity worn on the body of members. They advertised to others who these people were and where they stood in the hierarchy. The wearing of livery was only partially about the performance of self; it was more an allegiance of belonging to a group. The outfits of those wearing the livery of the mayor and other officials informed the public of their official positions; they empowered the wearers.

One might wonder why the hierarchical order did not result in protests. Partly, it was the unquestioned and presumed social order of a Christian society. More importantly, social status in London was fluid. London did not create a hereditary elite with wealth and businesses that passed from one generation to the next, as was typical on the Continent. Wealth could be destroyed by misfortune or bad business decisions. Sons did not necessarily follow in the same business as fathers, and some of the successful businessmen bought land in the countryside and blended into the landed gentry. Disease, as well, opened up new opportunities as possible heirs died or men died without issue. New men, such as Richard Whittington, could rise to wealth and prominence in city and gild politics. With such potential for opportunity to move up there was little reason to question the social arrangements.

The model of the gild permeated London male society. It was the organizing principle that they understood well. At all levels of male civic engagement, whether that of bachelors and yeoman, parish confraternities, or craft or merchant misteries, the organization was based on that of the gild. Even the bachelors and yeomen, who might have had the most reason to break ranks and think of a different way to achieve their ends of higher wages, relied on the model of a religious gild to bring their members together. The society was one that did not think in terms of throwing over the old hierarchical system, but of how to become part of it. Although it may seem to modern historians that attempts to challenge the mayor and the gild system were the stirrings of modern democracy, the rebels themselves were quite conservative.

City governance, although limited to a small group of elites, was openly on view. In modern terms, they conducted their business with transparency. The sheriff's court and the mayor's court were held in the Guildhall. The assessment of grain to determine the price of loaves of bread was done openly by elites who became skilled at their assaying work. The public nature of oaths from the basic one of joining the frankpledge in a ward to the oaths of citizenship were binding on the oath taker and required loyalty to the mayor as well as the king and obedience to the laws of the city. In a society that was still largely oral and visual, oaths were serious matters. In London, a man could clear his good name if he had a sufficient number of men who would swear an oath to his good repute.

Urban space was crucial to the performance of ceremony and ritual. In addition to the enclosed structures of the Guildhall, St. Paul's, gildhalls, and parish churches, the area around the Guildhall, the open area of the Cheap, and the processional space to St. Paul's were all part of the routine area of civic ceremonial. Other routes were added as needed, such as the Bridge, the passage of the hurdle to the pillory on Cornhill, the royal progress from the Tower through London to Westminster, the barge on the Thames to Westminster. All of these passages could be packed with symbolic significance. But even the side streets could be used for local processions, including funeral processions to the parish church, gild processions on the gild's saint's day, and parish processions. All of these took the display of hierarchy into public space, where much of life was lived in medieval cities. Music accompanied processions. It might be horns for the mayor and sheriffs, or funeral dirges for the departed, or tabors for the miscreants taken to the pillory. Or the street could be turned into festival as at Christmas or at the Midsummer Watch when the officials turned out to police the wards. Urban space was adaptable to ritual practice. Residents could expect to be entertained and instructed frequently in the streets.

By the first quarter of the fifteenth century London had acquired sufficient stability in its own institutions and loyalty from its inhabitants to avoid being drawn into disputes over royal succession. While not all went smoothly, the mayor and aldermen managed to control the city. The fifteenth-century *Journals* show that citizens increasingly relied on the mayor's arbitration in their many disputes. This trust reflects a confidence in the government. The collection of cartularies and chronicles that proliferated among the citizens in the fifteenth century attest to the pride that they felt in their city and their own sense of continuity. Following the anthropologist Catherine Bell's suggestion, the repetition of rituals, such as the annual election of the mayor, created a seasonal cycle to the year and reinforced a renewal of power and a sense of the orderliness.[2] Carpenter praised the well-being of the city in an entry in *Letter Book I* in 1412. "Of all cities in the West, this City of London, the most ancient, is rendered praiseworthy and famous by the governors thereof, men known to be and to have been persons of experience and reflugent by their discreetness; and, more especially, because that at the present day its rulers do unweariedly labor to end what is for private advantage only, and to increase the public weal."[3]

Glossary

Alderman. Elected official in charge of governing one of London's twenty-five wards. He took oaths of frankpledge, held wardmotes, and was responsible for peace-keeping in his ward. He was a member of the aldermanic council and worked closely with the mayor.

Attach. To legally arrest someone or take property.

Beadle. A man of good standing in the ward. He duties included keeping peace in the ward and reporting cases of immorality and infractions of the city ordinances to the alderman and motecourt.

Calendar. List of documents that included summaries of their contents.

Cartulary. A manuscript containing transcriptions of original documents, such as charters, letters from the king, and other matters relating to the privileges or history of London.

Chamberlain. The chief financial officer of the city. He collected and spent city revenues, kept city records, protected the property of orphans, and reviewed the qualifications of those entering the freedom of the city. He was elected, but with the strong input of the mayor and aldermen. Andrew Horn was elected chamberlain in 1320.

Common Clerk. Elected official, usually served a number of terms. He was charged with overseeing the clerks who recorded the business of the city courts, elections, and keeping the official documents of the city. John Carpenter was elected common clerk in 1417.

Common Pleader. *See* Serjeant-at-Arms.

Constable. A ward official and a subordinate of the beadle, to whom he reported. Wards could have more than one constable depending on their size. The constable's duties included pursuing offenders and arranging for panels of jurors.

Currency 1d. = 1penny, 1s.[shilling] = 12d [denarius or one penny]., £1 = 20s., 1 mark = 13s. 4d.

Distraint. The seizure of someone's property in order to secure money that they owed.

Frankpledge. System by which males over the age of twelve were required to take an oath in the ward to uphold the laws of the city and to participate in the governance and policing of the ward.

Gild or mistery. Corporation of merchants or craftsmen who regulated apprenticeships, the quality of their services or products, requirements for membership, and the behavior of members. Also parish gilds devoted to religious needs of members and yeoman gilds of wage workers.

Livery. Distinctive dress (not a uniform) worn by the mayor of London, the aldermen, and other officials that identified them with their office. The outfits were styled in the fashion of the day but had distinctive color combinations. Gilds also had liveries that identified them with their corporate bodies. The name "livery companies" derives from the livery the gilds wore to distinguish them from other gilds.

Measures tun = 252 gallons; pipe or butt = half a tun; barrel = 1/8 of a tun; cask = 9 gallons.

Serjeant-at-Arms. An elected official who served as the Common Pleader for the commons in the election of the mayor. He was also the Crier and announced the city ordinances, injunctions from the king, terms of wills in Hustings Court, and the charges against people led to the pillory. He also bore the city's mace of civic occasions.

Surety. A person who takes responsibility for someone's appearance in court or payment of a bond or debt.

Thew. A special pillory for women that permitted them to sit.

Ward. Administrative unit in the city. London had twenty-four wards until 1394, when one of the biggest wards was divided into two. The alderman was in charge of the ward. The business of the ward was to take frankpledge, hold wardmotes, and generally to keep the peace and oversee street cleaning.

Wardmote. Court held by the alderman of a ward to hear local pleas made against the offenders for misdemeanors and property offenses.

Abbreviations

CCorR	*Calendar of Coroners' Rolls*
CEMCR	*Calendar of Early Mayor's Court Rolls*
CPMR	*Calendar of Plea and Memoranda Rolls of the City of London*
EETS	Early English Text Society
Jour	*Journals of the Common Council.* Manuscript series in LMA
GL	Guildhall Library
LBA–LBL	*Calendar of Letter Books of the City of London, vols. A–L*
LMA	London Metropolitan Archives
TNA	The National Archives (London)

Notes

INTRODUCTION

1. Anthony Black, *Guilds and Civil Society in European Political Thought from the Twelfth Century to the Present* (Ithaca, NY: Cornell University Press, 1984), chap. 3. Black has argued that using the medieval term is preferable to more modern terms of Hegel and Habermas because those imply a later bourgeois society. I prefer this formulation of the concept of civil society to that of Frank Rexroth, *Deviance and Power in Late Medieval London*, trans. Pamela Selwyn (Cambridge: Cambridge University Press, 2007), 96–110. He used the terms "purity" and "transparency." He amalgamates the various terms used in the ordinances and the court cases for the wholeness of the city into the concept of "purity." "Transparency" is a modern term that does little for our understanding of civic culture in medieval London.
2. James Davis, *Medieval Market Morality: Life, Law and Ethics in the English Market Place* (Cambridge: Cambridge University Press, 2012). See particularly chapter 1 in which he discusses the various influences on market morality, including sermons, poems, church wall paintings, and devotional literature.
3. Martha C. Howell, *Commerce before Capitalism in Europe, 1300–1600* (Cambridge: Cambridge University Press, 2010), 194. See particularly chapter 4, on the sumptuary legislation in Europe. In northern Europe and particularly in England, the concern that the upwardly mobile could appear in the clothing above their rank threatened the hierarchical status quo. Hence the need arose to legislate the appropriate attire for various social ranks. The statutes were very hard to administer.
4. Victor Turner, *The Ritual Process: Structure and Anti-Structure* (Ithaca, NY: Cornell University Press, 1969).
5. Clifford Geertz, *Negara: The Theater State of Nineteenth-Century Bali* (Princeton, NJ: Princeton University Press, 1980), 102, 124, 131.

6. Catherine Bell, *Ritual Perspectives and Dimensions* (New York: Oxford University Press, 1997).
7. Richard Trexler, *Public Life in Renaissance Florence* (New York: Academic Press, 1980); Edward Muir, *Civic Ritual in Renaissance Venice* (Princeton, NJ: Princeton University Press, 1981); Andrew Brown, *Civic Ceremony and Religion in Medieval Bruges c. 1300–1520* (Cambridge: Cambridge University Press, 2011); Peter Arnade, *Realms of Ritual: Burgundian Ceremony and Civic Life in Late Medieval Ghent* (Ithaca, NY: Cornell University Press, 1996).
8. Marcello Fantoni, "Symbols and Rituals: Definition of a Field of Study," in *Late Medieval and Early Modern Ritual: Studies in Italian Urban Culture*, ed. Samuel Cohen Jr., Marcello Fantoni, Franco Fraceschi, and Fabrizio Ricciardelli (Turnhout, Belgium: Brepols, 2013), 15–40. Philippe Buc, in *The Dangers of Ritual: Between Early Medieval Texts and Social Scientific Theory* (Princeton, NJ: Princeton University Press, 2001), cautions about using the word at all, although he has resolved the problem by putting it in quotes.
9. Barbara A. Hanawalt, *The Wealth of Wives: Women, Law and the Economy in Late Medieval London* (New York: Oxford University Press, 2007), esp. chaps. 3 and 4. Men tended to marry women younger than themselves in their first marriages; and consequently many widows survived them and remarried. The inheritance laws were generous to widows, who could take their dower into a second marriage. The practice of remarriage of widows tended to concentrate wealth in the hands of fewer and fewer elites.
10. Muir, *Civic Ritual in Renaissance Venice*, 3
11. Brown, *Civic Ceremony and Religion in Medieval Bruges*, see especially the Introduction. He argues that the civic authorities tried to establish their own power by allying with religious ceremony.
12. Trexler, *Public Life in Renaissance Florence*, 2–3.
13. Mervyn James, "Ritual Drama and Social Body in the Late Medieval Town," *Past and Present* 98 (1983): 3–29; Charles Phythian Adams, "Ceremony and the Citizen: The Communal Year in Coventry, 1450–1550," in *Crisis and Order in English Towns, 1500–1700*, ed. Peter Clark and Paul Slack (London: Routledge, 1972). A very considered reply to Mervyn James is the essay by Sarah Beckwith, "Ritual, Theater, and Social Space in the York Corpus Christi Cycle," in *Bodies and Disciplines: Intersections of Literature and History in Fifteenth-Century England*, ed. Barbara Hanawalt and David Wallace. Medieval Cultures 9 (Minneapolis: University of Minnesota Press, 1996), 63–86. The arguments against the inclusivity of city ceremony are numerous. See, for instance, Sheila Lindenbaum, "Ceremony and Oligarchy: The London Midsummer Watch," in *City and Spectacle in Medieval Europe*, ed. Barbara A. Hanawalt and Kathryne L. Reyerson, Medieval Studies at Minnesota 6 (Minneapolis: University of Minnesota Press, 1994), 171–88; Ben R. McRee, "Unity and Division? The Social Meaning of Guild Ceremony

in Urban Communities," in Hanawalt and Reyerson *City and Spectacle*, 189–207. McRee notes how important it was to the gildsmen to make distinctive dress and ceremonies, so that their members stood out from the rest of the population. In so doing, they created tensions within the Norwich community.

CHAPTER 1

1. *Memorials of London*, 492.
2. Derek Keen, "A New Study of London before the Great Fire," in *Urban History* 11, (1984): 11–21; B. M. S. Campbell, J. A. Galloway, D. Keen, and M. Murphy, *A Medieval Capital and Its Grain Supply: Agrarian Production and Distribution in the London Region c. 1300*, Historical Geography Research Group, 30 (Lancaster, 1993), 172, estimated the population at 100,000 based on a survey of property ownership in Cheapside. Pamela Nightingale, however, disputed this estimate in "The Growth of London in the Medieval Economy," in *Progress and Problems in Medieval England*, ed. Richard H. Britnell and John Hatcher (Cambridge: Cambridge University Press, 1996), 89–106, esp. 97–98. She cited evidence that the food consumption of the city was not consistent with a population of 100,000 and that Cheapside was heavily populated in the beginning of the fourteenth century, but large portions of the city were not heavily populated.
3. For a discussion of medieval housing in London, see John Schofield, *Medieval London Houses* (New Haven, CT: Yale University Press, 1994).
4. Caroline M. Barron, "London 1300–1540," in *The Cambridge Urban History of Britain*, ed. D. M. Palliser (Cambridge: Cambridge University Press, 2000), 395–440. This essay provides a very useful overview of London, covering population, topography, the economy, and governance.
5. Sylvia L. Thrupp, *The Merchant Class of Medieval London*, (Chicago: University of Chicago Press, 1948), chap. 5. Thrupp pointed out that the merchants who became wealthy tended to buy country property and marry into the gentry rather than remain in London. See also Barbara A. Hanawalt, *The Wealth of Wives: Women, Law, and the Economy in Late Medieval London* (New York: Oxford University Press, 2007), chap. 5. I pointed to another factor as well in that widows tended to outlive their husbands and then married other London merchants, so that the emphasis was on horizontal ties in the gilds rather than the vertical ones that are typical of Ghent, Florence, and Venice. Patrilineal ties seemed much less important to Londoners than to men on the continent.
6. Caroline M. Barron, "Richard Whittington: The Man behind the Myth," in *Studies in London History Presented to Philip Edmund Jones*, ed. A. E. J. Hollaender and William Kellaway (London: Hodder and Stoughton, 1969), 197–250.

7. *Calendar of Coroners' Rolls of the City of London, 1300–1378*, ed. Reginald R. Sharpe. (London: Richard Clay and Sons, 1913), 40, 44, 46, 48, 51, 52, 54 (three deaths, one due to starvation), 56, 65 (three deaths), 67–68 (five deaths, one due to starvation), and 80. These all took place during the famine years of 1321–23. In 1325–26 four deaths .124, 126 (two deaths), 128, 136, 139, 152, 153 (two deaths), 154 (three deaths).
8. *Memorials of London*, 677; A. H. Thomas, "Sidelights on Medieval London Life," *Journal of the British Archaeological Association*, 3rd ser., 2 (1937): 107–10, for a discussion of British prisons.
9. Kevin G. T. McDonnell, *Medieval London Suburbs* (London: Phillimore, 1978).
10. For a discussion of the attempts to control filth in London streets, see a series of articles by Ernest Sabine: "Butchering in Mediaeval London," *Speculum* 8 (1933): 335–53; "City Cleaning in Mediaeval London," *Speculum* 12 (1937): 19–43; and "Latrines and Cesspools of Mediaeval London," *Speculum* 9 (1934): 303–21. For a more recent study of health measures in England, see Carole Rawcliffe, *Urban Bodies: Communal Health in Late Medieval English Towns* (Woodbridge, UK: Boydell, 2013).
11. Caroline M. Barron, *London in the Later Middle Ages: Government and People 1200–1500* (Oxford: Oxford University Press, 2004), chaps. 4 and 5, for the overseas and redistributive trades.
12. Barron, *London in the Later Middle Ages*. chap. 3. For the ordinary shopper buying from markets and hucksters, see Martha Carlin, "Putting Food on the Table in Medieval London," in *London and the Kingdom: Essays in Honour of Caroline M. Barron*, ed. Matthew Davis and Andrew Prescott, Harlaxton Medieval Studies 16 (Donnington: Shaun Tyas, 2008), 58–77.
13. Lawrence Manley, *Literature and Culture in Early Modern London* (Cambridge: University of Cambridge Press, 1995), 223–29.
14. Manley, *Literature and Culture*, 226–27 for his map for these itineraries.
15. *Ecclesiastical London*, ed. Mary C. Erler, Records of Early English Drama (Toronto: University of Toronto Press, 2008); Hannes Kleineke, "Civic Ritual, Space and Conflict in Fifteenth-Century Exeter," in *Ritual and Space in the Middle Ages: Proceedings of the Harlaxton Symposium 2009*, ed. Frances Andrews, Harlaxton Medieval Stuties 21 (Donington, UK: Shawn Tyas, 2011), 165–78. The area in Exeter for ceremonial use was so small that fights frequently broke out over access to the space.
16. *LBD*, 35–96.
17. *LBD*, 197. The oath at this time (1318) was in French. See also *LBG*, 179–80, for further elaboration in the late 1360s. Masters should testify that the apprentice has served faithfully and at least seven years. Citizens could buy and sell wholesale within the city or without. But they could sell retail in the city only those goods that belonged to their own gilds. A further recommendation was that only apprentices who could pay 60 s. should be admitted. The others would have to work as hired labor (journeymen) so that there would not be an undue increase in the number of masters in the city.

18. *LBG*, 179–81; *CPMR: 1323–1364* 10–11.
19. *LGK*, 34 (1423), 180 (1434).
20. *LBK*, 290 (1443). The reason for extending this franchise was to foster divine worship without injuring anyone in the city.
21. LMA, Jour 5, fol. 260. Jour 7, fol. 89. reinforced the ancient custom regarding women.
22. *LBK*, 108 (1429), 337 (1451); *LBI*, 257–258 (1421).
23. LMA, Jour 1, fols. 47–47v., 71; Jour 4, fols. 18, 54v.; Jour 5, fol. 184.
24. LMA, Jour 1, fol. 76v.
25. LMA, Jour 7, fol. 48v., 149.
26. Barbara A. Hanawalt, *Growing Up in Medieval London: The Experience of Childhood in History* (New York: Oxford University Press, 1993), 89–108; Hanawalt, *Wealth of Wives*, 69–115.
27. TNA, Just. 2/194A, ms. 2, 3, 5 for the years of the 1315–16 famine.
28. TNA, Just. 2/194A, ms. 5; *CCorR*, 61, for the famine years of 1322–23.
29. Barbara Hanawalt, "Reading the Lives of the Illiterate: London's Poor," *Speculum* 80 (2005): 1067–86, for a more complete discussion. On poverty and poor relief in England more generally, see Marjorie Keniston McIntosh, *Poor Relief in England, 1350–1600* (Cambridge: Cambridge University Press, 2012).
30. Thrupp, *Merchant Class*, 14–18.
31. The term oligarchy has led to debate among historians. Susan Reynolds, "Medieval Urban History and the History of Political Thought," *Urban History* 9 (1982): 20–22. She argues that the term "oligarchy" implies democracy, which was certainly not a concept in the Middle Ages. Stephen H. Rigby, "Urban 'Oligarchy,'" in Late Medieval England," in *Towns and Townspeople in the Fifteenth Century*, ed. John A. F. Thomson (Gloucester, UK: Alan Sutton, 1988), 62–86; Stephen. H. Rigby and Elizabeth Ewan, "Government, Power, and Authority 1300–1540," in *The Cambridge Urban History of Britain*, vol. 1, ed. D. M. Palliser (Cambridge: Cambridge University Press, 2000), 291–312. Rigby and Ewan saw the control of the oligarchy as a general phenomenon, not simply for London. Jenny Kermode, "Obvious Observations on the Formation of Oligarchies in Late Medieval English Towns," in *Towns and Townspeople in the Fifteenth Century*, ed. John A. F. Thomson (Gloucester, UK: Alan Sutton, 1988), 87–106, uses the term without questioning it, as does David Gary Shaw, "Social Networks and the Foundations of Oligarchy in Medieval Towns," *Urban History* 32, no. 2 (2005): 200–222.
32. Caroline M. Barron, "The Political Culture of Medieval London," in *Political Culture of Late Medieval England*, ed. Linda Clark and Christine Carpenter (Woodrbidge, UK: Boydell, 2004), 4:128–31. Barron sees the revolt of Northampton and that of Ralph Holland as reflecting popular ideas on government that "all men were equal before the law." Reynolds, "Medieval Urban History," 21, found no evidence of ideological tracts. Peter Fleming, "Telling Tales of Oligarchy in the Late

Medieval Town," in *Revolution and Consumption in Late Medieval England*, ed. Michael Hicks (Woodbridge, UK: Boydell, 2001), 177–93. Fleming points out that protest against the oligarchy would require some ideology of power. He finds little evidence of discontent with oligarchy.

33. Elizabeth New, "Representation and Identity in Medieval London: The Evidence of Seals," in Davies and Prescott, *London and the Kingdom*, 246–565.
34. Barron, "Political Culture," 113–15, in Clark and Carpenter, *Late Medieval Britain*. *LBH* contains a description of the ceremony of the breaking of the old seal before the full congregation held in the upper chamber of the Guildhall. The new seal was unveiled. By common assent the new seal was "of honorable aspect and a work of art." *Memorials of London*, 447–48.
35. LMA, Jour 5, fols. 65v, 90v, 130.
36. Geoffrey of Monmouth, *The History of the Kings of Britain*, ed. Michael D. Reeve, trans. Neil Wright (Woodbridge, UK: Boydell, 2007), lviii.
37. Geoffrey of Monmouth, *History of the Kings of Britain*, 6–30.
38. Muir, *Civic Ritual in Renaissance Venice*, 67.
39. *The Brut or The Chronicles of England*, ed. Friedrich W. D. Brie, pt. 1, EETS, orig. ser. 131 (London: K. Paul, Trench, Trübner, 1906), 1–4, 5–16.
40. William Fitz Stephen, *A Description of London*, trans. H. E. Butler, in F. M. Stenton, *Norman London: An Essay*, Historical Association Leaflets 93, 94 (London: G. Bell and Sons, 1934), 55.
41. *Munimenta Gildhalle Londoniensis: Liber Albus, Liber Custumarum et Liber Horn*, edited by Henry Thomas Riley. (London: Rolls Series, 1860), 2, 2–15.
42. *Liber Albus: The White Book of the City of London*, comp. John Carpenter and trans. Henry Thomas Riley (London: Richard Griffin and Co, 1861), 54–55.
43. *LBK*, 80, 90. Trojan law was cited in this case since the brothers had lived peacefully, "with honest conversation and free condition," in London for forty years, but had been claimed as serfs.
44. *The Chronica Maiora of Thomas Walsingham (1376–1422)*, trans. David Preest, with introduction and notes by James G. Clark (Woodbridge, UK: Boydell, 2005), 262; Sheila Lindenbaum, "The Smithfield Tournament of 1390," *Journal of Medieval and Renaissance Studies* 20 (1990): 10.
45. Fitz Stephen, *Description of London*, 31–32.
46. Fitz Stephen, *Description of London*, 27.
47. Fitz Stephen, *Description of London*, 28–32.
48. Mary-Rose McLaren, *The London Chronicles of the Fifteenth Century: A Revolution in English Writing* (Cambridge: Cambridge University Press, 2002), 11, 15–39. McLaren writes that hundreds of these chronicles must have been written, but only forty-four survive. See also by the same author, "Reading, Writing and Recording: Literacy and the London Chronicles in the Fifteenth Century," in Davies and Prescott, *London and the Kingdom*, 346–65.

49. McLaren, *London Chronicles*, 51–63. For an alternative interpretation of Henry's procession on his return to the throne, see Paul Strohm, "Interpreting a Chronicle Text: Henry VI's Blue Gown," in Davies and Prescott, *London and the Kingdom*, 335–45.
50. McLaren, *London Chronicles*, 47–49.
51. McLaren, *London Chronicles*, 15, 25, 31–46.
52. McLaren, *London Chronicles*, 39–48.
53. Debbie Cannon, "London Pride: Citizenship and the Fourteenth-Century Custumals of the City of London," in *Learning and Literacy in Medieval England and Abroad*, ed. Sarah Rees Jones (Turnout, Belgium: Brepols, 2003), 188–98. For valuable insights into the role of London's civic writings on Thomas Moore, see Sarah Rees Jones, "Thomas Moore's *Utopia* and Medieval London," in *Pragmatic Utopias: Ideals and Communities, 1200–1630*, ed. Rosemary Horrox and Sarah Rees Jones (Cambridge: Cambridge University Press, 2001), 117–35.
54. Cannon, "London Pride," 181.
55. Paul Strohm, "Three London Itineraries," in *Theory and the Premodern Text* (Minneapolis: University of Minnesota Press, 2000), 3–19.
56. Derek Pearsall, "Langland's London," in *Written Work: Langland, Labor, and Authorship*, ed. Steven Justice and Kathryne Kerby-Fulton (Philadelphia: University of Pennsylvania Press, 1997), 185–207.
57. *England from Chaucer to Caxton*, ed. Henry Stanley Bennett (London: Methuen, 1952), 124–28.
58. *England from Chaucer to Caxton*, 109–11; *Chronicles of London*, ed. Charles Kingsford (Oxford: Clarendon, 1905), 253–55. The poem was recited at a banquet on the occasion of the Scottish ambassador's visit to London in 1501.

CHAPTER 2

1. *Liber Albus*, 119.
2. Barron, *London in the Later Middle Ages*, 9–29. She sees the basic problems with the crown as arising over money. London's role in king making declined in importance. In the fifteenth century, London very reluctantly supported the Yorkists, and by the accession of Henry Tudor, their role was negligible.
3. Ian W. Archer, *The Pursuit of Stability: Social Relations in Elizabethan London* (Cambridge: Cambridge University Press, 1991). In the Tudor period as well, crises led Londoners to seek ways of creating a stable environment in the city. Lorraine Attreed, "The Politics of Welcome: Ceremonies and Constitutional Development in Later Medieval English Towns," in Hanawalt and Reyerson, *City and Spectacle*, 208–31, also speaks of the need to provide shows for royal entries in order to seek stability.
4. Reginald R. Sharpe, *London and the Kingdom*, (London: Longsman Green, 1894), 1: 34–35.

5. Gwyn A. Williams, *Medieval London from Commune to Capital* (London: Athelon, 1963), 3.
6. Frank Rexroth, *Deviance and Power in Late Medieval England*, trans. Pamela E. Selwyn (Cambridge: Cambridge University Press, 2007), 34–43. Rexroth, coming to the study of London from the point of view of a continental historian, seemed to have found London's reliance on the crown to be strictly limiting. Williams's discussion of the commune is much more subtle.
7. Rexroth, *Deviance and Power*, 219–42.
8. Rexroth, *Deviance and Power*, 243–63.
9. Barron, *London in the Later Middle Ages*, 149.
10. Barron, 33. For the broader picture of London in the reign of Edward III, see W. Mark Omrod, *Edward III* (New Haven, CT: Yale University Press, 2011).
11. *Memorials of London*, 202–3. *LBH*, ccx. The claim that London was the model for other cities in the realm was not an idle boast. *The Calendar of the Letters from the Mayor and Corporation of the City of London, c. 1350–1370*, ed. R. R. Sharp (London: John Edwards Francis, 1885), contains correspondence with other cities in which they solicit advice on how to handle various situations.
12. Nightingale, *A Medieval Mercantile Community: The Grocers' Company and the Politics and Trade of London 1000-1485* (New Haven, CT: Yale University Press, 1989),169–72. She points to a general increase in disturbance of the peace in London as a result of the economic hard times.
13. Thomas, Introduction to *CPMR:1323–1364*, xxvi–xxviii.
14. Anne Lancashire, *London Civic Theater: City Drama and Pageantry from Roman Times to 1558* (Cambridge: Cambridge University Press, 2002), 48–49. The description of the first pageant comes from John Stow, *A Survey of London: Reprinted from the Text of 1603*, ed. C. L. Kingsford (Oxford: Clarendon Press, 1971), 1, 96. *Memorials of London*, 107, has a description of the ship.
15. *CPMR: 1323–1364*, 103–7, 128, 189.
16. *CPMR: 1323–1364*, 123.
17. William Herbert, *The History of the Twelve Great Livery Companies of London* (London: published by author, 1838), 2:11, 306.
18. *CPMR: 1323–1364*, 122–23, 126–27.
19. *CCorR*, 266–69.
20. *CPMR: 1324–1364*, 128–29. The charge from the king appears in *LBF*, 18–23, and the writ from the king exonerating and praising the mayor for his part in the execution is on 138. Nightingale, *A Medieval Mercantile Community*, 172–74, has a summary of the case and praise for Mayor Aubrey for his handling of the situation.
21. *LBF*, 95–96.
22. *Memorials of London*, 210–11.

23. Herbert, *Twelve Great Livery Companies*, 2:11–12. The Goldsmiths accounts show that the gild paid £3 6s. for seven yards of blue and murrey to give to the fishmongers for their hoods, 205.
24. Charles Welch, *History of the Cutlers' Company: From the Earliest Times to 1500*, vol. 1 (London: Printed privately, 1916), 107–9. For a dispute over the use of space in the city, see *CPMR: 1323–1364*, 222 (1345). The Poulterers and the Butchers were to divide the space where they could sell their products. *LBI*, 96 (1420–22) in which the mayor mediated a dispute between the Cordwainers and the Cobblers. *LBG*, 127–28 involved the mayor's mediation between the Fishmongers and Butchers.
25. *Memorials of London*, 156–162. For more on the Saddlers, see Kingsley M. Oliver, *Hold Fast, Sit Sure: The History of the Worshipful Company of Saddlers of the City of London, 1160–1960* (Chichester, UK: Phillimore, 1995).
26. For other examples, see *LBF*, 95–99, 138 (1343, 1345) between the Fishmongers and the Skinners; *LBG*, 279 (1370) between the Fletchers and Bowyers [also in *Memorials of London*, 348–50]; *LBI*, 176–77 (1417) among Hatters, Haberdashers, and Capers; *LBI*, 222–23 (1418) between Salters and Chandlers; *LBK*, 42 (1425) between Pinners and Cardmakers; *LBK*, 37 (1324) between the Fusters and Saddlers; *LBK*, 113 (1429), between the Cordwainers and Girdlers.
27. Barron, *London in the Later Middle Ages*, 237–39. Exact figures are difficult to find for the deaths in London. But judging from the wills entered into the Husting Court of Wills and Deeds, the number of enrolled wills increased sixteenfold in 1349. Again, with the re-appearance of the plague in 1361–62, the number of recorded wills increased eightfold. These figures are for citizens of London and therefore represent the wealthier inhabitants. The death toll among the poorer residents was probably even higher. See Barney Sloane, *The Black Death in London* (Stroud, UK: History Press, 2011) for the excavation of graves of the poor during the plague. On mortality and morbidity rates, as well as the unhealthy environment of London, see Maryann Kowaleski, "Medieval People in Town and Country: New Perspectives from Demography and Bioarchaeology," *Speculum* 89 (2014): 573–600.
28. *CPMR: 1323–1364*, 238 (1350).
29. Caroline M. Barron, "Revolt in London: 11th to 15th June 1381" (Museum of London, 1981). The chronicle accounts and indictments indicate that much of the violence in London had to do with the settling of old disputes. Ruth Bird, *The Turbulent London of Richard II* (London: Longsman Green, 1949), 44–62.
30. The Staple was established as an efficient way of collecting taxes on the export of raw wool. After the capture of Calais, in 1347, the trade was centered in that city and was very profitable for those engaged in it. Since the Fishmongers and Grocers had ships, they were very involved in the Staple and made considerable profits from this trade. Their rivals were the Mercers and Drapers, who traded

in finished cloth, and the Italian and Flemish merchants, who had access to the Staple.

31. For a detailed description of the economic factors leading to the strife, see Nightingale, *A Medieval Mercantile Community*, 194–262.
32. Bird, *Turbulent London*, emphasized the fight between the haves and the have nots in London, in which John of Northampton was the rabble rouser that mobilized the mob of Londoners. Nightingale, *A Medieval Mercantile Community*, 230, argued that the opposition labeled Brembre and two other men who had married the heiress daughters of a wealthy vintner as "victualers," connecting them with the high prices for food. It was a political smear campaign.
33. The two parties to the dispute have been called by various titles. Perhaps the most common term was the "party of the victulars," or "Brembre's party" (the Grocers, Fishmongers, etc.) and the "non-victualers" (Drapers, Mercers, and Goldsmiths), or "Northampton's party." These terms are not entirely accurate, and Northampton may even have used "the party of the victulars" for the Grocers as one of derision. See Rexroth, *Deviance and Power*, 139. Bird, *Turbulent London*, used the term "capitalists" for Brembre's party. In fact, the parties were a mixture. The "victulars" were mostly long-distance traders in wool, although they did provide some foodstuffs, such as fish and spices. The "non-victulars" were not made up solely of craftsmen.
34. Bird, *Turbulent London*, 17–43. Nightingale, *A Medieval Mercantile Community*, 244–47, 250–62.
35. Rexroth, *Deviance and Power*, chap. 4, has argued that the moral reforms, including punishment of bawds and prostitutes and sturdy beggars and the use of the public spectacle of the pillory for a number of offenses, were popular and helped to cement Northampton's power. The weakness of the argument is that when Brembre continued the reforms, he was criticized.
36. Nightingale, *A Medieval Mercantile Community*, 271–91.
37. Bird, *Turbulent London*, 81–85. For an idea of the individuals involved in the struggles, see Paul Strohm, "Horchon's Arrow," in *Horchon's Arrow: The Social Imagination of Fourteenth-Century Texts* (Princeton, NJ: Princeton University Press, 1992), 11–32.
38. Bird, *Turbulent London*, 86–101. Nightingale, *A Medieval Mercantile Community*, 306–17.
39. In 1391 a proclamation was made in the city that the struggle between Northampton and Brembre was causing strife in the city and threatening the peace. No one was to engage in fights over the two sides: "Let the folks of the said city be of one accord in love, without speaking, any person to another, in the said matter." If they did not, they would be sent to Newgate for a year without redemption. *Memorials of London*, 526–27.
40. Shiela Lindenbaum, "The Smithfield Tournament of 1390," *The Journal of Medieval and Renaissance Studies*, 20 (1990):1–20.

41. Caroline M. Barron, "The Quarrel of Richard II with London 1392–7," in *The Reign of Richard II: Essays in Honor of May McKisack*, ed. F. R. H. Du Boulay and Caroline M. Barron (London: Athelone Press, 1971), 173–89.
42. Nigel Saul, *Richard II* (New Haven, CT: Yale University Press, 1997), 342–43. Descriptions of the entry and pageants appear in Richard Maidstone's poem "Concordia inter regem Ric. II et civitatem London," in *Political Poems and Songs Relating to English History*, ed. Thomas Wright, Rolls Series (London, 1859), 1: 282–300; Richard Maidstone, *Concordia: The Reconciliation of Richard II with London*, trans. A. G. Rigg, ed. David R. Carlson (Kalamazoo, MI: TEAMS 2003; Glynne Wickham, *Early English Stages, 1300–1660* (London: Routledge and Kegan Paul, 1959), 64–71. Wickham provides a prose translation of Maidstone's poem. Maidstone was an eyewitness to the event. A personal letter in Anglo-Norman from another eyewitness to the event was edited by Helen Suggett, "A Letter Describing Richard II's Reconciliation with the City of London, 1392," *English Historical Review* 52, no. 143 (1947): 209–13. Suggett points to a passage in the letter in which the king and queen travel to Westminster by barge after their entry into London accompanied by other barges carrying Londoners. There was music, drink, and dancing, and the Londoners offered drinks to the royal party. The king graciously invited them to the palace to share a drink with him. As Suggett points out, the incident was a surprising departure from the scripted royal entry.
43. Barron, "Richard II and London," 191–201. She estimates that the reconciliation cost London about £30,000.
44. Nightingale, *A Medieval Mercantile Community*, 346–49; Barron, "Richard II and London," 201.
45. Barron, *London in the Later Middle Ages*, 26–29; C. L. Kingsford, *Prejudice and Promise in Fifteenth-Century England* (Oxford: Clarendon, 1925), 107–21. Kingsford covers the history of the city's approach to the upheavals of the fifteenth century and shows that the elite were astute in avoiding being drawn into dynastic wars and the appearance of imposters claiming rights to the crown.
46. Caroline M. Barron, "Ralph Holland and the London Radicals, 1438–1440," in *The Medieval Town: A Reader in English Urban History, 1200–1540*, ed. Richard Holt and Gervase Rosser (London: Longman, 1990), 160–83.
47. Robert Withington, *English Pageantry: An Historical Outline*, vol. 1 (Cambridge, MA: Harvard University Press, 1918), 104.
48. Lancashire, *London Civic Theater*, 54–55.
49. Wickham, *Early English Stages*, 35.
50. Wickham, *Early English Stages*, 20–21. See also Lancashire, *London Civic Theater*, 62–64.
51. For a complete discussion of royal entries in England and on the continent, see Gordon Kipling, *Theatre, Liturgy, and Ritual in the Medieval Civic Triumph* (Oxford: Oxford University Press, 1998). See also Paul Strohm, "Coronation as Legible Practice," in *Theory and the Premodern Text* (Minneapolis: University of Minnesota Press, 2000), 33–50.

52. Gordon Kipling, "The King's Advent Transformed: The Consecration of the City in Sixteenth-Century Civic Triumph," in *Ceremonial Culture in Pre-modern Europe*, ed. Nicholas Howe (Notre Dame, IN: University of Notre Dame Press, 2007), 89–91. The Jerusalem motif was a popular one for cities to adopt in their advent pageants for kings.
53. Lancashire, *London Civic Theater*, 43–46.
54. Withington, *English Pageantry*, 1:124–40, provides a useful summary of these processions.
55. Lawrence M. Bryant, "Configurations of the Community in Late Medieval Spectacles: Paris and London during the Dual Monarchy," in Hanawalt and Reyerson, *City and Spectacle*, 18–25. The entry of Henry VI is one of the best-documented medieval royal entries. John Lydgate wrote a poem about the event, "The Entry of Henry VI into London after His Coronation in France." See *A Selection of Minor Poems of Dan John Lydgate*, ed. James Orchard Halliwell, Percy Society, vol. 2 (London: C. Richards, 1840), 1–21. It is possible that Lydgate also wrote the script or at least the speeches for the pageants. See *LBK*, 137–39, for John Carpenter's account in a letter written in Latin and inserted in the letter book. The Common Council had objected to paying for the reception to for Henry because there was not sufficient money in the treasury and a poll tax would cause hardship. The chamberlain undertook to advance the money out of his own purse (£1000) and the participants were to pay for their own livery. The chamberlain was reimbursed with the profits from the city beam. *LBK*, 129–30.

CHAPTER 3

1. *Memorials of London*, 424.
2. Sheila Lindenbaum, "The Smithfield Tournament of 1390, 8; and Lindenbaum, "London Midsummer Watch," in Hanawalt and Reyerson, *City and Spectacle*, 171–88.
3. Pierre Bourdieu, *Outline of a Theory of Practice*, trans. Richard Nice (Cambridge: Cambridge University Press, 1977), 175–84.
4. *Chronicles of London*, vi–viii. In the introduction and in the appendices to the volume, Kingsford has done comparisons to show the extent of borrowing and to analyze probable authorship. Malcolm Richardson, in *Middle-Class Writing in Late Medieval London* (London: Pickering and Chatto, 2011), 74–80, analyzes the writing of Fitz Thedmar, Horn, and Carpenter.
5. The full text of the decision to burn it is in *Memorials of London*, 494. Sheila Lindenbaum, "London's Texts and Literate Practice," in *The Cambridge History of Medieval English Literature*, ed. David Wallace (Cambridge: Cambridge University Press, 1999), 288; *LBH*, 303.
6. McLaren, in *London Chronicles*, 16, 18–19, questions the authorship or perhaps the exclusive authorship of Fitz Thedmar. Ralph Hanna III, in *London Literature*,

1300–1380 (Cambridge: Cambridge University Press, 2005), 63, accepts that he is the author.

7. Fitz Thedmar, introduction to *Chronicles of the Mayors and Sheriffs of London*, trans. H. T. Riley (London: Trübner, 1863), viii–ix. Fitz Thedmar's personal account appears on 201–4. He knew both French and Latin and wrote his chronicle in Latin.
8. See Fitz Thedmar, 107–12, as examples of charters and letters from Henry III guaranteeing the specific rights and privileges of Londoners. See also 133–36, 165, 170–72.
9. Fitz Thedmar, 104–5.
10. Fitz Thedmar, 155–73.
11. *Munimenta Gildhallae, Liber Custumarum*, vol. 2, pt. 1, x, and Riley's introduction in general. See also Jeremy Catto, "Andrew Horn: Law and History in Fourteenth-Century England," in *The Writing of History in the Middle Ages: Essays Presented to Richard William Southern*, ed. R. H. C. Davis and J. M. Wallace-Hadrill (Oxford: Oxford University Press, 1981), 367–92.
12. Debbie Cannon, "London Pride: Citizenship and the Fourteenth-Century Custumals of the City of London," Rees Jones, *Learning and Literacy*, 182–86. Lynn Staley, *Languages of Power in the Age of Richard II* (University Park: Penn State University Press, 2006), 34–35, 58–59, 307–9.
13. Catto, "Andrew Horn," 387–391; Barron, "Political Culture," in Clark and Carpenter, *Late Medieval Britain*, 123–24.
14. *Munimenta Guildhalae, Liber Horn*, vol. 2, pt. 2, 517–28. Richardson, *Middle-Class Writing*, 79, suggests that if Horn hoped that a rhetorical tradition would develop in London along the lines suggested by Datini, he would be disappointed.
15. *Memorials of London*, 580. Carpenter tended to be a bit of a showoff about his erudition.
16. Thomas Brewer, *Memoir of the Life and Times of John Carpenter* (London: A. Taylor, 1856), 59–72. Brewer discusses the connections that he had with the intellectuals and elites of London. The books he distributed in his will are listed on pages 139–44. He gave some of his books to establish a library at the Guildhall "for the profit of students there and those discoursing to the common people." The books were to be chained to avoid theft. He also founded a grammar school.
17. William Kellaway, "John Carpenter's *Liber Albus*," *Guildhall Studies in London History*, 3 (1978): 67–84.
18. *Liber Albus*, 2–4.
19. *Liber Albus*, 11–13. In later medieval England the title of duke replaced that of earl, but Carpenter is citing old city records.
20. CPMR: *1413–1437*, 117. See note by the editor, A. H. Thomas. Sharpe, *London and the Kingdom*, 1:196–96, 217. Alfred B. Beaven, *The Aldermen of the City of London, Temp. Henry III–1912* (London: Eden Fisher, 1913), vol. 1:xxix. The origins of the title Lord Mayor are disputed; some say that in 1354 a charter

granted the mayor's serjeants the right to carry gilded or silver maces, indications of the status of earl. Although there were statutes that had prohibited cities from tipping maces in anything but base metals, London was an exception. The mace bearers were to carry them before the mayor as would be done before an earl. But the charter permitting this show of prestige did not use the term "lord mayor." In the poll tax of 1379, the mayor was assessed on the same scale as an earl and the aldermen, as barons.

21. Barron, *London in the Later Middle Ages*, 147–53, presents the history of the selection of the mayor. By 1415, the system was well established and the Common Council had a very limited representation. Nonetheless, the disputes continued till the end of the fifteenth century.
22. *Liber Albus*, 17.
23. *Memorials of London*, 560 from *LBI* (1404), fol. 33.
24. *Liber Albus*, 17–18.
25. Barron, *London in the Later Middle Ages*, 145–52. In 1315 the king had also mandated that the number of voters be limited to responsible members of the wards.
26. Thrupp, *Merchant Class*, 288. The body politic metaphor as applied to London also appeared in a bishop's sermon in which he likened the citizens and burgesses to the body's heart and the artisans to its hands.
27. See *LBF*, 304–6 (1346), for an earlier description of a mayoral election. *LBG*, 198 (1365). Eric Hobsbawm and Terence Ranger, *The Invention of Tradition* (Cambridge: Cambridge University Press, 1983), 1–6. The ceremonies surrounding the election of the mayor and his oath taking were already well established when Carpenter wrote the script for these events in the *Liber Albus*. The elite were not trying to establish a new tradition based on old ones, but rather wanted to record the traditional ceremonies as they had been performed in the past and to ensure, by recording them, that they would be performed in the same way in the future. The limited franchise was recorded in an official book kept in the Guildhall and could be referred to when a dispute arose.
28. Lindenbaum, "London Texts and Literate Practice," in Wallace, *Cambridge History*, 285, 293–95.
29. Edward Muir, "The Eye of the Procession: Ritual Ways of Seeing in the Renaissance," in *Ceremonial Culture in Pre-Modern Europe*, ed. Nicholas Howe (Notre Dame, IN: University of Notre Dame Press, 2007), 132.
30. Ilaria Taddei, "Between Rules and Ritual: The Election of the *Signoria* in Florence in the Fourteenth and Fifteenth Centuries," in Cohen Jr. et al., *Late Medieval and Early Modern Ritual*, 43–64. This essay shows much the same emphasis on the use of space, gesture, and formal language that was true of the election of the mayor in London.
31. *Liber Albus*, 17–18.
32. The election did follow tradition. In the election of 1328 an assembly in the Guildhall included the mayor, sheriffs, aldermen, and twelve, ten, or eight

commoners from each ward. The mayor and aldermen retired to the chamber and made the election among themselves. They then presented the candidate to the commons according to custom. When Chigwell's name was presented, all the assembled yelled "yea," but after a short silence some began to shout "Fulsam" and others "Chigwell." The assembly broke up, and the next day the wiser men of the city determined that neither should be mayor but that a third party be chosen. CPMR: 1323–1364, 72–73.

33. LBH, 50–51; LMA, Jour 3, fol. 85. The chamberlain was to have all the profits from the brokers and pay each alderman 100s. for his livery.
34. Liber Albus, 19–20.
35. LBK, 33, 191 (1435).
36. LBK, 301 (1444).
37. LBF, 304–6.
38. LBG, 240, 245; LBI, 42, 159 (1416). LBH, 59–60, had a provision for removing aldermen who did not perform their duties.
39. Memorials of London, 635–36.
40. LBK, 274, 286, 288, 301, 311. The accounts of these elections are more detailed because of the need to refresh the citizens' memory about the ancient procedures, since Holland had questioned their authenticity. Barron, "Ralph Holland," in Holt and Rosser, Medieval Town, 160–83.
41. LBI, 52–53. See Memorials of London, 565–66, for a description of the election of Richard Whittington.
42. Liber Albus, 18–20.
43. Barron, London in the Later Middle Ages, 151–152. Charles M. Clode, The Early History of the Guild of Merchant Taylors of the Fraternity of St. John the Baptist (London: Harrison and Sons, 1888), vol. 1:21–22.
44. Jean-Claude Schmitt, La raison des gesteur dans l'Occident medieval (Paris: Gallimard, 1990). For a brief English summary of the thesis, see "The Rationale of Gestures in the West: Third to Thirteenth Centuries," in The Cultural History of Gesture, ed. Jan Bremmer and Herman Roodenburg (Ithaca, NY: Cornell University Press, 1991), 59–70. Schmitt's approach has limitations for a more general applicability of gesture in that he was mostly concerned with those used in religious rituals, particularly those visually represented in artworks.
45. Liber Albus, 21–22.
46. Clode, Guild of Merchant Taylors, 1:26–27; Charles Pendrill, London Life in the Fourteenth Century (1925; Port Washington, NY: Kennikat, 1971), 51.
47. Barron, London in the Later Middle Ages, 152.
48. Liber Albus, 265–66, has the full text of the mayor's oath.
49. Liber Albus, 22–23. It became the custom, in 1434, for the mayor to return by barge.

50. *LBK*, 48. In 1425 the Duke of Gloucester interrupted the mayor's banquet and alerted him and the aldermen to keep watch in the city because the duke feared that there would be a clash between himself and Beaufort.
51. *Liber Albus*, 23–24.
52. *LBI*, 78–79. The hoods of the commons were to be red and white, the colors of the city.
53. Barron, *London in the Later Middle Ages*, 152. LMA, Jour 8, fols. 253v., 255, 257. A fine of £20 was to be imposed on the offenders.
54. Lancashire, *London Civic Theater*, 171–72.
55. Ben R. McRee, "The Mayor's Body," in *The Ties That Bind: Essays in Medieval British History in Honor of Barbara Hanawalt*, ed. Linda E. Mitchell, Katherine L. French, Douglass L. Biggs (Burlington, VT: Ashgate, 2011), 39–48.
56. Robert Rickart, *The Maire of Bristowe is Kalendar*, ed. Lucy Toulmin Smith, vol. 5 of Camden Society, New Series, 1872, 68–88.
57. *Liber Albus*, 25–27.
58. *Liber Albus*.
59. Clode, *Guild of Merchant Taylors*, 1, 26–27.
60. *Liber Albus*, 26, 31. On this occasion an acolyte was suspended from the ceiling as an angel. The mayor and aldermen were required to wear matching livery on these occasions.
61. *Liber Albus*, 26, 31. LMA, Jour 1, fol. 21v. (5 Henry 5), "The rector of St. Peter's Cornhill (which was formerly the principal church of the city) shall go behind all the other rectors in procession at Pentecost. And the Rectors of St. Magnus and St. Nicholas Cole Abbey shall go before with their crosses and the masters of the fishmongers of both streets of the Old and New Fisheries." There were fights for precedence among the parishioners of the three churches. *Memorials of London*, 651–53.
62. *LBH*, 108. The person responsible had to be granted a license to build a chapel outside his house abutting the Guildhall.
63. William Henry St. John Hope and G. Cuthbert F. Atchley, *English Liturgical Colours* (New York: Macmillan, 1918), 86–88, has a chart of the most usual colors. But even church celebrations did not carefully adhere to a particular pattern.
64. Sharpe, introduction to *LBL*, xxvi–xxvii. Liveries were granted to some pensioners who had served the city government. In addition, the serjeants and yeomen of the mayor received liveries.
65. *LBG*, 93; *Liber Albus*, 1, 31. The lining had to be silk for Pentecost, but the color was not specified.
66. Sharpe, introduction to *LBL*, xxvii.
67. LMA, Jour 1, fol. 18v.; Jour 3, fols. 87, 127v., 193v.; Jour 4, fols. 50v., 99, 149v., 177v.; LMA, Jour 6, fols. 54; LMA, Jour 7, 17, 20, 155, 181, 202v., LMA, Jour 8, fol. 98.

68. *Memorials of London*, 466.
69. Maura Nolan, *John Lydgate and the Making of Public Culture* (Cambridge: Cambridge University Press, 2005), 78–85. Nolan argues that mummings were elite entertainments rather than those of the populace as a whole, but this argument is hard to support since the origins are unknown. She is right that London elites used mummings at the royal court as a way of currying favor with the monarch. The disguises and the lavish gifts sweetened the monarch's relations with the city.
70. Lancashire, *London Civic Theater*, 41–43.
71. Lancashire, *London Civic Theater*, 50.
72. *Munimenta Gildhallae, Liber Custumarum*, vol. 2, pt. 1, 147–51, and pt. 2, 554–58.
73. Stow, *Survey of London*, 1: 99–104; Lindenbaum, "London Midsummer Watch," in Hanawalt and Reyerson, *City and Spectacle*, 171–88, has a complete discussion of the 1521 watch. The watch was much enjoyed by Henry VIII, who participated in it and partly took it over, but it disappeared with the Reformation.
74. *Memorials of London*, 419–20. For 1386, see 488.
75. Lindenbaum, "London Midsummer Watch," in Hanawalt and Reyerson, *City and Spectacle*, 173–78; Lancashire, *London Civic Theater*, 153–61, discusses the gradual use of pageants in the Midsummer Watch in the late fifteenth century. By the early sixteenth century it had become more of a civic holiday and one in which royalty and nobles participated.
76. *Memorials of London*, 414–15.
77. Betty R. Masters, "The Mayor's Household before 1600," in *Studies in London History Presented to Philip Edmund Jones*, ed. A. E. J. Hollaender and William Kellaway (London: Hodder and Stoughton, 1969), 95–116.
78. McRee, "Mayor's Body," in Mitchell et al., *Ties That Bind*, 51–53. The situation in Norwich eventually ended with one of the mayors being imprisoned. While he was in Flete prison, actions were taken in the name of the city, which the inhabitants declared illegal because the mayor had not been present. The case was an interesting legal one and was argued in the Letter Books. The lawyers argued that the mayor was not a particular person but that the corporation was the legal entity. But the counterargument was that if the head of the body politic was missing and in prison, then the action could not be legal. The office and the man had to go together.
79. *Memorials of London*, 603–5.
80. LMA, Jour 2, 1422–1429, fol. 46. The Duke of Gloucester, Protector of England, and the Earl of Suffolk and several peers and knights came to communicate certain business to the mayor. The mayor stood before the chair, supported with his sword; and the Duke with his sword stood at the right hand of the mayor.
81. *CPMR: 1323–1364*, 154–55, 206–7.

82. "The Boke of Nurture folowyng Englondis gise by John Russell," in *The Babees' Book: Medieval Manners for the Young*, ed. Frederick J. Furnivall (London: Chatto and Windus, 1923), 70–72, where the priorities of seating are listed.
83. "Gregory's Chronicle," in *The Historical Collections of A Citizen of London in the Fifteenth Century*, ed. James Gairdner (Camden Society, new ser. 17, 1876), 222–23. See also *LBL*, 7; Stowe, *Survey of London*, vol. 2:36; Sharp, introduction to *LBL*, ii, with a version from the Drapers' Company. Different dates are given for this event in the various sources.
84. *LBK*, 103 (1429). Mayor William Estfeld bequeathed his cup to his grandson. The entry states that the mayor, aldermen, and sheriffs claimed, through the recorder, the right to serve the king his spiced wine and to receive the gold cup and ewer to take home with them. The petition to the Duke of Clarence, Steward of England, appears in a full English text in *LBL*, 5–6. LMA, Jour 9, fols. 18, 20, 21v., 33v., and 43 describe the cup ceremony for Edward V and Richard III.
85. For a complete discussion of the duties of the aldermen, see Barron, *London in the Later Middle Ages*, 136–46.
86. *Liber Albus*, 25.
87. Thrupp, *Merchant Class*, 65–74. Beaven, *Aldermen*, 2:xv–xx.
88. LMA, Jour 7, fol. 198.
89. Beaven, *Aldermen*, 1: xx–xxi. *LBI*, 42 (1414–15). John Gedeney refused to take Farringdon Without; he was put in prison and his property was confiscated. He agreed to serve as alderman the next day.
90. LMA, Jour 7, fol. 109. See also fol. 267, in which Henry Colet paid 200 marks for the repair of the cross on the Cheap. and John Fisher (LMA, Jour 9, fol. 27) paid 400 marks to do the same. See also Barron, *London in the Later Middle Ages*, 142–43.
91. LMA, Jour 4, fols. 95, 125v; LMA, Jour 5, fols. 4, 183v; LMA, Jour 6, fol. 279v.; LMA, Jour 8, fol. 1v. One alderman was able to retire because he was infirm, but he had to pay £50.
92. Barron, *London in the Later Middle Ages*, 146, says that they personally paid for their livery, but as we have seen, in 1389 the Chamberlain was to give 100s. toward the livery from taxes on foreign brokers.
93. *Memorials of London*, 502–3.
94. *Liber Albus*, 37–40; Barron, *London in the Later Middle Ages*, 159.
95. *LBH*, 347–48.

CHAPTER 4

1. *Memorials of London*, 605–6; *LBI*, 132.
2. Helen Carrel, "The Ideology of Punishment in Late Medieval English Towns," *Social History* 34 (2009): 301–20.

3. Sarah Rees Jones, "Thomas More's '*Utopia*'," in Horrox and Rees Jones, *Pragmatic Utopias*, 120–21, has pointed out that new laws and ordinances used a rhetorical form found in sermons. As she comments, "The need to represent the law as protecting the common good of all citizens resulted in the stories being generalized in the form of moral fables."
4. Richard Britnell, "Town Life," in *A Social History of England, 1200–1500*, ed. Rosemary Horrox and W. Mark Omrod (Cambridge: Cambridge University Press, 2006), 164–67; Richard Britnell, *The Commercialization of English Society, 1300–1500* (Cambridge: Cambridge University Press, 1993), 172–74; Davis, *Medieval Market Morality*, chapt. 1.
5. Jan Dumolyn and Jolle Haemers, "'A bad Chicken was Brooding': Subversive Speech in Late Medieval Flanders," *Past and Present* 214 (2012): 45–86. The authors note that the more public the setting, the more threatening the slanders were to the authorities.
6. *CPMR: 1381–1412*, 50–51 (1384). Because he was of a high status, being a member of the prestigious Grocers' Company, several aldermen and "good men of the city" prayed the mayor to allow him to avoid prison if he promised not to speak ill of the mayor again and to pay £40 if he did so. He got off paying only a half a mark.
7. *LBI*, 244 (1420). John Corbet, a goldsmith, was deprived of the freedom of the city for causing riots. He petitioned to have his rights restored. See also *CPMR: 1364–1381*, 28 (1365).
8. Barron, *London in the Later Middle Ages*, 144–45.
9. *Memorials of London*, 500–502.
10. *Memorials of London*, 207–8; *LBF*, 40.
11. Nightingale, *A Medieval Mercantile Community*, 171–72. Thrupp, *Merchant Class*, 333. *CPMR: 1323–1364*, 192 (1343).
12. *CEMR*, ed. Thomas, 261 (1307).
13. *CPMR: 1323–1364*, 69 (1328). For other cases, see *LBI* (1416–17), 170; *CPMR: 1381–1412*, 275 (1406); *LBH* (1378), 94.
14. *LBI* (1414–1415), 132. Also in *Memorials of London*, 605–6. See also *CPMR: 1364–1381*, 28 (1365), *CPMR: 1381–1412*, 199 (1375). Geoffrey Loveye, a mercer, slandered Thomas Fauconer and was put on a bond for good behavior, but he offended again. *LBI* (1411), 96–97 (also in *Memorials of London*, 576 (1413)).
15. Nightingale, *A Medieval Mercantile Community*, 376.
16. *LBG*, 53. *Memorials of London*, 275–77, for the complete case.
17. *CEMCR*, 3, 16 (1286).
18. Mario Damen, "Giving by Pouring: The Function of Gifts of Wine in the City of Leiden (14th–16th Centuries)," in *Symbolic Communication in Late Medieval Towns*, ed. Jacoba Van Leeuwen (Leiden: Leiden University Press, 2006), 83–100. In Leiden, special pitchers were used as gifts of wine for visiting officials. There

might on some occasions have been reciprocity in the wine gifts, but mostly they were meant to be persuasive with the officials.
19. *Memorials of London*, 663 (1418).
20. *Memorials of London*, 274–75; also in *LBG*, 23. For another case, see *LBG*, 62–63.
21. *CPMR: 1381–1412*, 50–51. On the other side of the political divide, John Filiol, a fishmonger, swore that for half a house of gold he would fight Mayor Northampton and called him a false scoundrel and harlot. *Memorials of London*, 473–74.
22. Nightingale, *A Medieval Mercantile Community*, 284–87.
23. See Sharpe, *London and the Kingdom*, 1:248–257, for a discussion of London and Lollardy.
24. *LBI*, 178–81. *CPMR: 1413–1437*, 43 (1416). *Memorials of London*, 630–34, has the complete case.
25. *LBG*, 176–77, has a discussion of the use of the whetstone as a punishment for liars. Other cases are found in that reference, as well as in *LBH*, 94 (1378). *Memorials of London*, 586–87, the punishment of whetstone was removed at the request of the victim of the slander.
26. *CPMR: 1381–1412*, 156–60, 170, 229, 230, 236, 242; *LBH*, 368, 34, 392, 394–96. For other cases of complaints by commoners against the mayor, see *CPMR: 1323–1364*, 103 (1339); *CPMR: 1364–1381*, 14, 17–18 (1365).
27. See A. H. Thomas, "Sidelights on Medieval London Life," *Journal of the British Archaeological Association*, 3rd ser. 2 (1937), 104–7, for a full description of the case and others against the jailor. *CPMR: 1381–1412*, 156–61, 228–30. Walpole's grievances had a history going back to 1389, when he and other prisoners had complained about the distribution of alms. He had put the matter in a bill and then asked that the bill be amended because he had not used a lawyer. He received a thorough runaround and had even appealed to the Duke of Lancaster. By 1395, when he made his assault on the mayor's dignity, he had some cause to be angry. See *LBH*, 368, 374, 392–93, 395–6. See *CPMR: 1381–1412*, 156–59 (1388). Evidence given by others who were in prison at the time confirmed his allegations.
28. *CPMR: 1364–1381*, 6, 14 (1364).
29. *Memorials of London*, 460, 476. In the latter case the man was to stand on the pillory for five days with a large whetstone around his neck for insulting the mayor and a smaller whetstone for insulting another man.
30. *CPMR: 1381–1412*, 211 (1375). In 1373 (150), a man was put in prison for drawing a knife and brandishing it at an alderman. See also *CPMR: 381, 5, 6, (1364), 28, 39 (1365). *CPMR: 1413–1437*, 97 , 130, 162, 197, 210–211.
31. *CPMR: 1364–1381*, 222–23 (1376).
32. *CPMR: 1413–1437*, 210.
33. *Memorials of London*, 352–53. See also *LBG* (1364), 176–77, in which a man was accused of spreading news that a conspiracy was being planned against the leading men of the city.

34. *Memorials of London*, 507–8.
35. John Watts, "Popular Voices in England's Wars of the Roses, c. 1445–c. 1485," in *The Voices of the People in Late Medieval Europe: Communication and Popular Culture*, ed. Jan Dumolyn, Jelle Haemers, Hipóito Rafael, Oliva Herrere, Vincent Challet, Urban History 33 (Turnhout, Belgium: Brepols, 2014), 107–20.
36. Rawcliffe, *Urban Bodies: Communal Health* presents a survey of the various measures towns and cities took to preserve the health of inhabitants.
37. Rexroth, *Deviance and Power*, 110–25, has a complete discussion of the sites of public humiliation and the categories of people who endured them.
38. *Liber Albus*, 228. *Munimenta Gildhallae, Liber Custumarum*: Translations from the Anglo-Norman, 12, pt. 3, 78.
39. Rexroth, in *Deviance and Power*, 96–110, has used the word "purity" to describe the physical and moral cleanness of the city, but this carries religious connotations that are not appropriate to the city. Purity is too strong a word for what the officials could hope to achieve. *Cleanness* is closer to the meaning of their goals. This term was also used in the records. He uses the word *transparency* to describe "a pattern of thought well known from everyday life of late medieval towns: A thing or transaction should be what it seems or seem to be what it is." This term, however, carries too much modern baggage to be useful to describe medieval market or governmental mentalities. See Davis, *Medieval Market Morality*, for a better take on the attitudes toward fraud.
40. *Liber Albus*, 266.
41. *Memorials of London*, 580. This passage was actually the preamble to an ordinance concerning the importation of eels by the Dutch. Carpenter was at the time a clerk in the Guildhall; he became town clerk five years after this date (1412).
42. James Davis, "Baking for the Common Good: A Reassessment of the Assize of Bread in Medieval England," *Economic History Review*, new ser., 57, no. 3 (2004): 481–85. Davis points out that the theory of just prices was not only a theological position but was also assumed by the royal government. Bakers had to make some profit, but not excessive profit.
43. Christopher Dyer, *Standards of Living in the Later Middle Ages: Social Change in England c. 1200–1520* (Cambridge: Cambridge University Press, 1989), 151–54. The nutritional need of an adult male by modern standards is 2,000 to 3,000 kilocalories per day, of which bread and ale made up a large proportion in the Middle Ages. See Bruce M. S. Campbell, James A. Galloway, Derek Keene, and Margaret Murphy, *A Medieval Capital and Its Grain Supply*, 1–36. The authors' estimate that 75 percent of the diet was grains. Ten percent of the grain calories were consumed as ale. Given the poor water quality, ale was a safe drink. It was often small ale of low alcohol content. In London, brown-bread bakers outnumbered white-bread makers, an indication that most of the population ate brown bread.
44. *Liber Albus*, 302–6; Riley, *Munimenta Gildhallae*, 3. Riley included the outstanding cases in appendix I, "Extracts from the *Assisa Panis*, 21 Edward I–16 Henry VI," 411–29. The writ appears in *LBA*, 213 (November 18, 1281)

45. *CPMR: 1323–1346*, 5. In 1298 the king ordered that all corn that was ground in mills within or outside the city was to be weighed before being ground and that the millers were to answer for light weight in flour coming from the mills. *Memorials of London*, 37. The mills were outside the city so that the weighing had to be done before grain left the city and after it had been milled to insure honest measures. Bakers who did not comply were imprisoned, as was John "Maywe," who refused to pay the presage for grinding and weighing his corn and flour. He used "opprobrious language" when detained. *LBK*, 368 (1455); *CPMR: 1323–1364*, 174 (1338). Thomas de Sharnebrok, a baker apparently eluded the pesage by taking his corn out by Aldgate and bringing his flour in by Cripplegate. On the subterfuge of putting good grain on top of bad, see *Munimenta Gildhallae, Liber Customarum* 1:326–33, 380: *LBG*, 212 (1366) and 261 (1370).
46. *Liber Albus*, 307.
47. Davis, "Baking for the Common Good," 469–71. For the legal background of the Assize, see Gwen Seabourne, "Assize Matters: Regulation of the Price of Bread in Medieval London," *Journal of Legal History* 27, no. 1 (2006): 29–52.
48. Seaboure, "Assize Matters," 35–36.
49. *Liber Albus*, 302.
50. Davis, "Baking for the Common Good," 71–76. Another entry permitted adjustments depending on the variation of the price of grain sold over the year. The assay of bread would not be done again that year, but bakers were given regulations that would permit them to adjust the quantity of loaves made per quarter of grain according to the price. If grain went up in price, bakers could produce loaves of bread at a lighter weight than was established for the year. *Liber Albus*, 304–5, 308.
51. *Munimenta Gildhallae, Liber Custumarum*, 2, pt. 2, 598–99. Seabourne, "Assize Matters," 47, found that some bakers did have their ovens torn down, but that expulsion did not follow. Perhaps the authorities were concerned about protecting the bread supply. She also concluded that the humiliation was intended to bring down a proud baker.
52. Sylvia Thrupp, *The Worshipful Company of Bakers: A Short History* (Croydon, UK: Galleon, 1933), 42–43.
53. Seabourne, "Assize Matters," 43–48. Seabourne found that some of the offenders rode the hurdle backward.
54. *Munimenta Gildhallae*, 3, 416–17. See also *CPMR: 1323–1364*, 44 (1326). *Memorials of London*, 162–65. The two women were to remain in Newgate prison until it was ascertained if their husbands were responsible for their actions.
55. *Liber Albus*, 308.
56. *Munamenta Gildhallae*, 3, 415–16, 420–21. John Gibbe inserted a piece of iron in a loaf to bring it up to weight (498).
57. *LBH*, 106–7, 140, gives the text of a proclamation to be made through the city concerning horse bread.

58. *Memorials of London*, 323.
59. *Munimenta Gildhallae*, 3, 424. See also page 425 for another case in which a foreigner was drawn on the hurdle through the Cheap to Temple Bar.
60. *Munimenta Gildhallae*, 3, 425–26.
61. *CEMCR*, (1298–1307), 67. *Memorials of London*, 180–83. In 1331, an ordinance complained that the bakers hid themselves in mills outside the city so that they could not be prosecuted for their false bread and that they had their servants bake and sell the loaves instead. The ordinance was proclaimed in the street so that people knew to mistrust bakers.
62. *Memorials of London*, 423.
63. *CPMR: 1323–1364*, 251 (1355).
64. *Memorials of London*, 266–67.
65. *CPMR: 1364–1381*, 163 (1373).
66. *Memorials of London*, 438.
67. *LBF*, 226–27 (1350–51), also in the *Memorials of London*, 266. *LBG*, 173 (1364), 175 (1364), 192 (1365); *LBH*, 110 (1378).
68. *LBG*, 176 (1365); *Memorials of London*, 328, 448.
69. *CPMR: 1323–1364*, 228 (1349). See above 225, n. 2.
70. *LBE*, 110–11 (1319); *Memorials of London*, 132–33.
71. *LBF*, 208 (1350); *LBG*, 8 (1353); *Memorials of London*, 270–71. *CPMR: 1323–1364*, 12 (1364) showed that fines of 20s. could also be required.
72. *Liber Albus*, 311.
73. *CPMR: 1323–1364*, 45, 246. For information about England, see Judith M. Bennett, *Ale Beer, and Brewsters in England* (New York: Oxford University Press, 1996), 137–38.
74. *Memorials of London*, 670–672. *LBI*, 214–15. The original ordinance is in Middle English.
75. *CPMR: 1413–1437*, 212 (1427). He was also accused of sophisticating 10 casks of unsound La Rochelle wine and also for having sophisticated 8 casks of old, sour-sweet Spanish wine. He was a "common sophisticator." *LBK*, 377 (1457). A foreign merchant and a couple "coupers" were accused of having "falsely and deceivably counterfeited colored dubbed and meddled vi pipes of white Rochelle wine old and feeble of color and taste then in the cellar of the said Austyn there being with red wine called teynt and with eggs alum gums and other horrible and unwholesome things for to induce and bring again a pleasant color to the sight and likely manner drinking of red wine to the smell and taste of the people" contrary to the ordinance. (original in Middle English, transposed by Barbara Hanawalt). In another case, a wine merchant sold wine that was so dense and impure that it could not be recognized by taste or sight. The merchant had assured the buyers that it was good. After a two weeks, however, it was putrid, and the scrutineers broke the casks and discharged the wine in the gutter. *CEMCR*, 262.

76. *LBK*, 114 (1430); *LBI*, 211–212, gives the ordinance of the city for false brokerage including the punishments mentioned.
77. *LBG*, 178 (1364).
78. *Memorials of London*, 181–83.
79. *LBK*, f. 11. Quoted in *A Book of London English, 1384–1425*, ed. R. W. Chambers and Marjorie Daunt (Oxford: Clarendon, 1931), 102–3.
80. *CPMR: 1364–1381*, 252, 66–67 (1366). *LBH*, 121. TNA: PRO C1/33/253. CLRO MC1/1/188. Marjorie McIntosh, *Working Women in English Society, 1300–1620* (Cambridge: Cambridge University Press, 2005), 130–32.
81. *LBG*, 175, 269 (1352–1374). See also *CPMR: 1413–1437*, 159.
82. *LBF*, 91–93 (1343).
83. *CPMR: 1413–1437*, 138 (1422). *LBG*, 259. John Wastelle, a poulterer, was charged with selling snipe, thrushes, and a woodcock that were unfit to eat. But John Smyth declared under oath that he had bought the birds elsewhere and had given them to the first man's wife to pluck. John Wastelle was sentenced to stand at the pillory as the birds were burnt under his nose, because it was determined that he owned them. John Smyth acknowledged that he was suborned by Wastelle's wife to "bear false witness on the promise of a pair of hose." Smyth was committed to prison, but soon released.
84. *LBK*, 230. Apparently, there was a crackdown on prostitution, which "Gregory's Chronicle" mentions, 183.
85. *Liber Albus*, 394–95. According to Rexroth, *Deviance and Power*, chap. 4, the punishment of bawds and prostitutes, in addition to the increased use of the pillory, rough music, and other humiliation rituals were part of John of Northampton's moral crusade during his years as mayor.
86. LMA, *Letter Book N*, 92. This Letter Book is in manuscript form and not published.
87. Consider the pictures that immediately spring to mind: Tacitus's description of the shearing of adulteresses' hair in *Germania* and the unforgettable pictures of the shaven heads of women who took Nazi lovers, including the designer Chanel, as they were paraded through the streets of Paris after World War II. *Liber Albus*, 395.
88. *A Book of London English*, ed. Chambers and Daunt, 103.
89. *Memorials of London*, 484–86.
90. *Memorials of London*, 534–35. Ruth Mazo Karras, *Common Women: Prostitution and Sexuality in Medieval England* (New York: Oxford University Press, 1996) for a full discussion of prostitution and its regulation.
91. *Memorials of London*, 458–59, specified that prostitutes were to wear hoods of ray and no fur decoration. *Liber Albus*, 247, records the prohibition of cortesans from wearing minever on her hood or cendal (a silk). Diane Owen Hughes, "Sumptuary Law and Social Relations in Italy," in *Disputes and Settlements: Law and Human Relations in the West*, ed. John Bossy (Cambridge: Cambridge University Press: 1983), 69–99, for a discussion of distinctions by dress. See

Notes to pages 102–104   193

also "Earrings for Circumcision: Distinction and Purification in the Italian Renaissance City," in *Persons in Groups: Social Behavior as Identity Formation in Medieval and Renaissance Europe*, ed. Richard C. Trexler (Binghamton, NY: Medieval and Renaissance Texts and Studies, 1985), 155–82. "Gregory's Chronicle," (1439–40), 182, says that the punishment of the ray hood was done "dyvers tymes."

92. *Liber Albus*, 395.
93. See, for instance, the case of Elizabeth Judele, *LBL*, 169. The church courts also used dress and undress as tools of humiliation and the drawing of boundaries. A prostitute convicted in a church court was to lead the Sunday procession dressed only in a smock and carrying a candle. This ritual was to be performed as a penance for two to three Sundays. Robert Wunderli, *London Church Courts and Society on the Eve of the Reformation* (Cambridge, MA: Medieval Academy of America, 1981), 50.
94. *Liber Albus*, 396. The symbol for the brawler or scold, of either sex, was a female symbol of the distaff dressed with flax. The usual parade occurred. For other offenses, parades with music and imprisonment in the Tun were mandated. The preamble to this whole section, on page 394, describes the need for cleanness and honesty in the city to win the favor of God and thereby preserve the city for the honest people of the wards.
95. *Liber Albus*, 32–33, 287–92. For ducks, see *LBC*, 119.
96. LMA, Portsoken, Ward Presentations 1465–1483, 266C ms. 1, 3–7. Although the series has gaps in it, the total number of recorded cases in this poor ward are 423. For the use of these wardmote presentments to investigate the economy of makeshift among the poor, see Barbara A. Hanawalt, "Reading the Lives of the Illiterate: London's Poor." *Speculum* 80 (2005): 1067–86.
97. Marjorie Keniston McIntosh, *Controlling Misbehavior in England 1370–1600* (Cambridge: Cambridge University Press, 1998).
98. See Rexroth, *Deviance and Power*, chap. 5, for a discussion of the wardmote.
99. Introduction to *London Assize of Nuisance, 1301–1431; A Calendar*, ed. Helena M. Chew and William Kellaway. London Record Society (London: Chatham and McKay, 1973) 10 (1974): ix–xii.
100. *Liber Albus*, 277.
101. *Introduction to London Assize of Nuisance*, ed. Chew and Kellaway , xiii–xxx, for a discussion of the full procedure. The introduction also has a discussion of the categories of cases that caused problems, xx–xxvi.
102. *London Assize of Nuisance*, 174

CHAPTER 5

1. Reddaway, T. F., and Lorna E. M. Walker. *The Early History of the Goldsmiths' Company, 1327-1509. The Book of Ordinances, 1478–83*. London: Edward Arnold, 1975, 212–13.

2. *CPMR: 1364–1381*, xv; Charles Gross, *The Gild Merchant: A Contribution to British Municipal History* (Oxford: Oxford University Press, 1890), 10; Mathew Davies, "Artisans, Guilds and Government in London," in *Daily Life in the Late Middle Ages*, ed. Richard Britnell (Stroud, UK: Sutton, 1998), 125–50, provides a useful discussion of gilds and the role they played as a complement to government.
3. Franco Franceschi, "The Rituals of Guilds: Examples from Tuscan Cities (Thirteenth to Sixteenth Centuries)," in Cohen Jr. et al., *Late Medieval and Early Modern Ritual*. See pp. 68–69 for a discussion of the literature on the subject.
4. See George Unwin, *The Gilds and Companies of London*, 4th ed. (New York: Frank Cass, 1966), for an extended discussion of the origins of gilds.
5. Herbert, *Twelve Great Livery Companies*, 1: 40–42, explains the way in which the charters gave the gilds a corporate status.
6. Unwin, *Gilds and Companies of London*, 370–71, prints the list of London gilds that was recorded in the Brewers' company records in 1422. See Elspeth M. Veale, "Craftsmen and the Economy of London in the Fourteenth Century," in *Studies in London History Presented to Philip Edmund Jones*, ed. A. E. J. Hollaender and William Kellaway (London: Hodder and Stoughton, 1969), 140. Barron, *London in the Later Middle Ages*, 218–23, has a list of crafts and companies that she compiled from some civic lists, but it only includes 102 gilds.
7. Herbert, *Twelve Great Livery Companies*, 1:43–44, gives the Grocers as an example of the early foundation structure of gilds.
8. Reddaway and Walker, *Goldsmiths' Company*, 69–70.
9. Reddaway and Walker, *Goldsmiths' Company*, 189–91.
10. Anne F. Sutton, *The Mercery of London: Trade, Goods and People, 1130–1578* (Aldershot: Ashgate, 2005), 176–77.
11. Herbert, *Twelve Great Livery Companies*, 1:51.
12. Herbert, *Twelve Great Livery Companies*, 1:52–53. Sutton, *Mercery of London*, 180–81.
13. Jean M. Imray, "'Les Bones Gentes de la Mercerye de Londres:' A Study of the Membership of the Medieval Mercers' Company," in *Studies in London History Presented to Philip Edmund Jones*, ed. A. E. J. Hollaender and William Kellaway (London: Hodder and Stoughton, 1969), 159. The Goldsmiths likewise admitted most of their members from those completing apprenticeships rather than redemption. Reddaway and Walker, *Goldsmiths' Company*, 107. Nightingale, *A Medieval Mercantile Community*, 433, 480–81.
14. *LBK*, 161–62. In the lists of freemen compiled by the city in 1309–12, the number gaining citizenship by redemption outnumbered those who achieved it by apprenticeship. As the gilds became more powerful, the balance shifted to apprenticeship. Barron, *London in the Later Middle Ages*, 205.
15. See Hanawalt, *The Wealth of Wives*, 181. See chapter 2 for girls in apprenticeship. Records of female apprenticeship are few, and most of the evidence from London arose from broken contracts.

16. See Bennett, *Ale, Beer and Brewsters*, chap. 3.
17. Nightingale, *A Medieval Mercantile Company*, 185–87. She points out that the recruits for the Grocers were often distant cousins or young men from the county from which the gild member came. They frequently married within the household of the master.
18. *CPMR: 1364–1381*, xxxiii–iv. For a more complete discussion of apprenticeship, see Barbara A. Hanawalt, *Growing Up in Medieval London: The Experience of Childhood in History* (New York: Oxford University Press, 1993), esp. chaps. 8 and 9.
19. *CPMR: 1364–1381*, xxi–xlvii, for a discussion of apprenticeship. Walter S. Prideaux, ed., *Memorials of the Goldsmiths' Company, Being Gleanings from Their Records* (London, 1896), 15. According to Imray, "Les Bones Genter do la Mercerye," 157–58, in 1347 entry into the Mercers' Gild required 2s., but the fee was raised in 1348 to 20s., and in 1357, the fee was raised to £3. Thrupp, *Merchant Class*, 214–15.
20. Clode, *Guild of Merchant Taylors*, 344, gives a full example of a contract.
21. Imray, "Les Bones Gentes do la Mercerye," 172. Mercers insisted that the apprentice be enrolled with the Mercers first and then with the city. Masters and gilds were lax in enforcing enrollment.
22. For an example of the oath, see Guildhall Library, MS 11592, Grocers' Company, Register of Freemen (1345–1481). For the church and the reading of the oath, see *Acts of the Court of the Mercers' Company*, ed. Laetitia Lyell and Frank D. Watney (Cambridge: Cambridge University Press, 1936), 105, 382.
23. TNA, C1/49/527.
24. *CPMR*: (1442), 50–51; *LBD*, 97, refers to the enrollment by wards.
25. *LBG*, 179–80, 211; Sharpe, introduction to *LBL*, xii–xiii. The mayor and aldermen agreed to the presence of gild members in addition to the master and apprentice, but did not approve setting aside a special day for enrollment.
26. *Acts of the Court of the Mercers*, 89, 105, 592. *Memorials of London*, 258, the Furbishers threatened to deny freedom of the city to anyone not enrolling an apprentice. See also Welch, *Cutlers' Company*, 141–42; *LBI*, 134. R. R. Sharp, in *LBD*, x, states that more apprentices than masters were cited for failing to enroll. Taking all the cases from various court records, I found that failures to enroll appeared to be equal for both parties.
27. Sutton, *Mercery of London*, 209–211. The Mercery was not unusual. Among the Goldsmiths and Skinners as well the number of apprentices enrolled who did not appear as freemen at the end of their term was significant. Reddaway and Walker, *Goldsmiths' Company*, 90–91.
28. Sutton, *Mercery of London*, 209–11.
29. Reddaway and Walker, *Goldsmiths' Company*, 212–13.
30. Charles Welch, *History of the Worshipful Company of Pewterers of the City of London Based Upon Their own Records*, vol. 1 (London: Blades, East and Blades, 1902), 31

(1463–64). See also A. H. Johnson, *History of the Worshipful Company of Drapers of London* (Oxford: Clarendon, 1914), 1:104. Brewers' gild 1418–1441, Guildhall Library, MS 5440 m. 20 has the oath in French.

31. Welch, *Pewterers*, 30–31.
32. Sharpe, introduction to *LBL*, xxviii–xxix; Unwin, *Gilds and Companies of London*, 190–91.
33. Sutton, *Mercery of London*, 210–11.
34. Unwin, *Gilds and Companies of London*, 190.
35. Howell, *Commerce before Capitalism*, esp. chap. 4.
36. See Howell, *Commerce before Capitalism*, 259, on the importance of the fungibility of clothing and the anxiety this caused in using clothing as status markers.
37. Unwin, *Gilds and Companies of London*, 191. Unwin points out that with the Reformation, the clothing became drab, much to the regret of Stow. Herbert, *Twelve Great Livery Companies*, 1:61–65, has an extensive discussion of liveries.
38. *French Chronicle of London, 1259–1342*, trans. H. T. Riley (London: Trübner, 1864), 253.
39. Herbert, *Twelve Great Livery Companies*, 1:28, found that liveries were generally adopted late in the reign of Edward III, when he granted charters.
40. Herbert, *Twelve Great Livery Companies*, 1:66–74, has a full description of the processions on the saint's day and at funerals.
41. Herbert, *Twelve Great Livery Companies*, 1:29.
42. Unwin, *Gilds and Companies of London*, 192; *Facsimile of the First Volume of the Ms. Archives of the Worshipful Company of Grocers of the City of London, A. D. 1345–1463, Pt. 1*, ed. and trans. John Abernethy Kingdom, (London: Richard Clay, 1886), 90–91. The company paid £43 8s. for fabric of verdulet (bright, bluish green). In addition. they paid a minstrel and his five companions including their hoods, their dinner and wine for two days.
43. Brewers Gild, 1418–1441, Guildhall Library, MS 5440.
44. *Memorials of London*, 612; Unwin, *Gilds and Companies of London*, 190–91.
45. *Facsimile of the first vol. of Grocers*, 91, 143; Welch, *Pewterers*, 32, 35, 49.
46. *Acts of the Court of Mercers' Company*, 101.
47. *Liber Albus*, 24–25.
48. *Acts of the Court of Mercers' Company*, 101.
49. *Liber Albus*, 25. Nightingale, *A Medieval Mercantile Company*, 551–52, says that the incident was indicative of the declining economic position of the Grocers in the late Middle Ages.
50. Herbert, *Twelve Great Livery Companies*, 2:319–20. The arrangement is a lengthy one, spelling out all eventualities.
51. Unwin, *Gilds and Companies of London*, 176–88. Clode, *Guild of the Merchant Taylors*, 82–109, had a description of the hall and its contents, as well as of the disappearance of the gilt statue of St. John the Baptist and a fine tapestry of the life of St. John in the aftermath of the Reformation.
52. Unwin, *Gilds and Companies of London*, 193–95; Brewers Gild, 1418–1441, Guildhall Library, MS 5440 fol. 22b, fol. 22, fol. 27b, fol. 50. The Brewers were

convinced that Whittington had taken offense at the "fat swans" served at the gild feast on the election of wardens. They tried to propitiate him by bribing a sheriff and other officials. Finally, they called off their feasts and did not change their livery until he was out of office. The next mayor was kinder to the Brewers and they resumed their elaborate breakfasts and changed their livery every year. But they continued to take the precaution of giving bribes to successive mayors. A few years later, they paid for a farce which "shows in the most striking manner the malice of the late Mayor Whittington in English" (fol. 69b).

53. Sharpe, introduction to *LBL*, xxiv–xxv.
54. *Memorials of London*, 542. Riley suggests that this term is probably short for young man and should not be confused with *yeoman* which connoted a certain rank in society.
55. *Memorials of London*, 542–44. The Bakers also complained about their journeymen organizingm and the mayor called the Bakers' leaders in for a discussion in 1441. *LBK*, 263.
56. *LBH*, 431–32; *LBI*, 187–88, 609–12, 653. Clode, *Guild of the Merchant Taylors*, 1:60–64 gives a full account of the yeomen's revolt and their gild. Mathew Davies, "Governors and Governed: The Practice of Power in the Merchant Taylor's Company in the Fifteenth Century," in *Guilds, Society and Economy in London, 1450–1800*, ed. Ian Anders Gadd and Patrick Wallis (London: Center for Metropolitan History, Institute of Historical Research, 2002), 68–69. The Taylors tried to impose the rule that an apprentice would have to serve with a master for several years after finishing his apprenticeship. They were also concerned that some of these freshly minted apprentices were setting up shop on their own in chambers and stairways and producing inferior clothing.
57. Unwin, *Gilds and Companies of London*, 224–28. He has an extended discussion of the transformation of the yeoman or bachelor groups from the late fourteenth century to the sixteenth century. Barron, *London in the Late Middle Ages*, 211–14.
58. Sharpe, introducion to *LBK*, xvii–xxi.
59. Davis, *Medieval Market Mentality*, 159–62, has a discussion of the distrust of outsiders by the burgesses of English towns.
60. Reddaway and Walker, *Goldsmiths Company*, 123–24.
61. Davies, "Power in the Merchant Taylors' Company," 74–76. Reddaway and Walker, *Goldsmiths Company*, 120–39.
62. *LBK*, 61, for the Joiners' complaint and for the Cordwainers' complaint, 335.
63. Reddaway and Walker, *Goldsmiths Company*, 120–39.
64. Davies, "Power in the Merchant Taylors' Company," 74.
65. Jonathan Good, "The Alien Clothworkers of London, 1337–1381," in Mitchell, French, and Biggs, *Ties That Bind*, 7–20.
66. *Wardens' account and Court Minute Books of the Goldsmiths' Mistery of London*, ed. Lisa Jefferson (Woodbridge, Suffolk: Boydell, 2003).
67. Davis, *Medieval Market Morality*, 169–73.
68. Welch, *Cutlers' Company*, 253.

69. Welch, *Pewterers*, 53, 55. Carole Rawcliff, "'That Kindliness Should be Cherished More, and Discord Driven Out': The Settlement of Commercial Disputes by Arbitration in Later Medieval England," in *Enterprise and Individuals in Fifteenth-Century England*, ed. Jennifer Kermode (Wolfeboro Falls: Boydell, 1991), 99–117.
70. *LBG*, 174. *Munimenta Gildhallae*, 3, 196. The rise of the political power of the gilds has been traced by Unwin, *Gilds and Companies of London*, 72–92.
71. Davies, "Power in the Merchant Taylor's Company," 73.
72. The gild charters spelled out the rules that applied to the governance of the gilds, the quality of the product, and the other ordinances. These were recorded with the mayor and appear in the Letter Books and the *Journals*. The copy of the Goldsmiths' Gild is reprinted in *Wardens' Accounts and Minute Books of the Goldsmiths' Mistery*, 126–39.
73. Reddaway and Walker, *Goldsmiths Company*. This book provides a readable overview of the company.
74. *Wardens' Accounts and Minute Books of the Goldsmiths' Mistery*, 77 (1360), 109. When Thomas Burnham drew a knife in the assembly in 1368, his humble submission to the wardens included two tuns of wine. This was reduced to a fine of £4. John Burnham had a supporter in Thomas Raynham, who came to the court and "made a great denouncement" against the wardens, thereby breaking his oath to the gild. He had to pay 7s. 4d. But Burnham got off with paying £1 and the rest to be collected if he offended again. Raynham was taken to the Court of Arches, an ecclesiastical court, because he broke his oath to the gild. Unwin, *Gilds and Companies of London*, 93–109, explained that many of the gilds maintained an existence as fraternities and registered their charter with the Bishop of London, as well as with the city. This gave them flexibility and in a case such as Raynham's, they could use the ecclesiastical court as part of the disciplinary action.
75. *Wardens' Accounts and Minute Books of the Goldsmiths' Mistery*, 111.
76. *Wardens' Accounts and Minute Books of the Goldsmiths' Mistery*, 74–75, 108–11, 125–26, 140–44.
77. *Wardens' Accounts and Minute Books of the Goldsmiths' Mistery* (1365), 99–101.
78. *Wardens' Accounts and Minute Books of the Goldsmiths' Mistery*, 142–43.
79. *Wardens' Accounts and Minute Books of the Goldsmiths' Mistery*, 151–53.
80. Davis, *Medieval Market Morality*.
81. Davies, "Governors and Governed," 72.

CHAPTER 6

1. *LBE*, 12–14.
2. Cannon, "London Pride: Citizenship in the Fourteenth Century," in Rees Jones, *Learning and Literacy*, 182, citing *Chronicles of the Reigns of Edward I and Edward II*, ed. W. Stubbs, 2 vols (London, 1882). Rolls series 76, I, 325 from *Annles Paulini*.

3. Cannon, "London Pride," in Rees Jones, *Learning and Literacy*, 188, citing Stubbs, *Annales Londoniensis*, 175–76.
4. *CPMR: 1323–1364*, 220–21(1345); PRO CI 67/38.
5. *CPMR: 1364–1381*, 88. For a larger suspected rebellion, see *CPMR: 1381–1412*, 78 (1406).
6. Guildhall Library, Consistory Court, 9064/1 m. 133 (1470–73).
7. *Liber Albus*, 234; *The London Eyre of 1244*, ed. Helena M. Chew and Martin Weinbaum, London Record Society 6 (London: Chatham, W. & J. MacKay, 1970), 25.
8. *Statutes of the Realm*, ed. Alexander Luders et al (London: Dawsons of Pall Mall, 1810) vol 1, 102.
9. *CPMR: 1364–1381*, 218–19. The churches that rang curfew were St. Mary le Bow, Kerkyngcherche, St. Bride, and St. Giles without Cripplegate. The hours of curfew were nine or ten o'clock to prime depending on the season.
10. *Statutes of the Realm*, 1:104. Felicity Heal, *Hospitality in Early Modern England* (Oxford: Clarendon, 1990), 1–22, discusses the shifting attitude toward foreigners and extending them hospitality.
11. *Liber Albus*, 234–35.
12. *CPMR: 1364–1381*, 151.
13. *CPMR: 1381–1412*, 78–79. "Whereas larcenies and divers evil deeds are commonly perpetrated more openly, notoriously and frequently in this present than in past times in the city of London, its suburbs and neighbourhood, which would not have been possible, if the thieves and evildoers had not been maintained and harboured by persons dwelling in the city and suburbs and residing with innkeepers, who cared little what kind of men they received, to the great damage of the citizens of the city and those repairing there to the great disgrace and scandal of the same, and in order to prevent such damage and scandal of the same, it was agreed that Sir Nicholas Brembre, Mayor, and the Aldermen that the innkeepers within the liberty should be sworn to harbour no one longer than a day and a night unless he were willing to answer for them and their acts, nor to receive at their tables any strangers called "travaillyngmen" or others, unless they had good and sufficient surety from them for their good and loyal behavior, under penalty."
14. *LBA*, 127; *CPMR: 1323–1364*, 18, 45, 154, 156, 163; *LBG*, 294.
15. *CPMR: 1381–1412*, 146. The proclamation was that no one was to carry arms in the city except the valet of a noble carrying his master's sword in his presence and the king's serjeants-at-arms, prince, and officers of the city.
16. *CPMR: 1323–1364*, 220–21; *CPMR: 1364–1381*, 260–61. Sappy claimed loss of £18 6s. 8d. from two chests when the door of his room was broken open. The innkeeper tried to blame Sappy's servants, but the mayor and aldermen viewed the evidence of the broken door and sided with Sappy, making the hostiller responsible under "the common custom of the realm that the keeper of a

17. *CPMR: 1323–1364*, 45, 235; *CPMR: 1413–1437*, 119, 121, 125, 131, 135–136, 139–40, 145, 159; *LBF*, 19, 77.
18. Barbara A. Hanawalt, "The Host, the Law, and the Ambiguous Space of Medieval London Taverns," In *Medieval Crime and Social Control*, ed. Barbara A. Hanawalt and David Wallace (Minneapolis, University of Minnesota Press, 1999), 204–23; repr. Barbara A. Hanawalt, *"Of Good and Ill Repute": Gender and Social Control in Medieval England* (New York: Oxford University Press, 1998), 104–23. See *CPMR: 1364–1381*, 30, in which Isabel de Chepsted complained that William Dyne, taverner, had beaten and wounded her in 1365 to her damage of 40s. He confessed to the assault and was mainprised by John Chaucer.
19. *LBK*, 132.
20. *Liber Albus*, 34, 80, 234, 273.
21. Caroline M. Barron, "Lay Solidarities: The Wards of Medieval London," in *Law, Laity and Solidarities: Essays in Honour of Susan Reynolds*, ed. Pauline Stafford, Janet L. Nelson, and Jane Martindale (Manchester: Manchester University Press, 2001), 223.
22. There were twenty-four wards until 1394, when Farringdon was divided into two. See Barron, "Lay Solidarities," 121–27, for a brief history of wards.
23. Barron, "Lay Solidarities," 218–24.
24. *Liber Albus*, 34, 272.
25. Barron, "Lay Solidarities," 226–27.
26. Barron, "Lay Solidarities," 220.
27. Eamon Duffy, *Stripping of the Altars: Traditional Religion in England, c. 1400–c. 1580* (New Haven, CT: Yale University Press, 1992), 136–39.
28. The chantries could be very well endowed so that the priests could live a luxurious and not well-regulated life. This led to resentments against them. Sharpe, *London and the Kingdom*, 1:255. Between 1400 and 1440 sixty some clerks in holy orders were found guildy of adultery and were taken to the Tun. The *Journals of the Common Council* sometimes marked these trips to the Tun with a drawing of a barrel by the entry.
29. Clive Burgess, "Shaping the Parish: St Mary at Hill, London, in the Fifteenth Century," in *The Cloister and the World: Essays in Medieval History in Honour of Barbara Harvey*, ed. John Blair and Brian Golding (Oxford: Clarendon, 1996), 246–74. See also Clive Burgess, "London Parishes: Development of a Context," in *Daily Life in the Late Middle Ages*, ed. Richard Britnell (Stroud, UK: Sutton, 1998), 151–74. In this essay, he has contrasted the poorer parish of St. Andrew Hubbard with St. Mary at Hill.
30. *LBI*, 48, 72, 85, 124, 161, 194, 211; *LBK*, 28, 49, 59, 69, 96, 140, 186, 217.
31. Katherine L. French, *The Good Women of the Parish: Gender and Religion after the Black Death* (Philadelphia: University of Pennsylvania Press, 2008), 162–79. For

a complete description of the role of women in parishes, this book is excellent. "'To Free Them from Binding': Women in the Late Medieval Parish," *Journal of Interdisciplinary History* 27, no. 3 (1997): 387–412.
32. *Ecclesiastical London*, ed. Erler, xxix–xxxi.
33. *Ecclesiastical London*, ed Erler, xxxi.
34. *The Medieval Records of a London Parish*, ed. Henry Littlehales, EETS, old. ser. 5. nos. 125, 128, 89, 110, 121, 141, 154, 167, 179, 191, 204. For the bread and ale provisions, see 134, 155, 180, 192, 204.
35. *Medieval Records of a London Parish*, 148, 147, 162.
36. *Medieval Records of a London Parish*,129, 171, 241. Sir John Plommer's bell, 246.
37. *Ecclesiastical London*, ed. Erler, xxv–xxviii.
38. Burgess, "Shaping the Parish," in Blair and Golding, *Cloister and the Parish*, 11–12.
39. *The Church Records of St. Andrew Hubbard Eastcheap, c. 1450–c1570*, ed. Clive Burgess, London Record Society, 34 (1999), 4, 6, 12, 15, 17,19, 20, 22, 27.
40. Barbara A. Hanawalt, "Keepers of the Lights: Late Medieval English Parish Gilds." *Journal of Medieval and Renaissance History* 14 (1984): 21–37.
41. Duffy, *Stripping of the Altars*, 142.
42. *English Gilds: The Original Ordinances of More Than One Hundred Early English Gilds*, ed. Toulmin Smith and Lucy Toulmin Smith, EETS (London, N. Trübner,1870), 3–10.
43. Unwin, *Gilds and Companies of London*, 122.
44. *English Gilds*, 3; F. P. Westlake, *The Parish Gilds of Mediaeval England* (London: Macmillan, 1919), p. 180.
45. *English Gilds*, 6–8. Gild of SS. Fabian and Sebastian had a similar ritual.
46. *English Gilds*, 11. Garlekhith permitted the miscreant back in if he amended his behavior, 4.
47. Unwin, *Gilds and Companies of London*, 123.
48. *English Gilds*, 4; Unwin, *Gilds and Companies of London*, 121; Westlake, *Parish Gilds*, 180–84.
49. Ben McRee, "Religious Gilds and Regulation of Behavior in Late Medieval Towns," in *People, Politics, and Community in the Later Middle Ages*, ed. Joel Rosenthal and Colin Richmond (New York: St. Martin's Press, 1987), 108–22.
50. *Parish Fraternity Register: The Fraternity of the Holy Trinity and SS Fabian and Sebastian in the Parish Church of St. Botolph without Aldergate*, ed. Patricia Basing (London Record Society, 1992), xxi–xxv. See Thrupp, *Merchant Class*, 34–35, for other gilds and occupations of members.
51. *Parish Fraternity Register*, 5–17.
52. Charles Phythian-Adams, *Desolation of a City: Coventry and the Urban Crisis of the Late Middle Ages* (Cambridge: Cambridge University Press, 1979), 118–27; Gervase Rosser, *Medieval Westminster, 1200–1540* (Oxford: Clarendon, 1989), 287–89; Ben R. McRee, "Religious Gilds and Civil Order: The Case of Norwich in the Late Middle Ages," *Speculum* 67, no. 1 (1992): 69–97. The Norwich case

was one of considerable conflict before a peaceful transition to civic government was arrived at.

53. Caroline M. Barron, "Parish Fraternities of Medieval London," in *The Church in Pre-Reformation Society: Essays in Honour of R. R. H. Du Boulay*, ed. Caroline Barron and C. Harper Bill (Woodbridge, UK: Boydell, 1985), 29–30. Although the information is not as complete for other gilds, the membership was mostly craftsmen. The gild of the Virgin in the church of All Hallows Barking attracted royal officials and wealthy merchants. This area of eastern London was developing in the fifteenth century.

54. *Parish Fraternity Register*, xi–xii; Unwin, *Gilds and Companies of London*, 123.

55. *English Gilds*, 4; Westlake, *Parish Gilds*, 185, 187.

56. Barbara A. Hanawalt. "Medieval Banquets: Celebration and Social Control." in *Råtten: En Festshrift til Bengt Ankereloo*, ed. Lars M. Anderson, Anna Jansdotter, Bodil E. B. Persson, Charlotte Tornbjer (Lund, Sweden: Nordic Academic Press, 2000), 147–57.

57. Unwin, *Gilds and Companies of London*, 114–18.

58. Unwin, *Gilds and Companies of London*, 117–18.

59. Hanawalt, "Keepers of the Lights," Late Medieval English Parish Gilds:" 21–37.

60. Unwin, *Gilds and Companies of London*, 119–20.

61. *English Gilds*, 6, 8, 9, 10.

62. Barron, "Parish Fraternities of Medieval London," 26–27. Ben R. McRee, "Charity and Gild Solidarity in Late Medieval England, *Journal of British Studies* 32, no. 3 (1993): 195–225.

63. Gervase Rosser, "Party List: Making Friends in English Medieval Gilds," in Davies and Prescott, *London and the Kingdom*, 118–34; and Roesser, "Big Brotherhood: Guilds in Urban Politics in Late Medieval England," in *Guilds and Associations in Europe, 900–1900*, ed. Ian A. Gadd and Patrick Wallis (London: Centre for Metropolitan History, University of London, 2006),: 27–42. Miri Ruben, "Identity and Solidarity in the Late Middle Ages," in *Enterprise and Individuals in Fifteenth-Century England*, ed. Jennifer Kermode (Wolfeboro Falls: Boydell, 1991), 132–50, has argued that they provided a continuity between the living and dead in the gild.

64. Barron, *London in the Later Middle Ages*, 190–91.

65. *LBG*, 33.

66. *London English,*, 93, 96–97; *LBI*, 208–9.

67. *LBK*, 240, for a series of proclamations for similar public injunctions on holidays.

68. *London English*, 92–93. Popular feeling went against Richard II when the Lords Appellant were victorious in 1387. Richard reacted by threatening action against Londoners who put up notices.

69. Sharpe, *London and the Kingdom*, 256; V. J. Scattergood, *Politics and Poetry in the Fifteenth Century, 1399–1485* (New York: Barnes and Noble, 1971), 25–23.

70. Scattergood, *Politics and Poetry*, 26, 178.

71. *CCorR*, 14–15, 34–35; *CEMCR*, 255 (1307).
72. "Gregory's Chronicle," 132, 134, 137.
73. "Gregory's Chronicle," 162.
74. "Gregory's Chronicle."
75. "Gregory's Chronicle," 146–47.
76. "Gregory's Chronicle," 148–49. See also *Chronicles of London*, 148–49.
77. "The Lament of the Duchess of Gloucester," in *Political Poems and Songs Relating to English History Composed During the Period from the Accession of Edward II to that of Richard III*, ed. Thomas Wright, Rolls Series 14 (London, 1861), 2: 205–8. Barbara A. Hanawalt, "Portraits of Outlaws, Felons, and Rebels in Late Medieval England," in *British Outlaws of Literature and History: Essays on Medieval and Early Modern Figures from Robin Hood to Twm Shon Catty*, ed. Alexander L. Kaufman (Jefferson, NC: McFarland, 2011), 45–64.
78. Kenneth Hotham Vickers, *Humphrey Duke of Gloucester: A Biography* (London: A. Constable, 1907), 164–205.
79. *LBK*, 68.
80. For two of the more detailed fifteenth-century London Chronicle accounts, see *The Great Chronicle of London*, ed. A. H. Thomas and I. D. Thornley (London, 1919; repr. Gloucester, UK: Sutton, 1983), 175–76; *The Brut or the Chronicles of England*, 78–79.
81. Ralph A. Griffiths, "The Trial of Eleanor Cobham: An Episode in the Fall of Duke Humphrey of Gloucester," *Bulletin of the John Rylands Library* 51 (1968): 381–99. I have used his broad outline of events, but he has taken the accounts of the chroniclers as an accurate description of the allegations against her and of her trial. He supplemented these with record sources so that it is as reliable an account as can be made.
82. Griffiths, "Trial of Eleanor Cobham," 386–93. Bollingbroke was drawn and quartered; one of the accused died in prison; another was pardoned, and the Witch of Eye was burned at the stake.
83. Griffiths, "Trial of Eleanor Cobham," 395–99.
84. "Lament of the Duchess of Gloucester," 2:206.
85. "Lament of the Duchess of Gloucester," 2:206–7.
86. "Lament of the Duchess of Gloucester," 2:208.
87. Peter Burke, "Popular Culture in Seventeenth-Century London," *London Journal* 3, no. 2 (1977): 143–62. There is so much more available in writing for the seventeenth century than for the late fourteenth and fifteenth centuries from which to form an understanding of the popular culture of London, or what Burke called the "blue apron" culture. Some continuity existed, or course, but it is much harder to penetrate. One of his observations must also have been true about the official processions in the fifteenth century. They had to appeal to the elites as well as the masses, otherwise they would have lost their efficacy.

88. *Political Poems and Songs Relating to English History Composed During the Period from from the Accession of Edward III to that of Richard III*, ed. Thomas Wright, 1 and 2 (London, 1859-61); *Historical Poems of the XIVth and XVth Centuries*, ed. Rossell Hope Robbins (New York: Columbia University Press, 1959); *Secular Lyrics of the XIVth and XVth Centuries*, ed. Rossell Hope Robbins (Oxford: Clarendon, 1952).
89. Scattergood, *Politics and Poetry*, 28–29. He suggests that the song might have alluded to the mayor's frequent visits to the brothels in Southwark.
90. Lancashire, *London Civic Theater*, 54–62. The lack of theater in London is in contrast to theater in Arras. See Carol Symes, *Theater and Public Life in Medieval Arras* (Ithaca, NY: Cornell University Press, 2007). In Ghent, there were public contests of rhetoricians. See Arnade, *Realms of Ritual: Burgundian Ceremony and Civic Life*, 159–88.
91. Barron, "Political Culture," in Clark and Carpenter, *Late Medieval Britain*, 121–22. London's secular symbolism was in marked contrast to Bruges, where the civic authorities paid for religious statutes in civic space. See Brown, *Civic Ceremony and Religion in Medieval Bruges*, 8.
92. Barron, "Political Culture," in Clark and Carpenter, *Late Medieval Britain*, 119–20. She suggests that Carpenter, drawing on his extensive knowledge of classical authors found in his library, may have chosen the program for the statues. See also by the same author, *The Medieval Guildhall of London* (London: Corporation of London, 1974), 27.

CONCLUSION

1. Thrupp, *Merchant Class*, 188.
2. Bell, *Ritual Perspectives and Dimensions*, 129, 135.
3. *Memorials of London*, 580.

Bibliography

Archer, Ian W. *The History of the Haberdashers' Company*. Chichester, UK: Phillimore, 1991.

———. *The Pursuit of Stability: Social Relations in Elizabethan London*. Cambridge: Cambridge University Press, 1991.

Ashdown, Charles H. *The History of the Glaziers' Company; Otherwise the Glaziers and Painters of Glass, A. D. 1328–1918*. London: Blades, 1918.

Attreed, Lorraine. "The Politics of Welcome: Ceremonies and Constitutional Development in Later Medieval Towns." In *City and Spectacle in Medieval Europe*, edited by Barbara A. Hanawalt and Kathryn Reyerson, 208–31. Minneapolis: University of Minnesota Press, 1994.

Arnade, Peter. *Realms of Ritual: Burgundian Ceremony and Civic Life in Late Medieval Ghent*. Ithaca, NY: Cornell University Press, 1996.

Baker, Timothy. *Medieval London*. New York: Praeger, 1970.

Ball, Mia. *The Worshipful Company of Brewers: A Short History*. London: Hutchinson Benham, 1977.

Barron, Caroline M. "Chivalry, Pageantry and Merchant Culture in Medieval London." In *Heraldry, Pageantry and Social Display*, edited by Peter Cross and Maurice Keen, 219–41. Woodbridge, UK: Boydell, 2002.

———. "Lay Solidarities: The Wards of Medieval London." In *Law, Laity and Solidarities: Essays in Honour of Susan Reynolds*, edited by Pauline Stafford, Janet Nelson, and Jane Martindale, 218–33. Manchester: Manchester University Press, 2001.

———. "London 1300–1540." In *The Cambridge Urban History of Britain 600–1540*. Vol. 1, edited by D. M. Palliser, 395–440. Cambridge: Cambridge University Press, 2000.

———. *London in the Later Middle Ages: Government and People, 1200–1500*. Oxford: Oxford University Press, 2004.

———. *The Medieval Guildhall of London*. London: Corporation of London, 1974.

---. "The Parish Fraternities of Medieval London." *The Church in Pre-Reformation Society*, edited by Caroline M. Barron and Christopher Harper-Bill, 13–37. Woodbridge, UK: Boydell, 1985.

---. "The Political Culture of Medieval London." in *Political Culture in Late Medieval Britain: Fifteenth Century*, vol. 4, edited by Linda Clark and Christine Carpenter, 108–33. Woodbridge, UK: Boydell, 2004.

---. "The Quarrel of Richard II with London, 1392-7." In *The Reign of Richard II: Essays in Honour of May McKisack*, edited by F. R. H. Duboulay and Caroline M. Barron, 173–201. London: Athelone, 1971.

---. *Revolt in London: 11th to 15th June 1381*. London, Museum of London, 1981.

---. "Richard Whittington: The Man behind the Myth." In *Studies in London History Presented to Philip Edmund Jones*, edited by A. E. J. Hollaender and William Kellaway, 197–250. London: Hodder and Stoughton, 1969.

---. "Ralph Holland and the London Radicals, 1438–1444." In *The Medieval English Town: A Reader in English Urban History*, edited by Richard Hold and Gervase Rosser, 160–83. London: Longman, 1990.

---. *The Parish of St. Andrew Holborn*. With Penelope Hunting and Jane Roscoe. London: Diamond Trading Co.,1979.

---., and Nigel Saul, eds. *England and the Low Countries in the Late Middle Ages*. Stroud, UK: Alan Sutton, 1995.

Beaven, Alfred B. *The Aldermen of the City of London, Temp. Henry III–1912*. 2 vols. London: Eden Fisher, 1913.

Beckwith, Sarah. "Ritual, Theater, and Social Space in the York Corpus Christi Cycle." In *Bodies and Disciplines: Intersections of Literature and History in Fifteenth-Century England*, edited by Barbara Hanawalt and David Wallace, 63–86. Medieval Cultures 9, Minneapolis: University of Minnesota Press, 1996.

Bell, Catherine. *Ritual Perspectives and Dimensions*. New York: Oxford University Press, 1997.

Bellamy, John G. *The Law of Treason in England in the Later Middle Ages*. Cambridge: Cambridge University Press, 1970.

Bennett, Judith M. *Ale, Beer, and Brewsters in England: Women's Work in a Changing World*. New York: Oxford University Press, 1996.

Binski, P. *Westminster Abbey and the Plantagenets: Kingship and the Representation of Power, 1200–1400*. New Haven, CT: Yale University Press, 1995.

Bird, Ruth. *The Turbulent London of Richard II*. London: Longmans, Green, 1949.

Black, Anthony. *Guilds and Civil Society in European Political Thought from the Twelfth Century to the Present*. Ithaca, NY: Cornell University Press, 1984.

Bourdieu, Pierre. *Outline of a Theory of Practice*. Translated by Richard Nice. Cambridge: Cambridge University Press. 1977.

Brewer, Thomas. *Memoir of the Life and Times of John Carpenter*. London: A. Taylor, 1856.

Britnell, Richard. *The Commercialization of English Society, 1300–1500*. Cambridge: Cambridge University Press, 1993.

———. "Town Life." In *A Social History of England, 1200–1500*, edited by Rosemary Horrox and W. Mark Ormrod, 134–78. Cambridge: Cambridge University Press, 2006.

Brown, Andrew. *Civic Ceremony and Religion in Medieval Bruges, c. 1300–1520*. Cambridge: Cambridge University Press, 2011.

Bryant, Lawrence M. "Configurations of the Community in Late Medieval Spectacles: Paris and London during the Dual Monarchy." In *City and Spectacle in Medieval Europe*, edited by Barbara Hanawalt and Kathryn Reyerson, 3–33. Minneapolis: University of Minnesota Press, 1994.

Buc, Philippe. *The Dangers of Ritual: Between Early Medieval Texts and Social Scientific Theory*. Princeton, NJ: Princeton University Press, 2001.

Burgess, Clive. "London, the Church and the Kingdom." In *London and the Kingdom: Essays in Honour of Caroline M. Barron*, edited by Matthew Davies and Andrew Prescott, 118–34. Harlaxton Medieval Studies 16. Donington: Shaun Tyas, 2008.

———. "London Parishes: Development in Context." In *Daily Life in the Late Middle Ages*, edited by Richard Britnell, 151–74. Stroud, UK: Sutton, 1998.

———. "Shaping the Parish: St. Mary at Hill, London, in the Fifteenth Century." In *The Cloister and the World: Essays in Medieval History in Honor of Barbara Harvey*, edited by John Blair and Brian Golding, 246–86. Oxford: Clarendon, 1996.

Burke, Peter. "Popular Culture in Seventeenth-Century London." *London Journal* 3, no. 2 (1977): 143–62.

Campbell, B. M. S., J. A. Galloway, D. Keen, and M. Murphy. *A Medieval Capital and Its Grain Supply: Agrarian Production and Distribution in the London Region c. 1300*. Lancaster, UK: Historical Geography Research Group, no. 30, 1993.

Cannon, Debbie. "London Pride: Citizenship in the Fourteenth-Century Custumals of the City of London." In *Learning and Literacy in Medieval England and Abroad*. edited by Sarah Rees Jones, 179–98. Turnhout, Belgium: Brepols, 2003.

Carlin, Martha. *Medieval Southwark*. London: Hambledon, 1996.

———. "Putting Dinner on the Table in Medieval London." In *London and the Kingdom: Essays in Honour of Caroline M. Barron*, edited by Matthew Davies and Andrew Prescott, 58–77. Harlaxton Medieval Studies 16. Donington, UK: Shaun Tyas, 2008.

Carrel, Helen. "The Ideology of Punishment in Late Medieval English Towns." *Social History* 34 (2009): 301–20.

Catto, Jeremy. "Andrew Horn: Law and History in the Fourteenth Century." In *The Writing of History in the Middle Ages: Essays Presented to Richard William Southern*, edited by R. H. C. Davis and J. M. Wallace-Hadrill, with the assistance of R. J. A. I. Catton and M. H. Keen, 367–92. Oxford: Clarendon, 1981.

Clode, Charles M. *The Early History of the Guild of Merchant Taylors*. 2 vols. London: Harrison and Sons, 1888.

Coote, H. C. "The Ordinances of Some Secular Guilds of Medieval London." *Transactions of the London and Middlessex Archaeological Society*. Vol. 4. London (1875): 1–59.

Coss, P., and Maurice Keen, eds. *Heraldry, Pageantry and Social Display in Medieval England*. Woodbridge, UK: Boydell, 2002.

Carras, Ruth Mazo. *Common Women: Prostitution and Sexuality in Medieval England*. New York: Oxford University Press, 1996.

Damen, Mario. "Giving by Pouring: The Function of Gifts of Wine in the City of Leiden, 14th–16th Centuries." In *Symbolic Communication in Late Medieval Towns*, edited by Jacoba Van Leeuwen, 83–100. Leiden: Leiden University Press, 2006.

Davis, James. "Baking for the Common Good: A Reassessment of the Assize of Bread in Medieval England." *Economic History Review*, 2nd ser. 57 (2004): 465–502.

———. *Medieval Market Morality: Life, Law and Ethics in the English Market Place*. Cambridge: Cambridge University Press, 2012.

Davies, Matthew. "Artisans, Guilds and Government in London." In *Daily Life in the Late Middle Ages*. edited by Richard Britnell. Stroud: Sutton, 1998. 125–50.

———. "Governors and Governed: The Practice of Power in the Merchant Taylor's Company in the Fifteenth Century." In *Guilds, Society and Economy in London 1450–1800*, edited by Ian Anders Gadd and Patrick Wallis, 67–84. Centre for Metropolitan History, Institute of Historical Research 2002.

———., and Ann Saunders, *The History of the Merchant Taylor's Company*. Leeds: Maney, 2004.

———., and Andrew Prescott, eds. *London and the Kingdom: Essays in Honour of Caroline M. Barron*. Harlaxton Medieval Studies 16. Donington, UK: Shaun Tyas, 2008.

Duffy, Eamon. *The Stripping of the Altars: Traditional Religion in England, c. 1400–c. 1580*. New Haven, CT: Yale University Press, 1992.

Dummelow, John. *A Short History of the Worshipful Company of Wax Chandlers of London*. London: Phillimore, 1973.

Dumolyn, Jan, and Jolle Haemers,. "'A Bad Chicken was Brooding': Subversive Speech in Late Medieval Flanders." *Past and Present* 214, no. 1 (2012): 45–86.

Dyer, Christopher. *Standards of Living in the Later Middle Ages: Social Change in England c. 1200-1520*. Cambridge: Cambridge University Press, 1989.

Egan, Geoff. *The Medieval Household Daily Living c. 1150–1450*. London: The Stationery Office. 1998.

Fleming, Peter. "Telling Tales of Oligarchy in the Late Medieval Town." In *Revolution and Consumption in Late Medieval England*, edited by Michael Hicks, 177–93. Woodbridge, UK: Boydell, 2001.

Franceschi, Franco. "The Rituals of Guilds: Examples from Tuscan Cities (Thirteenth to Sixteenth Centuries)." In *Late Medieval and Early Modern Ritual: Studies in*

Italian Urban Culture, edited by Samuel Cohen Jr., Marcello Fantoni, Franco Franceschi, and Rabrizio Riciardelli, 65–92. Turnhout, Belgium: Brepols, 2013.

French, Katherine L. *The Good Women of the Parish: Gender and Religion after the Black Death*. Philadelphia: University of Pennsylvania Press, 2008.

Geertz, Clifford. *Negara: The Theater State of Nineteenth-Century Bali*. Princeton, NJ: University Press, 1980.

Girtin, Tom. *The Mark of the Sword: A Narrative History of the Cutler's Company, 1189–1975*. London: Hutchinson, 1975.

Good, Jonathan. "The Alien Clothworkers of London, 1337–1381." In *The Ties That Bind: Essays in Medieval British History in Honor of Barbara Hanawalt*, edited by Linda E. Mitchell, Katherine L. French, Douglas L. Biggs, 7–20. Burlington, VT: Ashgate, 2011.

Griffiths, Ralph A. "The Trial of Eleanor Cobham: An Episode in the Fall of Duke Humphrey of Gloucester." *Bulletin of the John Rylands Library* 51 (1968): 381–99.

Gross, Charles. *The Gild Merchant: A Contribution to British Municipal History*. 2 vols. Oxford: Clarendon, 1890.

Hanawalt, Barbara A. *Growing Up in Medieval London: The Experience of Childhood in History*. New York: Oxford University Press, 1993.

———. "The Host, the Law, and the Ambiguous Space of Medieval London Taverns." In *Medieval Crime and Social Control*, edited by Barbara A. Hanawalt and David Wallace, 204–23. Minneapolis: University of Minnesota Press, 1999.

———. "Keepers of the Lights: Late Medieval English Parish Gilds." *Journal of Medieval and Renaissance History* 14 (1984): 21–37.

———. "Medieval Banquets: Celebration and Social Control." In *Råtten: En Festshrift til Bengt Ankereloo*, edited by Lars M. Anderson, Anna Jansdotter, Bodil E. B. Persson, and Charlotte Tornbjer, 147–57. Lund, Sweden: Nordic Academic Press, 2000.

———. *"Of Good and Ill Repute": Gender and Social Control in Medieval England*. New York: Oxford University Press, 1998.

———. "Portraits of Outlaws, Felons, and Rebels in Late Medieval England." In *British Outlaws of Literature and History: Essays on Medieval and Early Modern Figures from Robin Hood to Twm Shon Catty*, edited by Alexander L. Kaufman, 45–64. Jefferson, NC: McFarland, 2011.

———. "The Power of Word and Symbol: Conflict Resolution in Late Medieval London." In *"Of Good and Ill Repute": Gender and Social Control in Medieval England*, 35–54. New York: Oxford University Press, 1998.

———. "Reading the Lives of the Illiterate: London's Poor." *Speculum* 80 (2005): 1067–86.

———. "Remarriage as an Option for Urban and Rural Widows in Late Medieval England." In *Wife and Widow in Medieval England*, edited by Sue Sheridan Walker, 141–64. Ann Arbor: University of Michigan Press, 1993.

———. "Rituals of Inclusion and Exclusion: Hierarchy and Marginalization in Medieval London." In *"Of Good and Ill Repute": Gender and Social Control in Medieval England*, 18–34. New York: Oxford University Press, 1998.

———. *The Wealth of Wives: Women, Law, and the Economy in Late Medieval London*. New York: Oxford University Press, 2007.

———., and Ben R. McRee. "The Guilds of Homo Prudens in Late Medieval England." *Continuity and Change* 7 (1992): 163–79.

———., and Michal Kolbialka, eds. *Medieval Practices of Space*. Minneapolis: University of Minnesota Press, 2000.

Hanna, Ralph III. *London Literature, 1300–1380*. Cambridge: Cambridge University Press, 2005.

Hazlitt, W. Carew. *The Livery Companies of the City of London: Their Origin, Character, Development and Social and Political Significance*. London: S. Sonnenshein, 1882.

Herbert, William. *The History of the Twelve Great Livery Companies of London; Principally Compiled from Their Grants and Records*, 2 vols. London: Published by author, 1837, 1838.

Hobsbawm, Eric, and Ranger, Terence. *The Invention of Tradition*. Cambridge: Cambridge University Press, 1983.

Hope, William St. John, and Atchley, G. Cuthbert F. *English Liturgical Colours*. New York: Macmillan, 1918.

Howell, Martha C. *Commerce before Capitalism in Europe, 1300–1600*. Cambridge: Cambridge University Press, 2010.

Hughes, Diane Owen. "Earrings for Circumcision: Distinction and Purification in the Italian Renaissance City." In *Persons in Groups: Social Behavior as Identity Formation in Medieval and Renaissance Europe*, edited by Richard C. Trexler, 155–82. Binghamton, NY: Medieval and Renaissance Texts and Studies, 1985.

———. "Sumptuary Law and Social Relations in Italy." In *Disputes and Settlements: Law and Human Relations in the West*, edited by John Bossy, 69–99. Cambridge: Cambridge University Press, 1983.

Humphrey, Chris. *The Politics of Carnival: Festive Misrule in Medieval England*. Manchester: Manchester University Press, 2001.

Imray, Jean M. "'Les Bones Gentes de la Mercerye de Londres': A Study of the Membership of the Medieval Mercers Company." In *Studies in London History Presented to Philip Edmund Jones*, edited by A. E. J. Hollaender and William Kellaway, 155–80. London: Hodder and Stoughton, 1969.

James, Mervyn. "Ritual, Drama and Social Body in the Late Medieval English Town." *Past and Present* 93 (1983): 3–29.

Johnson, A. H. *The History of the Worshipful Company of Drapers of London*. Vol. 1 Oxford: Clarendon Press, 1914.

Jones, Malcolm. *The Secret Middle Ages*. Stroud, UK: Alan Sutton, 2002.

Karras, Ruth Mazo. *Common Women: Prostitution and Sexuality in Medieval England*. New York: Oxford University Press, 1996.

Keen, Derek. "A New Study of London before the Great Fire." *Urban History* 11 (1984): 11–22.

Kellaway, William, "John Carpenter's Liber Albus." *Guildhall Studies in London History* 3 (1978): 67–84.

Kermode, Jennifer I. "Obvious Observations on the Formation of Oligarchies in Late Medieval English Towns." In *Towns and Townspeople in the Fifteenth Century*, edited by John A. F. Thomson, 87–106. Wolfboro, NH: Alan Sutton, 1988.

Kipling, Gordon. *Enter the King: Theater, Liturgy and Ritual in Medieval Civic Triumph, 1300–1660*. New York: Oxford University Press, 1998.

———. "The King's Advent Transformed: The Consecration of the City in the Sixteenth-Century Civic Triumph." In *Ceremonial Culture in Pre-Modern Europe*, edited by Nicholas Howe, 89–127. Notre Dame, IN: University of Notre Dame Press, 2007.

Kowaleski, Maryanne. "Medieval People in Town and Country: New Perspectives from Demography and Bioarchaeology." *Speculum* 89 (2014): 573–600.

Lancashire, Anne. *London Civic Theater: City Drama and Pageantry from Roman Times to 1558*. Cambridge: Cambridge University Press, 2002.

Lefebvre, Henri. *The Production of Space*. Translated by Donald Nicholson-Smith. Oxford: Blackwell, 1991.

Lindenbaum, Sheila. "Ceremony and Oligarchy: The London Midsummer Watch." In *City and Spectacle in Medieval Europe*, edited by Barbara A. Hanawalt and Kathryn L. Reyerson, 171–88. Medieval Studies at Minnesota 6. Minneapolis: University of Minnesota Press, 1994.

———. "London's Texts and Literary Practice." In *Cambridge History of Medieval English Literature*, edited by David Wallace, 284–315. Cambridge: Cambridge University Press, 1999.

———. "The Smithfield Tournament of 1390." *Journal of Medieval and Renaissance Studies* 20 (1990): 1–20.

Loach, Jennifer. "The Function of Ceremonial in the Reign of Henry VIII." *Past and Present* 124 (1994): 41–68.

McDonnel, Kevin. *Medieval London Suburbs*. London: Phillimore. 1978.

McIntosh, Marjorie Keniston. *Controlling Misbehavior in England, 1370–1600*. New York: Cambridge University Press, 1998.

———. *Poor Relief in England, 1350–1600*. Cambridge: Cambridge University Press, 2012.

———. *Working Women in English Society, 1300–1620*. Cambridge: Cambridge University Press, 2005.

McLaren, Mary Rose. *The London Chronicles of the Fifteenth Century: A Revolution in English Writing*. Woodbridge, UK: Boydell, 2002.

———. "Reading, Writing and Recording: Literacy and the London Chronicles in the Fifteenth Century." In *London and the Kingdom: Essays in Honour of Caroline M. Barron*, edited by Matthew Davies and Andrew Prescott, 346–65. Harlaxton Medieval Studies 16. Donington, UK: Shaun Tyas, 2008.

McRee, Ben R. "Charity and Gild Solidarity in Late Medieval England." *Journal of British Studies* 32, no. 3 (1993): 195–225.

———. "The Mayor's Body." In *The Ties That Bind: Essays in Medieval British History in Honor of Barbara Hanawalt*, edited by Linda E. Mitchell, Katherine L. French, Douglas L. Biggs, 39–54. Burlington, VT: Ashgate, 2011.

———. "Peacemaking and Its Limits in Late Medieval Norwich." *English Historical Review* 109, no. 433 (1994): 831–66.

———. "Religious Gilds and Civil Order: The Case of Norwich in the Late Middle Ages." *Speculum* 67 (1992): 69–79.

———. "Religious Gilds and Regulation of Behavior in Late Medieval Towns." In *People, Politics and Community in the Later Middle Ages*, edited by Joel Rosenthal and Colin Richmond, 108–22. New York: St. Martin's Press, 1987.

———. "Unity and Division? The Social Meaning of Guild Ceremony in Urban Communities." In *City and Spectacle in Medieval Europe*, edited by Barbara A. Hanawalt and Kathryn L. Reyerson, 189–207. Medieval Studies at Minnesota 6. Minneapolis: University of Minnesota Press, 1994.

———., and Barbara Hanawalt. "The Guilds of Homo Prudens in Late Medieval England." *Continuity and Change* 7 (1992): 163–79.

Manley, Lawrence. *Literature and Culture in Early Modern London*. Cambridge: Cambridge University Press, 1995.

Masters, Betty R. "The Mayor's Household before 1600." In *Studies in London History Presented to Philip Edmund Jones*, edited by A. E. J. Hollaender and William Kellaway, 95–116. London: Hodder and Stoughton, 1969.

Muir, Edward. *Civic Ritual in Renaissance Venice*. Princeton, NJ: Princeton University Press, 1981.

———. "The Eye of the Procession: Ritual Ways of Seeing in the Renaissance." In *Ceremonial Culture in Pre-Modern Europe*, edited by Nicholas Howe, 129–53. Notre Dame, IN: University of Notre Dame Press, 2007.

———. *Ritual in Early Modern Europe*. Cambridge, Cambridge University Press, 1997.

New, Elizabeth. "Representation and Identity in Medieval London: The Evidence of Seals." In *London and the Kingdom: Essays in Honour of Caroline M. Barron*, edited by Matthew Davies and Andrew Prescott, 246–565. Harlaxton Medieval Studies 16. Donington, UK: Shaun Tyas, 2008.

Nightingale, Pamela. "Capitalists, Crafts and Constitutional Change in Late Fourteenth-Century London." *Past and Present* 124 (1989): 3–35.

———. "The Growth of London in the Medieval Economy." In *Progress and Problems in Medieval England,*. edited by Richard H. Britnell and John Hatcher, 89–106. Cambridge: Cambridge University Press, 1996.

———. *A Medieval Mercantile Community: The Grocers' Company and the Politics and Trade of London, 1000–1485*. New Haven, CT: Yale University Press. 1995.

Nolan, Maura. *John Lydgate and the Making of Public Culture*. Cambridge: Cambridge University Press, 2005.

Oliver, Kingsley M. *Hold Fast, Sit Sure: The History of the Worshipful Company of Saddlers of the City of London, 1160–1960*. Chichester, UK: Phillimore, 1995.
Ormrod, W. Mark. *Edward III*. New Haven, CT: Yale University Press, 2011.
Pearsall, Derek. "Langland's London." In *Written Work: Langland, Labor, and Authorship*, edited by Steven Justice and Kathryn Kerby-Fulton, 185–207. Philadelphia: University of Pennsylvania Press, 1997.
Pendrill, Charles. *London Life in the Fourteenth Century*. Port Washington, NY: Kennikat, 1971. First published in London, 1925.
Phillips, Seymour. *Edward II*. New Haven, CT: Yale University Press, 2011.
Phythian-Adams, Charles. "Ceremony and the Citizen: The Communal Year at Coventry, 1450–1550." In *Crisis and Order in English Towns, 1500-1700: Essays in Urban History*, edited by Peter Clark and Paul Slack, 17–85. London: Routledge and Kegan Paul, 1972.
———. *Desolation of a City: Coventry and the Urban Crisis of the Late Middle Ages*. Cambridge: Cambridge University Press, 1979.
Prescott, Andrew, and Matthew Davies. *London and the Kingdom: Essays in Honour of Caroline M. Barron*. Harlaxton Medieval Studies 16. Donington, UK: Shaun Tyas, 2008.
Rappaport, Steve. *Worlds within Worlds: Structures of Life in Sixteenth-Century London*. Cambridge: Cambridge University Press, 1989.
Rawcliff, Carole. "'That Kindliness Should Be Cherished More and Discourd Driven Out': The Settlement of Commercial Disputes by Arbitration in Later Medieval England." In *Enterprise and Individuals in Fifteenth-Century England*, edited by Jennifer Kermode, 99–117. Wolfeboro Falls, NH: Alan Sutton, 1991.
———. *Urban Bodies: Communal Health in Late Medieval English Towns*. Woodbridge, UK: Boydell, 2013.
Reddaway, T. F., and Lorna E. M. Walker. *The Early History of the Goldsmiths' Company: 1327–1509; including the Book of Ordinances, 1478–83*. London: Edward Arnold, 1975.
Rees Jones, Sarah. "Thomas More's Utopia and Medieval London." In *Pragmatic Utopias: Ideals and Communities, 1200–1630*, edited by Rosemary Horrox and Sarah Rees Jones, 117–35. Cambridge: Cambridge University Press, 2001.
Reynolds, Susan. *Ideas and Solidarities of the Medieval Laity: England and Western Europe*. Aldershot, Hampshire: Variorum, 1995.
———. *Kingdoms and Communities in Western Europe, 900–1300*. 2nd ed. Oxford: Clarendon, 1997.
———. "Medieval Urban History and the History of Political Thought." *Urban History Yearbook* 9 (1982): 14–23.
Rexroth, Frank. *Deviance and Power in Late Medieval London*. Translated by Pamela Selwyn. Cambridge: Cambridge University Press, 2007.
Richardson, Malcolm. *Middle-Class Writing in Late Medieval London*. History of the Book 7. London: Pickering and Chatto, 2011.

Rigby, Stephen H. "Urban 'Oligarchy' in Late Medieval London." In *Towns and Townspeople in the Fifteenth Century*, edited by John A. F. Thomson, 62–86. Wolfboro Falls, NH: Sutton, 1988.

———, and Elizabeth Ewan. "Government, Power, and Authority, 1300–1540." In *The Cambridge Urban History of Britain*, vol. 1, edited by D. M. Palliser, 291–312. Cambridge: Cambridge University Press, 2000.

Rosser, Gervase. "Big Brotherhood: Guilds in Urban Politics in Late Medieval England." In *Guilds and Associations in Europe, 900–1900*, edited by Ian A. Gadd and Patrick Wallis, 27–42. London: Centre for Metropolitan History, University of London, 2006.

———. "Party List: Making Friends in English Medieval Guilds." In *London and the Kingdom: Essays in Honour of Caroline M. Barron*, edited by Matthew Davies and Andrew Prescott, 118–34. Harlaxton Medieval Medieval Studies 16. Donington, UK: Shaun Tyas, 2008.

———. *Medieval Westminster, 1200–1540*. Oxford: Clarendon, 1989.

Rubin, Miri. "Identity and Solidarity in the Late Middle Ages." In *Enterprise and Individuals in Fifteenth Century England*, edited by Jennifer Kermode, 132–50. Wofeboro Falls, NH: Sutton, 1991.

Sabine, Ernest. "Butchering in Mediaeval London." *Speculum* 8 (1933): 335–53.

———. "City Cleaning in Mediaeval London." *Speculum* 12 (1937): 19–43.

———. "Latrines and Cesspools of Mediaeval London." *Speculum* 9 (1934): 303–21.

Saul, Nigel. *Richard II*. New Haven, CT: Yale University Press, 1997.

Scattergood, V. J. *Politics and Poetry in the Fifteenth Century, 1399–1485*. New York: Barnes and Noble, 1971.

Schmitt, Jean-Claude. *La raison des gesterur dans l'Occident médiéval*. Paris: Gallimard, 1990.

———. "The Rationale of Gestures in the West: Third to Thirteenth Centuries." In *The Cultural History of Gesture*, edited by Jan Bremmer and Herman Roodengurg, 59–70. Ithaca, NY: Cornell University Press, 1991.

Schneider, Robert A. *The Ceremonial City: Toulouse Observed, 1738–1780*. Princeton, NJ: Princeton University Press, 1995.

Schofield, John. *Medieval London Houses*. New Haven, CT: Yale University Press, 1994.

Seabourne, Gwen. "Assize Matters: Regulation of the Price of Bread in Medieval London." *Journal of Legal History* 27, no. 1 (2006): 29–52.

Sharpe, Reginald R. *London and the Kingdom*. 3 vols. London: Longmans, Green, 1894.

Shaw, David Gary. "Social Networks and the Foundation of Oligarchy in Medieval Towns." *Urban History* 32, no. 2 (2005): 200–222.

Simon, Andre L. *The History of the Wine Trade in England*. London: Wyman, 1977.

Staley, Lynn. *Languages of Power in the Age of Richard II*. University Park: Penn State University Press, 2005.

Strohm, Paul. "Coronation as Legible Practice." In *Theory and the Premodern Text*, 35–50. Minneapolis: University of Minnesota Press, 2000.

---. "Horchon's Arrow." In *Horchon's Arrow: The Social Imagination of Fourteenth-Century Texts*, 11–32. Princeton, NJ: Princeton University Press, 1992.

---. "Interpreting a Chronicle Text: Henry VI's Blue Gown." In *London and the Kingdom: Essays in Honour of Caroline M. Barron*, edited by Matthew Davies and Andrew Prescott, 346–65. Harlaxton Medieval Studies 16. Donington, UK: Shaun Tyas, 2008.

---. "Three London Itineraries." In *Theory and the Premodern Text*, 335–45. Minneapolis: University of Minnesota Press, 2000.

Suggett, Helen. "A Letter Describing Richard II's Reconciliation with the City of London, 1392." *English Historical Review* 62, no. 243 (1947): 209–13.

Sutton, Anne F. *The Mercery of London: Trade, Goods and People, 1130–1578*. Aldershot, UK: Ashgate, 2005.

---. "The Tumbling Bear and Its Patrons: A Venue for the London Puy and Mercery." In *London and Europe in the Later Middle Ages*, edited by Julia Boffey and Pamela King, 85–109. London: Westfield Publications in Medieval Studies, University of London 9, 1995.

---. "The Women of the Mercery: Wives, Widows and Maidens." In *London and the Kingdom: Essays in Honour of Caroline M. Barron*, edited by Matthew Davies and Andrew Prescott, 160–78. Harlaxton Medieval Studies 16. Donington, UK: Shaun Tyas, 2008.

Symes, Carol. *Theater and Public Life in Medieval Arras*. Ithaca, NY: Cornell University Press, 2007.

Thomas, A. H. "Sidelights on Medieval London Life." *Journal of the British Archaeological Association*, 3rd ser., 2 (1937): 107–10.

Thomson, John A. F. *Towns and Townspeople in the Fifteenth Century*. Wolfboro, NH: Alan Sutton, 1988.

Thrupp, Sylvia L. "Aliens in and around London in the Fifteenth Century." In *Studies in London History Presented to Philip Edmund Jones*, edited by A. E. J. Hollaender and William Kellaway, 251–74. London: Hodder and Stoughton, 1969.

---. *The Merchant Class of Medieval London, 1300–1500*. Chicago: University of Chicago Press, 1948.

---. *A Short History of the Worshipful Company of Bakers of London*. Croydon, UK: Galleon, 1933.

Trexler, Richard C. *Public Life in Renaissance Florence*. New York: Academic Press, 1980.

Tucker, Penny. "London and 'The Making of the Common Law.'" In *London and the Kingdom: Essays in Honour of Caroline M. Barron*, edited by Matthew Davies and Andrew Prescott, 305–15. Harlaxton Medieval Studies 16. Donington, UK: Shaun Tyas, 2008.

---"Relationships between London's Courts and the Westminister Courts in the Reign of Edward IV. In *Courts, Counties, and the Capital in the Later Middle Ages*, edited by Diana E. S. Dunn, 117–38. Stroud, UK: Sutton, 1996.

Turner, Victor. *The Ritual Process: Structure and Anti-Structure*. Ithaca, NY: Cornell University Press, 1969.
Unwin, George. *The Gilds and Companies of London*, 4th ed. New York: Frank Cass, 1966.
Veal, Elspeth. "Craftsmen and the Economy of London in the Fourteenth Century." In *Studies in London History Presented to Philip Edmund Jones*, edited by A. E. J. Hollaender and William Kellaway, 133–54. London: Hodder and Stoughton, 1969.
Vickers, Kenneth Hotham. *Humphrey Duke of Gloucester: A Biography*. London: A. Constable, 1907.
Wadmore, J. F. "The Worshipful Company of Skinners, London." *Transactions of the London and Middlesex Archaeological Society* 59 (1876): 92–125.
Watts, John. "Popular Voices in England's Wars of the Roses, c. 1445–c.1485." In *The Voices of the People in Late Medieval Europe: Communication and Popular Culture*, edited by Jan Dumolyn, Jelle Haemers, Hipóito Rafael, Oliva Herrere, Vincent Challet, 107–20. Studies in European Urban History, 1100–1800 33. Turnhout, Belgium: Brepols, 2014.
Weissman, Ronald F. E. *Ritual Brotherhood in Renaissance Florence*. New York: Academic Press, 1982.
Welch, Charles. *History of the Cutlers' Company: From the Earliest Times to 1500*. Vol. 1. London: Privately printed, 1916.
———. *History of the Worshipful Company of Pewterers of the City of London Based upon Their Own Records*. Vol. 1. London: Blades, East and Blades, 1902.
Westlake, H. F. *The Parish Gilds of Medieval England*. London: Macmillan, 1919.
Wickham, Glynne. *Early English Stages, 1300–1660*. London: Routledge and Paul, 1958.
Williams, Gwyn A. *Medieval London: From Commune to Capital*. London: Athelon, 1963.
Withington, Robert. *English Pageantry: An Historical Outline*. Vol. 1. Cambridge, MA: Harvard University Press, 1918.
Wolffe, Bertram. *Henry VI*. 2nd ed. New Haven, CT: Yale University Press, 2001.
Wright, Laura. *Sources of London English: Medieval Thames Vocabulary*. Oxford: Clarendon, 1996.
Wunderli, Robert. *London Church Courts and Society on the Eve of the Reformation*. Cambridge, MA: Medieval Academy of America, 1981.

Manuscript Sources

Guildhall Library
Brewers Gild 1414–1441, MS 5440.
Grocers' Company, Register of Freemen (1345–1481), MS 11592.
London Metropolitan Archive
Journals of the Common Council, 1–9 COL/CC/01/01/
The National Archives (London)
Just. 2/94A Coroners' Rolls
C1 Chancery: Early Proceedings

Printed Primary Sources

Acts of Court of the Mercers' Company, 1453–1527. Edited by Laetitia Lyell and Frank D. Watney. Cambridge: Cambridge University Press, 1936.

De Antiquis Legibus Liber: Cronica Maiorum et Vicecomitum Londoniarum, curante Thoma Stapelton. London: Camden Society 34, 1908.

The Babees' Book: Medieval Manners for the Young. Edited by Frederick J. Furnivall. London: Chatto and Winduw, 1923.

A Book of London English, 1384–1425. Edited by R. W. Chambers and Marjorie Daunt. Oxford: Clarendon Press, 1931.

The Brut or The Chronicles of England. Edited by Friedrich W. D. Brie, pt. 1. Early English Test Society, orig. ser. 31. London: K Paul, Trench, Trübner, 1906, 1908. Repr. Woodbridge and Rochester, 2000.

Calendar of Coroners' Rolls of the City of London, 1300–1378. Edited by Reginald R. Sharpe. London: Richard Clay and Sons, 1913.

Calendar of the Early Mayor's Court Rolls, 1298–1307. Edited by A. H. Thomas. Cambridge: Cambridge University Press, 1924.

Calendar of Letters from the Mayor and Corporation of the City of London c. 1350–1370. Edited by Reginald R. Sharpe. London: John Edwards Francis, 1885.

Calendar of Letter Books of the City of London A–L. Edited by Reginald R. Sharp. London: John Edwards Francis, 1899–1912.

Calendar or Plea and Memoranda Rolls of the City of London. 4 vols. Edited by A. H. Thomas. 2 vols. Edited by Philip E. Jones. Cambridge: Cambridge University Press, 1889–1961.

The Chronica Maiora of Thomas Walsingham 1376–1422. Translated by David Preest. With introduction and notes by James G. Clark. Woodbridge, UK: Boydell, 2005.

Chronicles of the Mayors and Sheriffs of London, A. D. 1188–1274 and The French Chronicle of London, A. D. 1259–1343. Edited by and translated by Henry Thomas Riley. London: Trübner, 1863.

Chronicles of London. Edited by C. L. Kingsford. Oxford: Clarendon Press, 1903.

The Church Records of St. Andrew Hubbard Eastcheap, c. 1450–c1570. Edited by Clive Burgess. London Record Society, 34, 1999.

Civic London to 1558. 3 vols. Edited by Anne Lancashire, assistant editor David J. Parkinson. Records of Early English Drama. Cambridge: D. S. Brewer, 2015.

Ecclestical London. Edited by Mary C. Erler. Records of Early English Drama. Toronto: University of Toronto Press, 2008.

England from Chaucer to Caxton. Edited by Henry Stanley Bennett. London: Methuen, 1952.

English Gilds: The Original Ordinances of More Than One Hundred Early English Gilds. Edited by Joshua Toulmin Smith and Lucy Toulmin Smith. Early English Text Society, London: N. Trübner, 25, 1870.

Fitz Stephen, William. *A Description of London.* Translated by H. E. Butler. In F. M. Stenton, *Norman London: An Essay.* Historical Association Leaflets 93, 94. London: G. Bell and Sons, 1934.

Facsimile of the First Volume of Ms. Archives of the Worshipful Company of Grocers of the City of London, A. D. 1345–1463. Edited by and translated by John Abernathy Kingdom. London: Richard Clay, 1886.

The French Chronicle of London, 1259–1343. Translated by Henry Thomas Riley. London: Trübner, 1864.

Gesta Henrici Quinti: The Deeds of Henry the Fifth. Translated by F. Taylor and John S. Roskel. Oxford: Clarendon, 1975.

Geoffrey of Monmouth. *The History of the Kings of Britain*. Edited by Michael D. Reeve, Translated by Neil Wright. Woodbridge, UK: Boydell, 2007.

"Gregory's Chronicle." In *The Historical Collections of A Citizen of London in the Fifteenth Century*. Edited by James Gairdner. London: Camden Society, new ser. 17, 1876.

The Great Chronicle of London. Edited by A. H. Thomas and I. D. Thornley. London: G. W. Jones, 1938. Reprint: Gloucester, UK: Sutton, 1983.

Historical Poems of the XIVth and XVth Centuries. Edited by Rossell Hope Robbins. New York: Columbia University Press, 1959.

Liber Albus: The White Book of the City of London Compiled by John Carpenter. Translated by Henry Thomas Riley. London: Richard Griffin and Co., 1861.

Liber de Antiquis Legibus [Arnald Fitz-Thedmar]. In *Chronicles of the Mayors and Sheriffs of London, 1188–1274*. Translated by Henry Thomas Riley. London: Trübner, 1864.

London Assize of Nuissance, 1301–1431. Edited by Helena M. Chew and William Kellaway. London Record Society. London: Chatham, W. & J. MacKay, 1973.

The London Eyre of 1244. Edited by Helena M. Chew and Martin Weinbaum. London Record Society 6. London: Chatham, W. & J. MacKay, 1970.

Maidstone, Richard. *Concordia: The Reconciliation of Richard II with London*. Edited by A. G. Rigg, Translated by David R. Carlson. Kalamazoo, MI: TEAMS, 2003.

The Medieval Records of a London City Church (St. Mary at Hill), A. D. 1320–1559. Edited by Henry Littlehales, pt. 1 and 2. Early English Text Society, old ser., v. 125, 128. London, 1909.

Memorials of the Goldsmiths' Company Being Gleanings from Their Records. Edited by Walter S. Prideaux. London, 1896.

Memorials of the Guild of the Merchant Taylors of the Fraternity of St. John the Baptist in the City of London. Edited by Charles M. Clode. London: Harrison and Sons, 1875.

Memorials of London and London Life. Edited by Henry Thomas Riley. London: Longmans, Green, 1868.

The Merchant Taylors' Company of London: Court Minutes, 1486–93. Edited by Mathew Davies. Stamford, CT: Paul Watkins, 2000.

Munimenta Gildhalle Londoniensis: Liber Albus, Liber Custumarum et Liber Horn. Edited by Henry Thomas Riley. London: Rolls Series, 1860.

Parish Fraternity Register: Fraternity of the Holy Trinity and SS. Fabian and Sebastian in the Parish of St. Botolph without Aldergate. Edited by Patricia Basing. London Record Society 18, 1982.

Political Poems and Songs Relating to English History Composed during the Period from the Accession of Edward III to that of Richard III. Edited by Thomas Wright. 2 vols. Rolls Series, London, 1859–61.

Ricart's Kalendar: The Maire of Bristowe is Kalendar by Robert Rickart. Edited by Lucy Toulmin Smith, London: Camden Society, 1873.

Rotuli Parliamentorum 1278–1503. 6 vols. London, 1832.

Secular Lyrics of the XIVth and XVth Centuries. Edited by Rossell Hope Robbins. Oxford: Clarendon, 1952.

A Selection of Minor Poems of Dan John Lydgate. Edited by James Orchard Halliwell. Percy Society 2. London, 1840.

A Second History of the Worshipful Company of Cooks, London. Compiled by Frank Taverner Phillips. London: Privately printed, 1966.

Statutes of the Realm: Printed by the Command of His Majesty King George III in Pursuance of an Address to the House of Commons of Great Britain. Edited by Alexander Luders and others. Vol. 1. London: Dawson of Pall Mall, 1810.

Stow, John. *A Survey of London: Reprinted from the Text of 1603*. Edited by Charles Lethbridge Kingsford. 2 vols. Oxford: Clarendon, 1971.

Wardens' Accounts and Court Minute Books of the Goldsmiths' Mystery of London, 1334–1446. Edited by Lisa Jefferson. Woodbridge, Suffolk: Boydell, 2003.

Wardens' Accounts of the Worshipful Company of Founders of the City of London, 1487–1681. Edited by Guy Parsloe. London: Athlone, 1964.

Index

Abcock, John, 94
Accon, Mazera, 104
Accon, Robert, 104
Adams, Charles Phythian, 8
Aeneas of Troy, 26–27
Agas map, 49–50
Agincourt, 47, 49
aldermen, 2, 4, 15, 17, 77–80, 137–139, 186n89–186n92, 200n22
   Common Council election and, 44
   court of, 17, 44
   defined, 165
   financial burden on, 44
   livery of, 59, 64, 69–70, 78, 183n33
   responsibilities of, 60–61, 183n38
   retirement of, 78
   term length of, 47
Aldgate, 19–21
aliens/immigrants, 1, 11, 14, 22, 81, 97–98. *See also* foreign merchants
   gilds and, 123, 125–127
   legislation re, 136
   opportunities for, 2
   women, 9
All Saint's Day, 67–68
almsgiving. *See* charity/almshouses
Anne of Bohemia, 46, 117
apprenticeship, 10, 15, 110–116, 194n13–194n15, 195n17, 195n19, 195n21, 195n25–195n27
   chamberlains and, 113
   citizenship and, 21–22, 35, 110–114, 172n17, 194n14
   contracts for, 2, 10, 15, 22, 111–114, 123, 127, 130, 158
   cost of, 111–114, 195n19, 195n26
   women and, 110–111, 194n15
Archbishop of Canterbury, 74
Aristotle, 55
arms, 11, 136, 199n15
assault, 35–36, 137, 200n18
Asshecombe, Robert, 104
Asshewelle, William, 90
Assisa de Edificiis, 104
assistants within gilds, 110, 128, 145
Assize of Ale, 55, 97
Assize of Bread, 7, 55, 91–97
assize of buildings, 104
Assize of Nuisances, 10
atonement/contrition, 3–4
attach(ment), 85, 94, 135
   defined, 165
Aubrey, Andrew, 40, 84–85
authority. *See* rank

bachelors, 122–125, 172n17, 197n55, 197n56
Bagot, Sir William, 88
bakers
    fraud by, 5, 7, 91–97, 189n41–189n43, 190n45, 190n50, 190n51, 191n61
    price of bread and, 91–93, 189n42, 190n50
bareheadedness as punishment, 79, 82, 84, 86, 93–94
Barron, Caroline M., 173n32
"bars", 17
Barton, John, 101
Bassett, Beatrice, 89
bawds. *See* prostitutes/bawds
beadle, 89, 138
    defined, 165
bearbaiting, 18
"beating the bounds", 139
Beaubek, William, 136–137
Becket, Thomas, 19, 25, 28
Bedeham, John, 141
Bedford, John, Duke of, 72
begging, 103, 139, 142, 145, 178n35. *See also* charity/almshouses
Bell, Catharine, 162
Bird, John, 94–95, 190n54
Bishop of London, 8, 21, 34, 65
Bishop of Winchester, 74
Black, Anthony, 169n1
Black Death. *See* plague/Black Death
"blue apron" culture, 203n87
Bole, Richard, 78–79
Bolingbroke, Henry (Henry IV), 47
Bolingbroke, Roger, 203n82
bond. *See* surety/bond
Book of Treasure, The (Latini), 55
Boston, Alice, 102
"botchers", 127
Bothe, William, 113
Botlesham, John, 88
Bourdieu, Pierre, 53

Bowder, Edward of, 130–131
Boy Bishop festival, 142
brawling. *See* civil unrest/rebellion
bread. *See* Assize of Bread; bakers; victuals
Brekenhok, David, 124
Brembre, Nicholas, 28, 43–45, 47, 85, 87, 136, 178n32, 178n33, 178n35, 178n39, 199n13
Brewere, John le, 40
Bristol, elections in, 67
Bruges, John de, 129
Brut (Laymon), 28
Brut (prose version), 28
Brutus, founding myth of, 14, 26–29, 174n43
Buc, Philippe, 170n8
buildings, assize of, 104
burial, 24, 29, 42, 118, 139, 142, 145, 177n27
Burke, Peter, 203n87
Burnham, John, 198n74
Burnham, Thomas, 198n74
Bury, Margarete, 100
Busby, Sir John, 88

Cade, Jack, rebellion of, 29
calendars (kalendars), 62, 67
    defined, 165
Cambridge, Goodman, 142
Canterbury Tales, The (Chaucer), 31
Carpenter, John, 6, 10, 28, 53, 55–60, 79–80, 83, 91, 138, 162, 181n15, 181n16, 181n19, 182n27
cartularies, 6, 162
    defined, 165
Causton, John, 142
Caustone, Alice de, 100
Caustone, Robert de, 100
Caxton, William, 28
ceremony. *See* ritual/ceremony; symbols

Index 223

chamberlains, 17, 180n55, 183n33
   apprenticeship and, 113
   contracts and, 113
   defined, 165
   foreign merchants and, 115, 186n92
   as record-keepers, 53
   revocation of charter and, 46
Chancery, removal of court and, 46
Chanel, Coco, 192n87
Chapler, John, 129
charity/almshouses, 1, 15, 24, 29, 110–111, 120, 140–146. See also begging
charters, 4, 33–35, 107
Chaucer, Geoffrey, 14, 31
Chaucer, John, 200n18
Cheap, the (Cheapside), 19
   as ceremonial space, 19
   coronation processions and, 19–20
   mayoral oath-taking and, 20–21, 64–65
   payments for, 78
   population of, 171n2
Chepsted, Isabel de, 200n18
Chigwell, Hamo de, 85
children, 23, 111, 138, 142. See also apprenticeship
Chircheman, John, 90
Christmas, 70, 142, 185n69
chroniclers, 29–30
   "Gregory's Chronicle", 148–149
   language of, 181n7
   of ritual/ceremony, 53–59
churches, 2, 16. See also clergy; parishes; religious houses; specific church
   almsgiving and, 24
   as ceremonial space, 5–6, 9, 19
   feast days and, 8
   hierarchy in, 11
   liturgical time and, 7–8
   ritual/ceremony and, 67–70, 184n61–184n65
churchwardens, 11, 24, 139–141, 159

Cicero, 55
citizenship, 9–10, 21–25, 172n17, 173n20, 173n21, 173n31, 173n32
   apprenticeship and, 21–22, 35, 110–114, 172n17, 194n14
   benefits of, 21
   gilds and, 11, 14, 21–23, 34–35, 172n17
   loss of, 10, 22, 83, 187n7
   oath-taking and, 21–22, 172n17
   patrimony and, 21
   rank and, 13
   redemption and, 21–22, 110, 194n13, 194n14
   responsibilities of, 21–22
civil unrest/rebellion, 3–4, 10, 34, 193n94
   Nicholas Brembre and, 28, 43–45, 47, 85, 87, 136, 178n32, 178n33, 178n35, 178n39, 199n13
   within a gild, 127–133, 198n72, 198n74
   gild skirmishes and, 37–43, 177n23, 177n24
   John of Northampton and, 24, 43–45, 47, 173n32, 178n32, 178n33, 178n35, 178n39
   Peasant Revolt of 1381 and, 43, 177n29
   Southwark as entry point for, 18
Clarence, Duke of, 186n84
clergy, 14–15, 140, 200n28. See also churches; parishes; specific church
Clerk, Luce, 100
clothing/costuming, 4–5, 30, 49, 59, 69–72, 169n3, 184n60, 184n63–184n65. See also livery
   punishment for inappropriate, 70
   removal of, as punishment, 5, 84
coal, 18
Cobham, Eleanor, trial of, 29–30, 149–150, 203n82
Colet, Henry, 186n90
Colwythe, Robert, 113
Common Bench, 64

common clerk, 6, 17, 53, 56, 62
  defined, 165
Common Council, 17, 24, 60, 69, 72, 98, 144, 158, 182n21
  election of, 44
  Journals of the Common Council, 7, 26, 69, 77, 94, 162
  selection of sheriffs and, 79
common pleader. *See* serjeant-at-arms
constable, 35–36, 138, 148
  defined, 165
Constantin, John, 45, 87
contracts. *See* apprenticeship; marriage
contrition. *See* atonement/contrition
cookhouses, 18, 96–97
Corbet, John, 22, 187n7
Cornubia, John de, 39–40
coronation processions, 19–20
coroners' inquests, 15, 23, 39–40, 148
Coroners' Rolls, 7
Corpe, Gerald, 84–85
costuming. *See* clothing/costuming; livery
court of aldermen, 17, 44
Court of Arches, 198n74
craft gilds. *See* gilds
crown, 2, 9–10, 14–15, 33–51. *See also* nobility
  challenges to city government from, 4
  charters granted by, 4, 33–35, 107
  coronation processions and, 19–20
  economic dealings with, 14
  gilds and, 107
  mayoral oath-taking and, 64
  need for money by, 33, 45–46, 175n2
  Parliament and, 45–46
  privileges in dealing with, 76–77, 186n84
  royal entries by, 47–51, 179n42, 180n55
  slander of (*See* slander)

curfew, 11, 135–136, 199n9, 199n15
currency, 37, 92
  defined, 165

Darby, John, 22
Darby, Master, 128
Darci, Henry, 84
Datini, 81, 83, 181n14
Davy, Richard, 96
death, 42, 177n27
  coroners' inquests into, 15, 23, 39–40, 148
  Coroners' Rolls and, 7
  infant mortality and, 2
  in Newgate prison, 15, 172n7
  plague/Black Death and, 2, 7, 13, 42, 97, 177n27
  poverty and, 23–24
De Barton, John, 128
debtors' prison, 15, 172n7
De gestis Britonum (Geoffrey of Monmouth), 27
Derby, Earl of, 74–75
dialect, 1
distraint, 68
  defined, 165
drink. *See* victuals; water conduits; wine
Dunbar, William, 31–32, 175n58
Dyne, William, 200n18

Easter week, 68
Ecclesiasticus, 57
economy
  citizenship and, 22
  civil unrest and, 25, 37, 42–44
  currency shortages and, 37
  price of bread and, 91–93, 189n42, 190n50
  price of meat and, 97
education, 11, 134–137, 199n9
Edward I, 34, 38, 53
Edward II, 34–35, 37–38, 49, 55

Edward III, 35, 37–38, 40–41, 48–49, 74, 86, 117, 134, 149
Edward IV, 76, 126
Edward V, 186n84
elections, 183n40
    of beadles, 138
    of Common Council, 44
    within gilds, 108–110
    of mayors, 8, 9–10, 17, 34, 57–58, 61–67, 182n21, 182n25, 182n27, 183n40
    precedence in, 59, 182n32
    of sheriffs, 8, 17, 34
    of wardens, 108–110
elites
    as chroniclers, 53–59
    elections and, 61
    factions among, 3
    marriage among, 7, 170n9
    punishment of, 10
    slander against (*See* slander)
entertainments, 45–51, 179n42, 180n55
Estfeld, William, 60, 186n84
Exchequer, 34–35
    oath-taking and, 52, 62, 64, 67, 69, 79
    removal of court and, 46
exports. *See* foreign merchants; merchants; trade
Exton, Nicholas, 35
Eynesham, Robert de, 39

famine, 2, 15, 23–24, 29, 172n7
Fantoni, Marcello, 6
Farrington Without, 17, 77, 186n89
Fastolfe, Hugh, 90
Fauconer, Thomas, 87–88, 187n14
feast days, 8, 120–122
Feast of St. Michael, 91, 93
Feast of the Apostles Simon and Jude, 8, 61
Festival of the Pui, 55
fighting. *See* civil unrest/rebellion

Filiol, John, 188n21
Fisher, John, 186n90
Fitz Stephen, William, 28–29
Fitz Thedmar, Arnald, 53–57, 180n6, 181n7
Fleming, Peter, 173n32
food. *See* victuals
foreign merchants, 14, 18, 22, 125–127. *See also* aliens/immigrants
    chamberlains and, 115, 186n92
"forestalling", 99
frankpledge, 15, 17, 135, 137–139
    defined, 166
fraud, 5, 10, 84, 129–130
    by bakers, 5, 7, 91–97, 189n41–189n43, 190n45, 190n50, 190n51, 191n61
    by women, 95, 190n54
freemen by birth, 22. *See also* citizenship
French, Katherine, 141
French Chronicle, 117
Fressh, John, 88
Frossh, John, 38
Fruiterer, Margaret, 142
Fusterers guild, 42

Galganet, Gerard, 98, 191n75
Gascon family, 18
Gaunt, John of (Duke of Lancaster), 43–44
Gedeney, John, 186n89
Gedyngton, William, 89
Geertz, Clifford, 5
Geoffrey of Monmouth, 27–28
gesture, 59
Gibbe, John, 190n56
gildhalls, 4, 6, 10, 13, 21, 120–122, 138, 162. *See also* Guildhall
gilds, 2, 4, 37–45, 97–98, 106–133, 177n23, 177n24, 177n30
    aliens and, 125–127

almsgiving and, 24
apprenticeship and (See apprenticeship)
assistants within, 110, 128, 145
charter of, 107–108
citizenship and, 11, 14, 21–23, 34–35, 172n17
cost of, 111–122
defined, 166
elections within, 108–110, 109
enrollment in, 113–114, 195n25–195n27
governance by, 106, 144–145
governance within, 107–110
as government space, 9
hierarchy of, 23
journeymen and, 122–125, 197n55, 197n56
livery of, 4, 23, 64, 106–107, 116–117, 116–118, 171n13, 196n39, 196n42
marriage and, 23, 111, 195n17
masters of, 108
membership in, 110–116, 114–116, 194n13–194n15, 195n17, 195n19, 195n21, 195n25–195n27 (See also apprenticeship)
oath-taking in, 106, 112–113
parishes and, 107, 112–113, 143–146
patrimony and, 110
peacekeeping and, 106
punishment by, 10
rank within, 106
rebellion within, 127–133, 198n72, 198n74
redemption and, 110, 194n13, 194n14
ritual/ceremony and, 112, 195n21
rivalry among, 5
structure of, 10–11
symbols of rank for, 5
violence among, 3, 37–43, 119–120, 177n23, 177n24, 196n49
wardens of, 108–110
women and, 3, 110–111, 194n15
Gloucester, Humphrey, Duke of. See Humphrey, Duke of Gloucester
Goslin, Richard, 77
governance/officialdom, 146–148. See also specific office-holders, e.g. mayors
crown's challenges to, 4
dignity of office and, 72, 74–77, 185n78, 185n80, 186n84
by gilds, 106
within gilds, 107–110
insults against, 3
spaces of, 9
stability and, 33, 175n3
theories of, 53–59
women in, 3
Gower, John, 150
grain. See bakers; millers
Greater Conduit, 18
"Gregory's Chronicle", 148–149
Grymmesby, Adam, 136, 199n15
Guildhall, 15. See also gildhalls
atonement and, 3–4
John Carpenter and, 56, 181n16
as ceremonial space, 5–6, 19, 59, 182n32
coronation processions and, 19–20
Arnald Fitz Thedmar and, 54–55
as government space, 9
Andrew Horn and, 56
mayoral oath-taking and, 19–21
slander of (See slander)
statuary at, 151–154
Gurmyn, Richard, 87

Habermas, Jürgen, 169n1
hair cutting as punishment, 5, 101–102, 192n87
Halpenny, Robert, 39–40
Hanawalt, Barbara A., 171n5
Hanseatic League, 39
Hanse merchants, 18

Harwe, John de, 148
Haunsard, John, 39–40
Haunsard, Thomas, 39–40
head coverings/hoods, 4–5
　as livery, 23, 41, 52, 64, 78, 106,
　　116–118, 157, 177n23, 196n42
　prostitutes and, 102, 148, 192n91
　removal of as punishment, 79, 82,
　　84, 86, 93–94
health, 2. *See also* plague/Black Death
　filth and, 95, 104, 190n56
　moral, 10, 82, 90–92, 100–105,
　　192n84–192n87, 192n91, 193n94
　nutrition and, 91, 189n43
　victuals and, 100
Heaumer, Simon le, 89–90
Heed, Master, 128
Hegel, Georg W. F., 169n1
Henry III, 34, 53–54
Henry IV (Henry Bolingbroke), 47
Henry V, 49, 72, 118
Henry VI, 29, 47, 49, 69–70, 149
Henry VIII, 185n73
Hervy, Walter, 54
Heyne, Richard, 95
hierarchy, 2. *See also* rank
　in church, 11
　of gilds, 23
　in parishes, 11, 140–146
　ritual/ceremony and, 8–9
　urban, 2
　use of space and, 6
Hoccleve, Thomas, 31, 150
Holland, Ralph, 47, 173n32, 183n40
Hollar, Wenceslas, 15–16, 139
Holy Innocents' Day, 142
hoods. *See* head coverings/hoods
Horn, Andrew, 10, 28, 55–57, 80, 83,
　　134, 181n14
Horn, Richard, 86
Horold, William, 98
horse bread, 95, 190n57

Hostiller, Thomas, 136–137, 199n16
housing, 13, 15–18, 23–24, 42, 49–50
Howell, Martha, 4
hucksters, 99–100
Hughlot, William, 35–36
humiliation. *See* shaming rituals
Humphrey, Duke of Gloucester, 30,
　　72–73, 75, 90, 149,
　　184n50, 185n80
Hundred Years' War, 37, 74
hurdles, 4, 84, 94, 96, 190n53

immigrants. *See* aliens/immigrants
imports. *See* foreign merchants;
　　merchants; trade
inclusivity, 8, 170n13
infant mortality, 2
inns. *See* taverns/inns
insults. *See* slander, lies and insults
Isabella, Queen of England, 38

James, Mervyn, 8, 170n13
John, Duke of Bedford, 72
John, King of England, 33–34
Journals of the Common Council, 7,
　　26–27, 69, 77, 94, 162
journeymen, 122–125, 172n17,
　　197n55, 197n56
Jubilee Book, 53, 138
Judele, Elizabeth, 193n93
judiciary. *See* law/legislation; prisons;
　　punishment
Julius Caesar, 28, 31

Keen, Derek, 171n2
Kene, Margaret, 142–143
King's Bench, 64

Lancaster, Duke of (John of Gaunt),
　　43–44, 188n27
Langland, William, 31
Langourne, Beatrice, 89

language, 1
  of chronicles, 181n7
  emotive, civil unrest and, 3
  insulting, against officials, 3
  power and, 24
Latini, Brunetto (Bruno), 10, 55, 62
law/legislation, 11, 146–148, 169n3. *See also* Assize; *Journals of the Common Council*
  challenges to city's authority and, 64
  civil unrest and, 178n39
  Coroners' Rolls and, 7
  gilds and, 144–145
  Letter Books and, 6–7
  on oath-taking, 6
  public readings of, 134
  re aliens, 136
  removal of court and, 46
  re taverns/inns, 135–137, 199n9, 199n13, 199n15, 199n16, 200n18
lawsuits, 22
Laymon (Layamon), 28
Leadenhall, 19
Leche, Nicholas le, 39
Leggy, Thomas, 85
legislation. *See* law/legislation
Lesser Conduit, 18
Letter Books, 6–7
  Letter Book D, 21
  Letter Book F, 84
  Letter Book G, 147
  Letter Book H, 71
  Letter Book I, 91, 162
  Letter Book K, 28
Liber Albus (Carpenter), 6–7, 10, 21, 28, 47, 52–53, 55–58, 69, 77, 79, 91, 100, 104, 119, 135–136, 157
Liber Custumarum (Horn), 28, 91, 93
Liber de Antiquis Legibus (Fitz Thedmar), 53–57, 180n6, 181n7
Liber de Assisa Panis, 93
Liber Horn (Horn), 10

licensing, 102, 107, 126–127, 184n62
Lindenbaum, Sheila, 52
literacy, 1, 8
  public readings and, 134
  slander and, 89
liturgical time, 7–8, 170n11
livery, 69–72, 78, 106–107, 171n13, 184n60, 184n63–184n65. *See also* clothing/costuming
  of aldermen, 59, 64, 69–70, 78, 183n33
  defined, 166
  exchange of, 41, 177n23
  expense of, 59, 183n33
  of gilds, 4, 23, 64, 106–107, 116–118, 171n13, 196n39, 196n42
  head coverings/hoods as, 23, 41, 52, 64, 78, 106, 116–118, 157, 177n23, 196n42
  of mayors, 4, 59, 64–65, 183n33, 184n52
  rank and, 4–5, 169n3
  women and, 111
Livres dou trésor, Li (Latini), 55
Lollardy, 87, 148
London, 13–32
  Brutus founding myth of, 14, 26–29, 174n43
  crown's relationship to (*See* crown)
  population of (*See* population)
  seals of, 25–27, 34, 62, 64, 174n34
  secular nature of, 7–8
London Bridge, 15–16, 18–20, 46, 148
"London Lickpenny" (poem), 31
Loveye, Geoffrey, 187n14
Lud, 28
Ludgate prison, 15, 19–20
Lydgate, John, 150
Lylye, Katherine, 100

mainprise. *See* surety/bond
manufacturing, 13–14

Index

Margaret, Queen of England, 141
marriage, 2, 7, 29, 170n9
  among merchant class, 13, 171n5
  children and, 23
  gilds and, 23, 111, 195n17
  widowhood and, 23, 171n5
Martyn, Zenobius, 136
May Day, 141
Mayhew, William, 83, 87, 187n6
Mayneld, Thomas, 85
mayors, 2
  avoiding office of, 60–61, 183n38
  John Carpenter on, 57–58, 181n19, 181n20, 182n21, 182n25, 182n27
  challenges to, 33, 74–77
  as chroniclers, 29–30
  civil unrest and, 4
  crown's relationship with (*See* crown)
  election of, 8, 9–10, 17, 34, 57–58, 61–67, 182n21, 182n25, 182n27, 183n40
  expenses of, 59–61, 183n33
  Andrew Horn on, 55–56
  insults to, 3
  livery of, 4, 59, 64–65, 183n33, 184n52
  oath-taking of, 4–6, 14, 19–21, 52, 62–64, 67, 69, 182n27, 184n52, 184n53
  outgoing, 61–62
  power of, 35
  prerequisites for, 59
  privileges of, 76–77, 186n84
  procession of, 19–21, 64–67
  rank of, 2, 34, 57, 181n19, 181n20
  seals of London and, 25–27, 34, 62, 64, 174n34
  slander of (*See* slander)
  space of, 72, 74–77, 185n78, 185n80
  symbols of rank for, 5
  term of, 60
Maywe, John, 190n45

McIntosh, Marjorie, 103
McRee, Ben R., 171n13
measures, 34, 95, 97, 100, 137
  defined, 166
meat, 96–97
merchants. *See also* trade
  as chroniclers, 29–30
  citizenship and, 21, 172n17
  clothing/costuming of, 30
  foreign, 14, 18, 22
  "forestalling" and, 99
  Hanse, 18
  horizontal ties among, 13, 171n5
  housing of, 13
  hucksters and, 99–100
  marriage among, 13, 171n5
Merchants of the Staple, 43–44, 177n30
Middleton, John, 78
Midsummer Watch, 71–73, 185n73, 185n75
millers, 91–92, 190n45, 190n50
minstrels, 11, 65, 91
mistery. *See* gilds
moral health, 10, 82, 90–92, 100–105, 192n84–192n87, 192n91, 193n94. *See also* prostitutes/bawds
Moring, Elizabeth, 102
Moring, Henry, 102
mumming, 70, 185n69
music, 5, 11, 65, 91, 149–150

Newgate prison, 4, 15, 35–36, 40, 79, 83–85, 89, 101–102, 128–129, 159, 172n7, 178n39, 190n54
Nightingale, Pamela, 171n2
nobility, 2, 181n19. *See also* crown; *specific member*
  economic dealings with, 14
  housing of, 13
  rank of, 5
Nolan, Maura, 185n69
Norman, John, 150, 204n89

230 *Index*

Northampton, John of, 24, 43–45, 47, 53, 173n32, 178n32, 178n33, 178n35, 178n39, 188n21, 192n85
Norwich, 65, 67, 144, 185n78
nuisance, 10, 15, 84, 90

oath-taking
  citizenship and, 21–22, 172n17
  Exchequer and, 52, 62, 64, 67, 69, 79
  in gilds, 106, 112–113
  of mayors, 4–6, 14, 19–21, 62–64, 67, 69, 182n27, 184n52, 184n53
odor, 17–18
officials. *See* governance/officialdom; *specific office-holders, e.g.* mayors
Oldcastle, Sir John, 87
oligarchs, 2, 24, 44, 173n31. *See also* aldermen
Ordinance of Dutchmen, 126
Ordinance of Laborers (1349), 42
Orleans, Duke of, 25
overcrowding, 2
Oxford, John de, 39–40

pageants, 45–51, 179n42, 180n55
Palm Sunday, 142
Paris, Mathew, 25
parish clerks, 22, 173n20
parishes, 2, 139–146. *See also* churches
  almsgiving and, 24
  gilds and, 107, 112–113, 143–146
  hierarchy in, 11, 140–146
  rents and, 140
  women and, 3, 140
parish gilds. *See* gilds
Parliament, crown finances and, 45–46
Passelewe, Henry de, 96
patrimony, 21, 110
Paynter, Davy, 130–131

peacekeeping, 2, 11, 15, 17, 35–36
  Farrington Without and, 77, 186n89
  gilds and, 37–41, 106, 177n23, 177n24
  taverns and, 135, 137
Peasant Revolt of 1381, 43, 177n29
Pecche, Henry, 96
Pentecost, 68, 70
Perrers, Alice, 48
Phillippa, Queen of England, 48
Piers Plowman (Langland), 31
pillories, 4, 9, 10, 36, 82, 87–90, 93–101, 178n35, 188n29
plague/Black Death, 2, 7, 13, 42, 97, 177n27. *See also* health
Plommer, Sir John, 142
Pokebrokie, Robert de, 96
political rights, 21
poll taxes, 43
population, 2, 13, 171n2
  citizenship and, 21
  response to drop in, 42–43
  transient nature of, 14
Portsoken, 17
power
  display of, 8–9
  language and, 24
  of mayors, 35
  records of, 53–59
  regulation of space and, 59–67
  ritual and, 1–2, 4–5
  theories of, 53–59
prisons, 4, 9. *See also* punishment; *specific crime; specific prison*
  debtors', 15, 172n7
  removal of court and, 46
  surety/bond from, 3, 85–87, 89, 112, 129–130, 159, 187n14, 200n18
processions, 67–72, 184n61
  coronation, 19–20
  mayoral, 19–21, 64–67
proclamations, 147–148, 202n68

product regulation, 10
property, 136–137, 199n16
prostitutes/bawds, 5, 10, 84,
    90–91, 100–105, 178n35, 189n39,
    192n84–192n87, 192n91, 193n94
  hair cutting and, 5, 101–102, 192n87
  hoods of ray and, 102, 148, 192n91
  poverty and, 23
  in Southwark, 18
public readings, 11, 134
punishment, 83–84. *See also* prisons;
    specific crime
  atonement and, 3–4
  bareheadedness as, 79, 82, 84,
    86, 93–94
  hair cutting as, 5, 101–102, 192n87
  for inappropriate clothing, 70
  loss of citizenship as, 10, 22,
    83, 187n7
  symbols of, 5, 36, 84, 87–88,
    93–94, 188n25
  types of, 5, 10
  wine payments as, 10, 22, 41, 75, 83–86,
    97, 128–129, 132, 159, 187n18

Racheford, Henry, 100
rank. *See also* hierarchy
  challenges to, 33, 74–77
  citizenship and, 13
  within gilds, 106
  livery and, 4–5, 169n3
  of mayors, 2, 34, 57, 181n19, 181n20
  symbols of, 4–5, 169n3
  types of, 9
  of women, 9
Rawlins, Joan, 101
Raynham, Thomas, 198n74
rebellion. *See* civil unrest/rebellion
recorder, 17
redemption, citizenship and, 21–22,
    110, 194n13, 194n14

Refham, Richer de, 134
regnal years, 7
regulations. *See* law/legislation; product
    regulation
religious houses, 15, 19. *See also*
    churches
Rexroth, Frank, 103, 169n1
Ricart's Kalendar, 67
Richard, Duke of York, 148
Richard II, 36, 43–47, 48–49,
    51, 58, 88, 117, 179n42,
    179n43, 202n68
Richard III, 77, 186n84
ritual/ceremony, 52–53, 67–72,
    184n60–184n65, 185n69, 185n73,
    185n75. *See also* processions;
    symbols
  chronicles of, 53–59
  defining, 5–6, 170n8
  dramaturgy of, 5
  gesture as part of, 59
  gilds and, 112, 195n21
  hierarchy and, 8–9
  inclusivity of, 8, 170n13
  music and, 5
  pageants and, 45–51, 179n42, 180n55
  power and, 1–2, 4–5
  practice theory of, 5
  religious, 67–70, 184n61–184n65
  shaming, 1–2, 5
  spaces for, 5–6, 19–21,
    172n15, 177n24
  as theater, 5, 59
  written scripts for, 6
Rogation Day, 139
Roman de Brute (Wace), 28
Rote, John, 35–36
royalty. *See* crown; nobility
rumor, 90
Russell, John, 75, 87–88
Russelle, John, 97

St. Andrew Hubbard, 142
St. Andrew Undershaft, 141
St. Dunstan's church, 35–36
St. Martin le Grand, 19
St. Martin's Day, 147
St. Mary at Hill, 139–140, 200n28
St. Nicholas Day, 142
St. Paul's Cathedral, 6, 9, 15, 19, 25
    as ceremonial space, 19
    coronation processions and, 19–20
    mayoral oath-taking and, 19–21, 65–66
St. Thomas de Acon, 19–20, 65
St. Thomas of Canterbury, 65
sanctuary, 19
sanitation, 17–18
Sappy, John, 136–137, 199n16
Sely, John, 70
Seneca, 55
serfs
    citizenship and, 21
    Trojan practice and, 28, 174n43
serjeant-at-arms, 17, 25, 61, 62, 65, 68, 72, 146–147
    defined, 166
serjeant-at-law, 75
Sevenok, William, 85
shaming rituals, 1–2, 5, 8–9
Sharnebrok, Thomas de, 190n45
sheriffs, 2, 77, 79–80
    election of, 8, 17, 34
    symbols of rank for, 5
Shordiche, Robert de, 39
slander, lies and insults, 3, 5, 10, 35–36, 84–90, 187n6, 187n7, 187n14, 188n21, 188n25, 188n27, 188n29, 188n33
songs, 11, 65, 91, 149–150
space, ceremonial, 5–6, 19–21, 172n15, 177n24
    mayoral, 72, 74–77, 185n78, 185n80
    punishment and, 93

regulation of, power and, 59–67, 182n32
slander within, 84
social space and, 9
stability, 33, 175n3
Staffertone, Robert, 83–84
Stanbury, John, 124
Staplers, 43–44, 177n30
statuary, 11, 46, 151–154
Statute of Laborers (1351), 42, 43
Steelyard, 18
Steer, Elene, 100
Stow, John, 41, 71, 141
strangers. See aliens/immigrants; foreign merchants
Strengere, Alice le, 100
Strode, John de, 95
summer solstice, 70–71
surety/bond, 3, 85–87, 89, 112, 129–130, 159, 187n14, 200n18
    defined, 166
Surmyn, Richard, 87
symbols. See also ritual/ceremony
    of punishment, 5, 36, 84, 87–88, 93–94, 188n25
    of rank, 4–5, 169n3

tallages, 22
taverns/inns, 135–137, 199n9, 199n13, 199n15, 199n16, 200n18
    peacekeeping and, 135, 137
    regulation of, 99
    as sources of information, 11, 135–137, 199n9
taxation, 17, 33, 45–46, 175n2
    citizenship and, 21
    poll, 43
Temple Bar, 17, 19–20
Thame, Robert of, 86
Thames river, 15–16, 18
    as ceremonial space, 19
    mayoral oath-taking and, 20–21

"theater state", 5
theatrical performance, 8
thews, 94, 100
   defined, 166
Thorndon, Peter, 89
Thrupp, Sylvia L., 24, 171n5
time, marking of, 7–8, 170n11
Topesfeld, John, 90
Torold, Roger, 85
tournaments, 45–46, 48
Tower of London, 9, 14–15, 19, 25
town crier. *See* serjeant-
   at-arms
trade, 14. *See also* foreign merchants;
   merchants
  being barred from, 10
  Thames river as center of, 18
  by women, 22, 173n21
  wool, 7, 13–14, 18, 43,
    177n30, 178n33
trade gilds. *See* gilds
Trappe, Hugh, 39
Troy myth, 26–28, 174n43
Turk, John, 39
Turk, Ralph, 39
Turk, Walter, 40
Turk, William, 39
Turmyn, Richard, 87

unrest. *See* civil unrest/rebellion
urban environment. *See* London;
   specific city
Usk, Thomas, 31

victuals, 90–97, 189n39,
   189n41–189n43, 190n45, 190n50,
   190n51, 191n61
  ale as, 97
  bread as (*See* Assize of Bread; bakers)
  cost of, 91–93, 189n42, 190n50
  filth in, 95, 190n56
  meat as, 96–97

"victualers" and, 178n32, 178n33
  wine as (*See* wine)
vigilantism, 148
Vintry, the, 18, 20–21
violence
  among gilds, 3, 37–43, 119–120,
    177n23, 177n24, 196n49
  Coroners' Rolls and, 7

Wace, 28
Walcote, John, 83
Walmesford, Henry de, 96
Walpole, John, 88–89, 188n27
Walsingham, Thomas, 28–29
Walworth, William, 25–26
wardens, elections of, 108–110
wardmotes, 15, 137–139
  defined, 166
  moral offenses and, 103
  poverty and, 23–24
wards, 2, 15, 17, 137–139, 200n22
  defined, 166
Wars of the Roses, 11, 47
water conduits, 15, 18, 47
Wattling Street, 19
weights and measures, 34, 95, 97,
   100, 137
  defined, 166
Westminster, 5–6, 10, 14
  coronation processions and, 19–20
  mayoral oath-taking and, 19–21, 64
whetstone. *See* slander, lies and insults
White Tower, 25
Whittington, Richard, 13, 46, 60,
   122, 196n52
widowhood, 23, 171n5
William, Bishop of London, 21, 34, 65
William the Conquerer, 21, 34, 65
wine. *See also* victuals
  conduits for, 15, 18, 47
  gifts of, 86, 187n18
  import of, 14

234   Index

regulation of, 97–99, 191n74–192n76
as reparation, 10, 22, 41, 75, 83–86, 97, 128–129, 132, 159, 187n18
Wodham, Jonet, 100
women
   apprenticeship and, 110–111, 194n15
   citizenship and, 22, 173n21
   fraud by, 95, 190n54
   gilds and, 110–111, 194n15
   as immigrants, 9
   livery and, 111
   marriage and, 171n5
   parishes and, 140
   rank of, 9
   role of, 3
   as servants, 9
   trading by, 22, 173n21
Wood, Thomas, 129–130
wool trade, 7, 13–14, 18, 43, 177n30, 178n33
Wootone, William, 78
Worcester, Earl of, 76
Wottone, Nicholas, 86
Wycliff, John, 87
Wylde, Katherine, 100

York, Richard, Duke of, 148
Young, Richard le, 95

CPSIA information can be obtained
at www.ICGtesting.com
Printed in the USA
BVHW031333060119
537103BV00004B/99/P